# Writing Your Plan for Small Business Success

### 5th edition

### Ian Birt

ALLEN&UNWIN

First published in 2013

Allen & Unwin
83 Alexander Street
Crows Nest NSW 2065
Australia
Phone:    (61 2) 8425 0100
Email:    info@allenandunwin.com
Web:      www.allenandunwin.com

Cataloguing-in-Publication details are available
from the National Library of Australia
www.trove.nla.gov.au

ISBN 978 1 74331 614 6

*Disclaimer*
The author and all other persons involved in the publication of this book expressly disclaim absolutely all
and any liability and responsibility whatsoever to any person for any claim made based on the contents of
this book, or for any consequences arising from the use of this book. This disclaimer includes exclusion
from liability or responsibility for any errors or omissions. This publication is a general guide and not
intended as a substitute for expert advice. No person should rely on the contents of this publication
without obtaining advice from an appropriate professional person. If professional advice is required, the
services of a competent and qualified person should always be sought.

Set in 11/13.5 pt Minion Pro by Midland Typesetters, Australia
Printed and bound in Australia by SOS Print + Media Group

10  9  8  7  6  5  4  3  2  1

# University Centre at
# Blackburn
## College

**Telephone: 01254 292165**

Please return this book on or before the last date shown

| | |
|---|---|
| | |

# Contents

Preface     vii

## Part 1: How to build a business plan

### 1 Understanding business planning     2
What is a business plan?     3
Reasons for business planning     3
Benefits of business planning     4
The business goal     5
Managing operational functions     5
The plan-building process     6
Planning for business cycles     8
Personal attributes for planning     13
Quick quiz     14

### 2 The business profile     17
Business profile guidelines     18
A.1 The business activity     18
A.2 Ownership structure     19
A.3 Business name     22
A.4 Business location     24
A.5 Business history/entry strategy     25
A.6 Legal requirements     27
A.7 Business objectives     32
Business profile example     35
Quick quiz     37

### 3 The marketing plan     39
Reviewing the existing operation     40
SWOT analysis     42

Gathering environmental information     43
Marketing objectives     48
Marketing plan guidelines     50
B.1 Environmental trends     50
B.2 Industry conditions     54
B.3 Products/services     56
B.4 Competitors     57
B.5 Target customers     58
B.6 Marketing strategies     61
B.7 Marketing controls     72
Marketing plan example     75
Quick quiz     79

### 4 The production plan     82
Production objectives     83
Production plan guidelines     83
C.1 Production capacity     83
C.2 Output levels     85
C.3 Production method     87
C.4 Production quality controls     88
Production plan example     89
Quick quiz     91

### 5 The purchasing plan     92
Purchasing objectives     93
Purchasing plan guidelines     94
D.1 Suppliers     95
D.2 Purchasing policies     98
D.3 Purchasing controls     100
Purchasing plan example     100
Quick quiz     102

**6 The personnel plan**    **103**
Personnel objectives    104
Personnel plan guidelines    104
E.1 Management details    105
E.2 Organisation structure    105
E.3 Staffing strategies    110
E.4 Professional advisers    115
E.5 Personnel controls    116
Personnel plan example    119
Quick quiz    122

**7 The financial plan**    **123**
Financial objectives    124
Break-even analysis    126
Financial plan guidelines    129
F.1 Personal financial position    130
F.2 Establishment costs    132
F.3 Borrowing requirements    134
F.4 Financial forecasts    137
F.5 Financial records    153
F.6 Business insurances    155
F.7 Financial controls    156
Financial plan example    159
Quick quiz    165

**8 The completed business plan**    **168**
Presenting the plan    169
Evaluating the plan    171
Approaching lenders    171
Implementing the plan    172
Operational review    177
The contingency plan    177
Quick quiz    181

**Part 2: Sample business plans**

**Introduction**
Summary of different business circumstances for sample plans    184

**Sample Plan 1:** Business Plan of Carla's Café    185

**Sample Plan 2:** Business Plan of Kate's Bush Tours    207

**Sample Plan 3:** Business Plan of Mike's Building Co. Pty Ltd    229

**Appendix 1: Assessment activities**    **253**
Compulsory activity 1: Completed written business plan    254
Compulsory activity 2: Verbal presentation of business plan    255
Optional activity 3: Operational review schedule    256

**Appendix 2: The environmentally friendly small business**    **257**

Answers: Quick quizzes    259
Glossary: Business planning terms    260
Index    265

# Preface

This book shows you how to prepare and use a business plan for your own small operation. The book is a practical guide for anyone wanting to start or who is already in a small business. The book is also intended as an essential educational text for people studying small business management.

Research consistently indicates businesses that use formal planning outperform those that do not. Not only will you increase your business performance by planning, you will also improve your survival chances in the small business arena.

There are three good reasons to prepare a business plan for your small business:

1. A business plan enables you to set a growth direction for your business to follow and provides you with a comprehensive set of standards against which business performance can be measured.
2. Preparing and working through a business plan enables you to understand your business, as well as to determine the viability of any proposed small business.
3. The business proposal detailed in your plan is a vital selling tool to influence a lender to advance funds.

It is important to realise that you have to prepare your business plan personally to get the real benefits. The plan must reflect your own intentions for the development of your business, not those of someone else.

The book is divided into two parts, with two appendixes:

Part 1 provides guidelines for the step-by-step building of your business plan. Chapters 1 to 8 include examples to illustrate key points, as well as exercises and quick quizzes to test your understanding. Chapter 1 explains the significance of business planning for small businesses. Chapter 2 explains how to prepare a business profile describing the main features of your business for inclusion in the business plan. The business plan-building process involves preparing a series of coordinated plans for each relevant function of your operation. The first plan to prepare is the marketing plan (Chapter 3), followed by the production plan (Chapter 4), then the purchasing plan (Chapter 5), the personnel plan (Chapter 6) and finally the financial plan (Chapter 7). These component plans are combined to complete the business plan (Chapter 8). Chapter 8 further explains how to use your business plan, including approaching lenders and implementing the plan. Scheduling operational reviews and preparing contingency plans are also examined in Chapter 8.

Part 2 shows three sample plans for different kinds of small business situation. The introduction to this part will help you select an appropriate plan for your particular business circumstances. Note that these sample plans are intended for illustrative purposes only, **not to copy**.

There are two Appendixes. Appendix 1 shows suggested assessment activities with assessment criteria and rating scales. Appendix 2 suggests various ways in which a small business can become more environmentally friendly.

There are also answers to the quick quizzes plus a glossary of business planning terms at the back of the book.

By following the guidelines provided in this book, you should be able to prepare and use a sound business plan for your own small enterprise.

*Ian Birt*

# 1

# How to build a business plan

# Understanding business planning

## Objectives

After studying this chapter, you should be able to:

- define a business plan
- recognise the significance of business planning for business success
- set a business goal
- explain the functions found in any business operation.

## WHAT IS A BUSINESS PLAN?

Every business operation should have a business plan to which it can work. Any business operation has the following characteristics:

- systematic organisation of resources (inputs)
- repetitive selling of goods or services
- predominant profit-making purposes.

So, what is a business plan? A business plan is simply a formal written blueprint for an operation in the period ahead. It provides a roadmap for where the business is going. The plan contents are arranged in a structured format and logical sequence to cover all aspects of the operation. Each section of the plan is coordinated and consistent with other sections.

A business plan should anticipate growth and development of the business operation. In a small business, a business plan is a written expression of the owner's intentions for the development of the business in the medium to long term. It begins with an analysis of the existing situation so that realistic growth can be planned for in the future. The plan should ideally be for three years but should extend no longer than five years, because it is difficult to plan with any real certainty beyond this time. A business plan explains how to reach your business goals. The plan will set a direction for your business to follow by defining business objectives and outlining the methods (strategies) to achieve them. In other words, a business plan describes a course of action to follow in order to achieve specified objectives.

A completed business plan will enable you to determine:

- what to do
- why it is being done
- how to do it
- when to do it
- who will do it
- what resources are required
- where you will be.

---

**EXERCISE**

1.1    Define a business plan in one sentence.

---

## REASONS FOR BUSINESS PLANNING

Every small business should have a formal operational plan, although in reality most do not. Studies consistently indicate businesses that work to a prepared business plan for the entire operation significantly improve their survival ability, and thereby their chances of future business success.

Businesses that use formal planning have a head start and a good chance of outperforming businesses that use informal planning or no planning at all. However, business planning is only beneficial if it is done properly.

Apart from the incentive of improved business performance and survival chances, there are three good reasons for preparing a formal business plan in a small business:

1. A business plan enables you to set a growth direction for your business and provides you with a comprehensive set of standards against which to measure business performance.
2. Preparing and working through a business plan is an effective way of determining the viability of any proposed small business.
3. The business plan is an essential selling tool to influence lenders (or prospective partners) to advance funds.

**EXERCISE**

**1.2**    Give three reasons why a business plan should be prepared.

## BENEFITS OF BUSINESS PLANNING

One of the real benefits of putting together a business plan can be found in the process itself. It will force you to examine all aspects of your operation, and to think carefully about how each will be developed in the future. Whether the business is an existing or a proposed one, you will understand your operation better after you have completed a business plan.

Some of the benefits that have been identified as arising from business planning in a small business include:

- more accurate financial forecasts
- more alternatives explored
- more efficient allocation and organisation of resources
- cost savings
- increased sales
- improved competitiveness
- faster decision-making
- reduced feelings of uncertainty
- better employee morale
- overcoming cash flow problems.

In summary, your business plan will have two practical purposes. First, for management, a business plan helps you to analyse your business to plan future growth (or to establish viability). Second, for borrowing, a business plan provides detailed information about your business to a lender for evaluating the likelihood of future success.

**EXERCISE**

**1.3**    Explain the benefits of business planning for a small business owner.

## THE BUSINESS GOAL

You will need to have a business goal before you start preparing your business plan. A business goal is a desired outcome for your business. It is your expectation of where you want your business to be by a specified time.

Your business goal should be stated at the start of your business plan. Examples of business goal statements are:

My business goal is to sell my business for $500 000 in five years' time.

My business goal is to have a debt-free business at the end of six years.

My business goal is to operate a franchise outlet in every capital city within ten years.

Any acceptable business goal must be:

- measurable (to evaluate the success of results)
- clear and concise
- in writing
- attainable.

Any business plan should show how the business goal will be reached. Plan objectives are set to achieve your business goal. The more specific your goal is, the more specifically you can define your business objectives. The following example illustrates the difference between a goal and an objective.

---

**EXAMPLE**

Suppose you set a goal (or desired outcome) to be fit enough to run 1500 metres under five minutes by the end of the year.

To reach this goal, you set weekly training objectives (or targets) to achieve. Here, you can observe how a clearly defined goal determines what objectives to set to reach it.

---

**EXERCISES**

1.4    What is the difference between a goal and an objective? Give examples.

1.5    Comment on the acceptability of the following stated business goal:
My business goal is to double the size of my current operation next year.

1.6    What is your business goal for your existing or proposed operation?

---

## MANAGING OPERATIONAL FUNCTIONS

Business performance relates to the activities of the total operation. You will therefore need to consider all parts of your operation for business planning. A business operation can be broken down into five possible parts or internal functions (see Table 1.1). Each function is interdependent and interrelated. Each function, however, involves the carrying out of specific and distinct activities. The neglect of any function will adversely affect overall business performance.

**TABLE 1.1** Functions within an operation

| Operational function | Description of function | Management aim |
|---|---|---|
| Marketing | Formulating a business offer to customers | To maximise sales |
| Production | Making products to sell | To maximise output |
| Purchasing | Acquiring physical supplies for sale | To obtain the best supply terms for desired quality |
| Personnel | Employing people to be productive | To maximise labour productivity |
| Financial | Measuring financial results of the operation | To maximise profit and cash flow surpluses |

Effective management of the total operation requires planning as well as control of each operating function. Your management success will be measured by financial results and other reports of business performance.

**EXERCISE**

1.7     Identify the operating functions to be found in your small business.

## THE PLAN–BUILDING PROCESS

### The planning process

Business planning involves defining objectives and formulating strategies for your operation. Figure 1.1 shows the sequence of steps to follow in the business planning process.

**FIGURE 1.1** Planning steps

| Step 1 | Step 2 | Step 3 | Step 4 |
|---|---|---|---|
| Understand operating environment | Define business objectives | Formulate strategies to follow | Design controls to measure success |

The process in Figure 1.1 is sometimes described as strategic planning. This planning process is applicable to any operating function of the business. Planning begins by gathering environmental information to understand the internal and external operating environment—sometimes called a *situational analysis*. A situational analysis is like a reality check. This is necessary to plan for realistic growth. Once the existing situation is understood, attainable business objectives are defined for the planning period. Next, strategies (proposed actions) are formulated to achieve stated objectives. Strategies are often selected from competing alternatives. Finally, controls must also be designed for how and when results will be monitored.

## Plan building

A properly prepared business plan covers all parts (functions) of the operation. In effect, the business plan consists of separate plans for each operating function. The plan-building process, therefore, involves preparing a series of plans for the different functions of your operation. This ensures that planned growth is coordinated and balanced for all functions of the operation.

Figure 1.2 describes the order in which to prepare each component plan of the complete business plan.

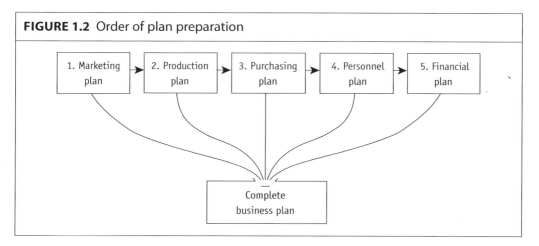

**FIGURE 1.2** Order of plan preparation

### 1. Marketing plan

The marketing plan is always the first plan to prepare. The marketing plan provides the foundation of the entire operation—it determines the nature of your business activities. The marketing plan describes what your business will offer to customers to create sales.

### 2. Production plan

If your business is manufacturing, the production plan comes next. The production plan must be closely coordinated with your marketing plan for product requirements. The production plan describes how the business will meet production volume targets.

### 3. Purchasing plan

A purchasing plan is required by businesses using physical supplies such as raw materials, component parts or trading stock. The purchasing plan explains how the requirements of the operation for physical supplies will be met.

### 4. Personnel plan

After you have prepared the above three plans, you can determine the personnel requirements for the operation. The personnel plan describes the proposed organisation of job roles within the operation.

### 5. Financial plan

The financial plan is always the last component plan to prepare. Financial planning forecasts are the financial expressions of the intended operating activities and resource requirements described in the marketing, production, purchasing and personnel plans.

### 6. Complete business plan

The component plans above are combined to construct the complete business plan (see Table 1.2).

## Business plan format

The suggested format of the complete business plan is shown in Table 1.2.

The individual sections of the business plan are examined in the following chapters.

**EXERCISES**

| | |
|---|---|
| **1.8** | What is strategic planning? |
| **1.9** | List the correct order in which to consider operating functions when business planning. |
| **1.10** | What should be the first plan prepared in the plan-building process? Why? |
| **1.11** | Why should the financial plan be the last component plan to prepare in the business plan-building process? |

## PLANNING FOR BUSINESS CYCLES

### The business cycle

You will need to take account of business cycle movements in your planning, and adopt different strategies for different stages of the cycle.

Business cycles are regular, periodic fluctuations in the general level of economic or business activity. They reflect the inevitable changes that occur in general economic activity. These economic changes are due to a wide and complex range of uncontrollable economic variables, such as production, consumption and investment, rather than government policies as some people seem to believe. Many of these variables, however, can be measured and their effects determined so that changes in economic activity can be predicted with some certainty. Whatever the reasons for economic changes, they must be expected and predicted.

**TABLE 1.2**  Business plan format

| | |
|---|---|
| TITLE PAGE | C.3   Production method |
| LIST OF CONTENTS | C.4   Production quality controls |
| BUSINESS GOAL STATEMENT | **D. Purchasing** |
| **A. Business Profile** | D.1   Suppliers |
| A.1   Business activity | D.2   Purchasing policies |
| A.2   Ownership structure | D.3   Purchasing controls |
| A.3   Business name | **E. Personnel** |
| A.4   Business location | E.1   Management details |
| A.5   Business history/entry strategy | E.2   Organisation structure |
| A.6   Legal requirements | E.3   Staffing strategies |
| A.7   Business objectives | E.4   Professional advisers |
| **B. Marketing** | E.5   Personnel controls |
| B.1   Environmental trends | **F. Financial** |
| B.2   Industry conditions | F.1   –Personal financial position |
| B.3   Products/services | F.2   Establishment costs |
| B.4   Competitors | F.3   Borrowing requirements |
| B.5   Target customers | F.4   Financial forecasts |
| B.6   Marketing strategies | F.5   Financial records |
| B.7   Marketing controls | F.6   Business insurances |
| **C. Production** | F.7   Financial controls |
| C.1   Production capacity | |
| C.2   Output levels | SUPPORTING DOCUMENTS |

Cycles are a major reason for you to do research and prepare a business plan. All businesses are affected to varying degrees by periodic fluctuations in the general level of economic activity. Changes in economic activity affect most but not all businesses in a similar way.

The stages of the business cycle are illustrated in Figure 1.3.

From Figure 1.3, it can be seen that the economy goes through a number of regular phases, which are different stages in the business cycle. The level of business activity alternates between boom peaks and recessionary troughs. In between are downward (contractionary) or upward (expansionary) trends. The business cycle in Figure 1.3 indicates a steady upward trend in the cycle to reflect population growth. The actual movements in the level of economic activity are, of course, a little more irregular than the perfect cycle shown in Figure 1.3.

**FIGURE 1.3** Stages of the business cycle

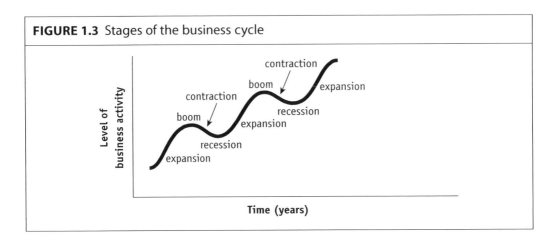

## Economic performance indicators

The general level of economic or business activity can be measured by many different specific variables, known as economic performance indicators. The behaviour of some of the more important performance indicators used to measure the level of business or economic activity is illustrated in Table 1.3.

Many of these indicators are available from the Australian Bureau of Statistics (<www.abs.gov.au>). Additionally, the Reserve Bank of Australia (<www.rba.gov.au>) also conducts economic research and provides regular commentaries on the performance of the general economy. A careful analysis of economic indicators will show the general level

**TABLE 1.3** Economic performance indicators

| Indicator | Boom | Recession |
|---|---|---|
| Rate of growth in gross domestic product (GDP— the national output measure) | Higher | Lower |
| Level of household expenditure | Higher | Lower |
| Level of retail sales/spending | Higher | Lower |
| Unemployment rate | Lower | Higher |
| Interest rates | Higher | Lower |
| New car registrations | Higher | Lower |
| New building construction | Higher | Lower |
| Housing loans granted | Higher | Lower |
| Consumer price index (CPI—an inflation measure) | Higher | Lower |
| Average weekly earnings (AWE) | Higher | Lower |

of business activity and offer projections into the future. This is useful for determining a suitable time to start a small business, and for planning business operations.

Many economic performance indicators can be interpreted in order to ascertain spending levels. For example, high spending levels are usually accompanied by higher interest rates, higher inflation rates, higher rates of growth in GDP and lower unemployment rates. The general level of spending is important because it is consumer spending that determines sales and business activity.

Confidence levels and expectations about the state of the economy and employment prospects are also relevant as underlying determinants of spending levels. Evidence of a widespread optimistic outlook can be a good indicator of healthy economic conditions emerging. Variations in the business cycle could well be the direct result of consumers' confidence levels and expectations for the future; performance indicators might well only measure them.

## Recessions

Recessions are low points or troughs in the business cycle. In a recession, most businesses are adversely affected by relatively low levels of general economic activity; sales turnover and profits are usually low. Not all businesses perform poorly during recessions, however. Those businesses that sell necessities at lower prices (e.g. secondhand furniture, whitegoods and clothing) can prosper in these conditions, as can repairers and takeaway fast-food businesses.

Generally, recessionary conditions are not favourable for starting many types of small business. However, the midst of a recession can be a good time to start some small businesses, because many business bargains become available. There can be good opportunities available, particularly if you have enough capital to take advantage of bargains and if an economic upturn is on the horizon. In these circumstances, the competition may also be at its weakest and most vulnerable.

Your main concern in your operational planning will be survival. Plan to have cash reserves in these periods by maximising net cash flows and minimising your debts. Keep tight controls on operating costs, stock levels and debtors. Marketing, production and purchasing activities, as well as personnel numbers, should also be restricted.

## Upward trends

In an upward trend or upturn in the business cycle, the general level of economic activity is rising. Sales turnover and the profits of many businesses should be increasing. This is generally a good time to start many types of small business, especially if the upturn is expected to last for a long period.

You should plan for growth and expansion in these periods. You could:

* expand your product or service range
* purchase larger stock quantities

- increase personnel
- purchase more or better long-term assets (e.g. plant and equipment) for use in the operation
- introduce new technology into the operation
- relocate or expand to larger premises
- buy another business operation
- purchase business premises
- increase the number of business locations.

Business expansion normally involves using more resources for increased marketing, production and purchasing activities. Plan to increase personnel to support your expansion program if sales volumes are sufficient. Take care to avoid excessive borrowings.

## Booms

Booms are high points or peaks in the business cycle. Boom conditions usually reflect an environment of economic prosperity, where the general level of economic activity is at relatively high levels. Many businesses experience high levels of sales turnover and profits in these conditions. This can be a good time to start many types of small business, if boom conditions are expected to be sustainable.

Your aim in operational planning will be to consolidate the growth achieved in the preceding upward trend. Maintain marketing, production and purchasing activities, as well as personnel, at peak levels. It is prudent not to expand the business further or enter into additional borrowings because boom conditions inevitably come to an end. Many established successful businesses fail in downward phases of the business cycle because of ambitious actions taken in preceding boom periods.

## Downward trends

A downward trend or downturn in the business cycle is where the general level of economic activity is reducing and sales turnover and the profits of many businesses are dropping. Generally, this is not a good time to start many types of small business.

Plan for the downturn in your operation and trim back your operating costs: reduce your marketing, production and purchasing activities and cut back personnel.

To plan for business cycle movements, you need an accurate knowledge of existing cycle conditions and likely movements. You will need to analyse economic performance indicators such as unemployment rates, consumer spending levels, inflation rates (measured by the consumer price index), interest rates and rates of economic growth, as well as gauging confidence levels in the community to know where the economy is in the cycle. This information gathering is examined further in Chapter 2.

**EXERCISES**

1.12   Which specific types of small business activity would you expect to perform well in recessions? Why?

1.13   What stage of the business cycle are we presently in? What are the expected business cycle phases for the next 3 years?

1.14   If you prepared a 3-year business plan today, what would be the aim in your operational planning, after considering the business cycle?

## PERSONAL ATTRIBUTES FOR PLANNING

Certain personal attributes are required to undertake effective business planning. Some important attributes are:

- *Analytical thinking.* You will need to be analytical in gathering and interpreting environmental information to use in your business plan, as well as analysing results in any control program.
- *Creativity.* The ability to think conceptually is required if you are to create ideas from your analysis of environmental information.
- *Forward thinking.* By thinking ahead, you will be able to set objectives and plan strategies for future periods.
- *Being realistic.* You will need to be realistic in your views of the future and avoid being over-optimistic.
- *Decisiveness.* In planning, you must be able to make decisions about future uncertainties, especially when alternatives are being considered.
- *Logical thinking.* Logical thinking is essential for devising strategies to meet objectives and for coordinating operational growth.
- *Being articulate.* You must be articulate, being able to express your intentions clearly and effectively, both orally and in writing.
- *Persuasiveness.* You will also need to be able to present your ideas in a persuasive manner, both orally and in writing.
- *Accuracy.* Planning requires attention to detail, especially for financial forecasting.
- *Flexibility.* A flexible attitude to planning is required if you are to be responsive to changes in business conditions that affect planned outcomes.
- *Alertness.* An alert attitude is also necessary if you are to be receptive to new ideas to identify opportunities and challenges occurring in the business environment, and to detect variations from your plan in operating performance.

## EXERCISE

**1.15**  Do the following self-evaluation of your personal attributes to determine whether you have the essential personal qualities to undertake effective business planning. For each attribute, rate yourself (tick a box) according to the scale indicated. Which personal attributes did you rate as below average? How will you improve your weaknesses?

**Rating scale**

| Personal attribute | Very weak | Weak | Average | Good | Very good |
|---|---|---|---|---|---|
| Analytical thinking | ☐ | ☐ | ☐ | ☐ | ☐ |
| Creativity | ☐ | ☐ | ☐ | ☐ | ☐ |
| Forward thinking | ☐ | ☐ | ☐ | ☐ | ☐ |
| Being realistic | ☐ | ☐ | ☐ | ☐ | ☐ |
| Decisiveness | ☐ | ☐ | ☐ | ☐ | ☐ |
| Logical thinking | ☐ | ☐ | ☐ | ☐ | ☐ |
| Being articulate | ☐ | ☐ | ☐ | ☐ | ☐ |
| Persuasiveness | ☐ | ☐ | ☐ | ☐ | ☐ |
| Accuracy | ☐ | ☐ | ☐ | ☐ | ☐ |
| Flexibility | ☐ | ☐ | ☐ | ☐ | ☐ |
| Alertness | ☐ | ☐ | ☐ | ☐ | ☐ |

## QUICK QUIZ

Each of the following multiple-choice items has one correct answer. Select the letter that corresponds to the correct answer.

1. The predominant purpose of any business operation is to:
   A. make a profit
   B. grow and expand
   C. survive
   D. reduce debt

2. A business plan is:
   A. a plan for future development
   B. a written expression of intentions
   C. a statement of objectives and methods
   D. all of the above

3.  The ideal period for a business plan is:
    A. 1 year
    B. 3 years
    C. 5 years
    D. 10 years

4.  The business plan for a small business should be prepared by its:
    A. accountant
    B. bank
    C. owner
    D. employees

5.  Which one of the following is a valid reason for preparing a business plan?
    A. to establish a competitive advantage
    B. to improve business credibility
    C. to determine business viability
    D. none of the above

6.  A business goal is:
    A. a planned action
    B. a target to achieve
    C. a desired outcome
    D. none of the above

7.  A strategy refers to a:
    A. set objective
    B. planned activity
    C. planned outcome
    D. direction to follow

8.  When building a business plan, the first component plan to be prepared is the:
    A. production plan
    B. marketing plan
    C. financial plan
    D. personnel plan
    E. purchasing plan

9.  When building a business plan, the last component plan to be prepared is the:
    A. production plan
    B. marketing plan
    C. financial plan
    D. personnel plan
    E. purchasing plan

10. The business cycle refers to:
    A. variations in economic activity
    B. life expectancies of businesses
    C. shifts in consumer confidence
    D. all of the above

11. Many economic performance indicators can be obtained from the:
    A. Australian Bureau of Statistics
    B. Reserve Bank of Australia
    C. federal Department of Treasury
    D. local council

12. When interest rates are low and falling, general economic conditions are likely to be:
    A. expansionary
    B. recessionary
    C. booming
    D. none of the above

13. An important determinant of general business activity is:
    A. income levels
    B. spending levels
    C. interest rates
    D. exchange rates

14. If consumer spending is generally increasing, the business cycle is probably in a phase of:
    A. boom
    B. expansion
    C. contraction
    D. recession

15. Any person undertaking effective business planning should be:
    A. conservative
    B. inflexible
    C. aware
    D. reflective

## CHAPTER 2

# The business profile

**Objectives**

After studying this chapter, you should be able to:

- prepare the business profile section of the business plan
- evaluate the acceptability of a business objective.

## BUSINESS PROFILE GUIDELINES

A business plan will contain a business profile section as well as plans for each function of the operation. The business profile section of the business plan should be prepared before the component plans for each operating function. This section of the plan summarises the key features of the operation. It describes the proposed operating structure of the business.

An outline of the business profile section of the business plan is shown in Table 2.1.

| **TABLE 2.1** Business profile outline |
|---|
| **Section A. Business profile** |

| | |
|---|---|
| **A.1 Business activity**<br>(Briefly describe the main business activity.)<br><br>**A.2 Ownership structure**<br>(Show the ownership structure chosen for the business, including brief reasons for the choice of ownership structure.)<br><br>**A.3 Business name**<br>(State the proposed name under which the business will trade and the business website name.)<br><br>**A.4 Business location**<br>(Identify the proposed business location and describe the premises. Emphasise any features of the location.) | **A.5 Business history/Entry strategy**<br>(For an existing business, give a brief history of the development of the business up to the present time. Alternatively, if commencing a new business, show the intended business entry method and proposed date of commencement.)<br><br>**A.6 Legal requirements**<br>(List the various types of licences, permits, approvals and registrations required to carry out the business and operate from the business location.)<br><br>**A.7 Business objectives**<br>(Summarise the main objectives of the business for each year of the plan period.) |

## A.1 THE BUSINESS ACTIVITY

A business activity can be described in terms of the generic products or services sold and the nature of the selling activity. The selling activity can be classified as follows:

- primary producer—growing livestock or crops to sell
- manufacturer—making products to sell
- wholesaler—selling trading stock to resellers
- retailer—selling trading stock to consumers
- service providers—selling services.
  Examples of descriptions of business activities are:
- a pest control service provider
- a leather goods retailer
- a computer consulting service provider
- an electrical goods wholesaler
- a gym equipment manufacturer.

## A.2 OWNERSHIP STRUCTURE

There are four main ownership structures to choose from for your small business:

- sole trader
- partnership
- joint venture
- small company.

### Sole trader

A sole trader is the simplest ownership structure to establish and operate. There are no registration requirements or documents to be prepared and record-keeping requirements are minimal.

A sole trader has exclusive control and ownership of the business. As a sole trader, you would be responsible for management decision-making and would take all the profit. A sole trader also has unlimited liability for the debts of the business. If debts could not be met from the assets of the business, you would be personally liable—that is, you would have to sell your personal assets to meet the debts.

Most small businesses operating as sole traders have limited cash capital and other business resources; their ability to expand is limited.

### Partnership

A general business partnership occurs when between two and 20 people agree to carry on a business and share the profits (or losses), according to a predetermined percentage. Partners can be silent or participating as long as all partners have a common business purpose.

Before entering a business partnership, you should assess the personal suitability of your partners. Is each partner trustworthy? Are you able to work together in a team? Can the partners communicate with each other? Do all the partners share the common objectives of the enterprise?

A partnership can be formed either orally or in writing. It is wise to have a partnership agreement (see Table 2.2), signed by all partners, to provide evidence of the terms of the partnership. This will protect each partner's interests and minimise misunderstandings or disputes. A typical partnership agreement will include each partner's share or interest in the partnership business, as well as each partner's roles and responsibilities in the operation.

In a partnership, there is joint ownership of partnership assets.

| **TABLE 2.2** Partnership agreement contents |
|---|
| 1.  The business name of the partnership |
| 2.  The commencement date of the partnership |
| 3.  The type of business of the partnership |
| 4.  The business address of the partnership |
| 5.  The name and address of each partner |
| 6.  The partnership bank account details, including authorised account signatories |
| 7.  The amount of capital contributed by each partner |
| 8.  The amount and frequency of drawings by each partner |
| 9.  The percentage share of profits (and losses) belonging to each partner |
| 10. The role of each partner in the business, including any limitations on authority |
| 11. The ways in which the partnership can be ended |
| 12. The process for settling disputes between the partners |
| 13. Partners' signatures |

Partners are jointly liable for partnership debts. Like a sole trader, each partner also has unlimited liability for the debts of the partnership business.

A major benefit of operating a business as a partnership is that partners can combine their capital, assets, technical know-how and expertise. Partnerships can also be used in some family situations to minimise tax by splitting income with eligible family members.

## Joint venture

As an alternative to a partnership, you could consider operating in a joint-venture arrangement. A joint venture is an agreement by two or more people to pool their separate resources and work together in a single venture, project or enterprise. A feature of a joint-venture arrangement is that each party maintains its separate identity, records and ownership of resources and debts, but business resources are combined to produce a large output. Each joint venturer has a distinct and separate share of the final output.

Joint-venture arrangements can be attractive because they can be constructed to avoid some of the pitfalls that occur with operating a partnership (e.g. unlike partners in a partnership, the parties can agree not to be jointly liable for the debts of the joint venture). Like partnerships, joint-venture agreements should be evidenced in writing to protect the separate interests of the parties involved. Any such agreement should clearly indicate the joint-venture intentions of the partners and emphasise the features of a joint-venture arrangement.

It is essential to use a solicitor to draw up a joint-venture agreement, particularly for any ongoing enterprise, because, depending on the facts, joint ventures can be legally interpreted as partnerships despite any declarations you make to the contrary. If you decide on a joint venture, you need to be constantly aware of how to conduct the business to avoid slipping into a partnership arrangement.

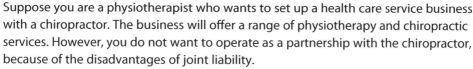

**EXAMPLE**

Suppose you are a physiotherapist who wants to set up a health care service business with a chiropractor. The business will offer a range of physiotherapy and chiropractic services. However, you do not want to operate as a partnership with the chiropractor, because of the disadvantages of joint liability.

As an alternative, both you and the chiropractor decide to operate separate businesses under a joint-venture arrangement. Under the joint-venture agreement, you will lease the business premises and pay the rent. Both of you will occupy the same premises for the performance of services. The chiropractor will employ and pay a secretary/receptionist who will work for both parties at the premises. You both agree to maintain your own record systems and pay your own operating expenses incurred. You will each charge and be entitled to receive your own fees for services performed.

## Small company

You could choose to carry on your business as a company. This is the most complex ownership structure of the four main forms. Companies are regulated by the *Corporations Act 2001* (Cth), which is administered by the Australian Securities and Investments Commission (ASIC) (see <www.asic.gov.au>).

All companies must be registered with ASIC. You can buy an existing company that is already registered or register a new company. There are different types of company. The relevant kind of company for a small business is the small proprietary company limited by shares. A small proprietary company can be operated by one person as the sole director and shareholder. The maximum number of shareholders allowed is 50.

In a company, there is a clear distinction between ownership and control. Shareholders own the company and directors manage or control it. Shareholders in the company also have limited liability. The shareholders' liability is limited to the issued value of their shares—for example, $1 or $2 per share. In contrast, directors have strict legal duties imposed under the *Corporations Act*. For example, directors are under a legal duty to be honest and competent in the management of the company.

A company comes into legal existence at the date of its registration. The main reason people choose to use a company structure for their business is that a company is recognised under the law as a legal entity, separate from its directors and shareholders. For legal purposes, a company is capable of doing most things a human being can. A company can, in its own name and right, own property and assets, enter into contracts, pay tax, incur debts, sue and be sued. A company also lasts forever unless formal steps are taken to end it.

The main practical advantage of a company being a separate legal entity is that personal assets cannot be called upon to pay company debts. Creditors dealing with the business can only recover debts from assets of the company. In reality, however, major creditors such as lenders, landlords and suppliers usually require personal guarantees from directors before entering into any agreements. Directors can also be personally liable under law for any company debts incurred during trading periods of insolvency.

Companies offer legitimate tax-minimising possibilities because they are separate legal entities. However, they must maintain extra records and lodge annual reports of operations and a fee with ASIC. These requirements significantly increase accountancy fees. The information contained in the reports lodged with ASIC is also available to the public.

## Comparison of ownership structures

The advantages and disadvantages of each main ownership structure are summarised in Table 2.3.

Some of the factors to consider when making your choice of ownership structure include:

- the number and nature of the persons involved
- the nature and extent of the business
- your capital, borrowings and expertise needs
- the degree of financial exposure and risk acceptable
- the extent of control and ownership of the business required
- the costs of establishing and maintaining the ownership structure
- the desire for confidentiality
- the need to minimise taxes legitimately.

Evaluate each ownership structure to determine which one suits your circumstances.

**EXERCISE**

2.2    Choose an appropriate ownership structure under which to operate. Give reasons for your choice.

## A.3 BUSINESS NAME

Whichever ownership structure you choose, the business needs a name under which to trade. A national business names registration system regulates the use of business names. The national business names register is administered and managed by ASIC (<www.asic.gov.au>). If the business trades under a name other than its owner's name, the business name must be registered for a fee with ASIC.

You can also determine the availability of business names (or proposed company names) by doing an online search of the national names register maintained by ASIC (<www.asic.gov.au>).

**TABLE 2.3** Advantages and disadvantages of ownership structures

**SOLE TRADER (one owner)**

| Advantages | Disadvantages |
|---|---|
| • Simple to set up and operate<br>• Sole control, decisions and ownership | • Unlimited liability for debts<br>• Limited resources for growth<br>• Business isolation |

**PARTNERSHIP (two to 20 partners)**

| Advantages | Disadvantages |
|---|---|
| • Benefits from combining resources for capital, know-how, etc.<br>• Tax minimisation by splitting income with family members | • Joint and unlimited liability for debts<br>• Sharing decisions may lead to disputes<br>• Increased administration to account for eligible separate interests<br>• Partners need to be trustworthy |

**JOINT VENTURE (two or more persons)**

| Advantages | Disadvantages |
|---|---|
| • Benefits from combining separately owned resources<br>• Responsibility for own liabilities<br>• Separate ownership of assets and resources<br>• Possible avoidance of liabilities under partnership law | • Usually of limited duration<br>• Sharing resources may lead to disputes<br>• Care needed to avoid being legally interpreted as a partnership |

**SMALL COMPANY (one to 50 shareholders and minimum of one director)**

| Advantages | Disadvantages |
|---|---|
| • Separate legal entity<br>• Personal assets can be protected from business risks<br>• Limited liability of shareholders<br>• Can be operated by one person<br>• Distinct division between ownership and control (i.e. shareholders and directors)<br>• Can be flexibly used to minimise taxes<br>• Lasts forever unless formally wound up | • Costly to set up<br>• Costly ongoing reporting requirements<br>• Public disclosure of information<br>• Strict legal duties for directors<br>• Expensive to wind up |

**EXAMPLE**

Jim Jones intends to operate a cleaning business as a sole trader. He proposes five possible business names to trade under. The registration requirements for each proposed name are stated.

| Proposed business name | Registrable |
| --- | --- |
| Jim Jones | No |
| J. Jones | No |
| Jim Jones & Co. | Yes |
| Jim Jones Cleaning | Yes |
| Betta Cleanz | Yes |

A proposed business name will only be registered if it is original and not misleading, deceptive or offensive.

The benefits of using a trading name include:

- It helps the business to project the desired image to customers.
- It can be easier to remember than a person's name.
- It is more practical for a partnership than using all the partners' names.
- It can describe the business activity.
- It can give the business a professional and credible appearance.
- It will be associated with the goodwill of the business.

A business name should be brief, descriptive of the business activity, catchy and easy to remember, and it should project the desired image.

Any business website address should also be disclosed in your business plan. Registration requirements for domain (website) names are outlined later in this chapter.

**EXERCISES**

2.3    Design an effective business name under which to trade.
2.4    Where is the business name to be registered?

## A.4 BUSINESS LOCATION

The choice of physical business location is a marketing decision that is considered in the marketing plan. A description of the business location chosen should be part of the business profile.

A description of the business location should include:

- the address of the business
- the size (square metres) of the premises
- a layout floor plan of the premises
- a location map.

Any location features such as exposure or accessibility should be emphasised in the description.

If applicable, also describe key lease terms negotiated for the premises. Key lease terms include:

- rent and frequency
- annual rent
- rent reviews
- contributions to outgoings
- lease period
- option period.

## A.5 BUSINESS HISTORY/ENTRY STRATEGY

### Business history

For an existing operation, provide a brief history of the development of the business from its starting date to the present time. You could include a summary of key measures of business performance to highlight growth (see Table 2.4).

**TABLE 2.4**  Business history summary—key measures

| Past annual period | Annual sales | Annual net profit | Number of personnel |
|---|---|---|---|
| | $ | $ | (full-time equivalents) |
| Year 1 | _____ | _____ | _____ |
| Year 2 | _____ | _____ | _____ |
| Year 3 | _____ | _____ | _____ |
| Year 4 | _____ | _____ | _____ |
| Year 5 | _____ | _____ | _____ |
| Year … | _____ | _____ | _____ |

A demonstrated history of business growth provides a lender with evidence of management ability.

### Entry strategy

You must select an entry strategy and start date for a proposed business. There are three main ways for you to enter small business:

- starting up
- buying an existing business
- obtaining a franchise outlet.

### Starting up

Starting up a small business will appeal to you if you seek total independence and control in the way your business is developed; you will have more scope to apply your own ideas. Starting up a business is also usually cheaper than buying an existing business because you do not have to pay for goodwill—the established reputation of the business. Starting up a small business carries the highest risk of failure, however, because sales are uncertain. There is also more time and effort required to procure resources and set up your operation.

The best times to consider starting up a small business are:

- when general business activity and demand is increasing (e.g. there is an upward trend in the business cycle)
- when there is an under-supply of the specific products or services of the business
- when the business offers a unique product or service.

### Buying an existing business

Buying an existing business as a going concern means you are buying an established operation. This avoids many of the problems associated with starting up, and ensures instant sales and receipts. The downside of this entry method is that it is often a costly way to enter small business. You must pay for goodwill (established business reputation) as well as other business assets. If you choose this entry strategy, include the business price payable in your plan.

When buying a business, decisions about retaining existing employees, collecting existing debtors and paying existing creditors may also be necessary.

The best times to buy an existing business are:

- when general business activity and demand is increasing (e.g. on an upward trend in the business cycle)
- when there is increasing demand for the specific product or service of the business.

### Obtaining a franchise outlet

Obtaining a franchise outlet as a franchisee in a well-known franchise system (see Figure 2.1) can be a good way to get into a proven business, provided you assess the franchise carefully. Training is often provided by the franchise system owner. You will not be as independent in a franchise outlet; you will need to comply with standardised policies and procedures of the franchise system owner. You operate in an agreed market area. You may also pay to the franchise system owner an upfront entry fee, a regular royalty based on turnover as well as other levies, depending on the franchise. If this entry strategy is chosen, show these various fees payable to the franchise owner in your plan.

You can obtain an outlet in a franchise system with an established and well-known business name at any stage of the business cycle.

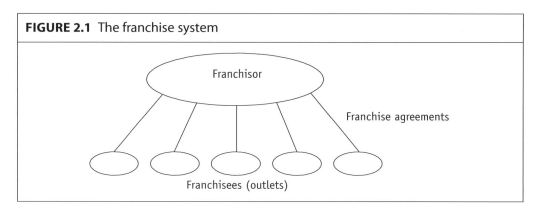

**FIGURE 2.1** The franchise system

The Franchise Council of Australia (<www.fca.com.au>) has more information on franchising.

### *Comparison of entry methods*

The advantages and disadvantages of each entry method are summarised in Table 2.5.

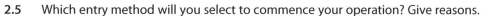

**EXERCISES**

2.5    Which entry method will you select to commence your operation? Give reasons.
2.6    On what date will you commence your operation? Justify your choice.

## A.6 LEGAL REQUIREMENTS

There may be specific legal requirements to be met when carrying out your business. Legal requirements may be in the form of business licences, approvals and permits, or compulsory registrations. A useful gateway website for finding out about general legal requirements for business is <www.business.gov.au>. Some of the main legal requirements are outlined below.

## Business licences

Some business activities will require a licence to be granted by your local consumer protection authority (see Table 2.6) before they can be carried out. The relevant licence will normally be granted if you satisfy prescribed qualification and experience prerequisites and pay the fee. Check with the Business Licence Information Service (BLIS) of your local authority to determine whether a licence is required to carry out your business activity. A gateway website to the BLIS in each state and territory is <www.bli.net.au>.

A national licensing system is currently being introduced to regulate specific occupations—mainly for building-related services. This system will be administered by the National Occupational Licensing Authority—NOLA (<www.nola.gov.au>).

**TABLE 2.5** Advantages/disadvantages of entry methods

**STARTING UP**

| Advantages | Disadvantages |
|---|---|
| • The business can be set up and developed as you wish.<br>• The cost of purchasing goodwill is avoided.<br>• The risk of inheriting existing business ill-will is avoided. | • There is a higher risk of failure because of uncertain customer demand.<br>• Customer demand and goodwill have to be built up.<br>• The business has to be promoted actively for it to be known.<br>• There may be teething problems encountered in setting up operating systems and procedures.<br>• Supplier relationships need to be established.<br>• Staff have to be found and trained.<br>• Borrowings are more difficult to obtain.<br>• There is often a time lag before sufficient sales are generated.<br>• Time and effort are required to set up the operation. |

**BUYING AN EXISTING BUSINESS**

| Advantages | Disadvantages |
|---|---|
| • The success of the business can be evaluated from its records.<br>• Immediate sales receipts occur.<br>• Time and effort are saved in having to set up the operation.<br>• Trained and experienced staff may come with the business.<br>• The business has an established location and relationships with customers and suppliers.<br>• It can sometimes be cheaper than starting up.<br>• It is easier to borrow.<br>• There is a reduced risk of failure. | • You inherit poor decisions of the previous owner (e.g. unsaleable stock, outdated equipment, unsuitable staff or poor location).<br>• You may pay too much for goodwill in the purchase price.<br>• You inherit any ill-will or poor business reputation. |

**TABLE 2.5** continued

| OBTAINING A FRANCHISE OUTLET | |
|---|---|
| **Advantages** | **Disadvantages** |
| • Training is usually provided for inexperienced operators.<br>• Loans are easier to get for well-known franchises.<br>• Large and well-known franchise names have instant pulling power.<br>• Assistance is given by the franchise system owner to set up the business.<br>• Standardised, proven operating systems and procedures are used.<br>• Cheaper stock is available through bulk purchasing power.<br>• Ongoing business training is usually provided by the franchise system owner.<br>• There are lower failure rates in well-known franchises.<br>• Group advertising can mean better promotions. | • There is a loss of some business independence in conforming to standardised procedures.<br>• Only the franchise business name can be used.<br>• Business policies are set by the franchise system owner, for example product range, prices.<br>• Customer areas are defined.<br>• There is usually an entry fee and ongoing royalty fee (based on sales) to pay to the franchise system owner.<br>• You share any ill-will with the franchise name.<br>• There is a risk that the franchise system owner's business will collapse if the franchise is new or not well known, or the business idea is just a passing fad. |

**TABLE 2.6** Consumer protection authorities

| State/territory | Authority name | Website address |
|---|---|---|
| New South Wales | NSW Office of Fair Trading | www.fairtrading.nsw.gov.au |
| Victoria | Consumer Affairs Victoria | www.consumer.vic.gov.au |
| Queensland | Office of Fair Trading | www.fairtrading.qld.gov.au |
| Western Australia | Department of Commerce—Consumer Protection | www.commerce.wa.gov.au |
| South Australia | Office of Consumer and Business Affairs | www.ocba.sa.gov.au |
| Tasmania | Consumer Affairs and Fair Trading | www.consumer.tas.gov.au |
| Australian Capital Territory | Office of Regulatory Services | www.ors.act.gov.au |
| Northern Territory | Consumer Affairs | www.consumeraffairs.nt.gov.au |

Professional occupations (e.g. health professionals) usually have specific state/territory licensing boards to regulate them.

Liquor sellers will also require a special licence for a fee from their local liquor-licensing authority.

## Approvals and permits

There could be several approvals and permits required to operate legally at a business location. Each approval and permit requires payment of a fee.

Local council approval is usually required to operate a business legally at any location. Approval is sought by lodging a development application (DA) with your local council (or equivalent authority in the ACT). Council approval will also indicate at what hours you can legally operate the business.

If you propose to make structural alterations or improvements to the premises, you will also need to lodge a building application (BA) with the local council (as well as get the landlord's permission) to obtain approval to do the work.

Food businesses require a health clearance permit from the local council, saying that the premises are clean and healthy. Specific local council permits may also be required to use external advertising signs or to operate on roadsides or walkways.

Businesses producing trade waste may require a waste permit to dispose lawfully of the waste. Relevant local authorities to consider include the water authority, the environmental protection authority, local council, as well as other authorities, depending on the kind of waste.

The use of some types of equipment or handling of dangerous goods may also require an operating permit from the local environmental protection authority or work health and safety authority (see Table 2.7).

Playing music in a business requires a special licence (permission) from the authorised collection agency that collects licence fees on behalf of music copyright owners. Collection agency websites are <www.apra.com.au> and <www.ppca.com.au>.

## Business name registration

If you use a business name other than your own to trade under, you will need to register it for a fee with ASIC (<www.asic.gov.au>). The business name will normally be registrable if it is original and not misleading or offensive.

## Domain name registration

If your business intends using a unique website address (a domain name) on the internet, you must register it for a fee with a registration authority.

Registration authorities for registering an Australian domain name can be found at the website <www.auda.org.au>. For global domain names, visit <www.icann.org>.

You can check the availability of Australian names (those ending in .au) at <www.ausregistry.com.au>; or global names at <www.whois.net>.

| TABLE 2.7  Work health and safety authorities | | |
| --- | --- | --- |
| **State/territory** | **Local authority** | **Website address** |
| New South Wales | WorkCover NSW | www.workcover.nsw.gov.au |
| Victoria | WorkSafe Victoria | www.worksafe.vic.gov.au |
| Queensland | Workplace Health and Safety Queensland | www.justice.qld.gov.au |
| Western Australia | Department of Commerce—WorkSafe | www.commerce.wa.gov.au |
| South Australia | SafeWork South Australia | www.safework.sa.gov.au |
| Tasmania | Workplace Standards Tasmania | www.wst.tas.gov.au |
| Australian Capital Territory | WorkSafe ACT | www.worksafe.act.gov.au |
| Northern Territory | NT Worksafe | www.worksafe.nt.gov.au |

## Taxation registration

Taxpayers (e.g. individuals, companies) must apply once only to the Australian Taxation Office (ATO) for a tax file number. A tax file number is required to lodge income tax returns and receive assessment notices from the ATO (<www.ato.gov.au>).

Additionally, business entities (e.g. sole traders, partnerships, companies) require an Australian Business Number (ABN) for various dealings with the ATO. A business will require an ABN to:

- register for GST
- lodge business activity statements
- withhold income tax from employee payments under the Pay As You Go (PAYG) system
- pay income tax by instalments.
  An ABN is also required to register a business name.
  The ABN can be applied for online (<www.business.gov.au> or <www.abr.gov.au>).
  Taxation registrations do not require the payment of any fees.

## Factory registration

Operators of factory premises may have to register their premises with the local work health and safety authority (see Table 2.7). This is to ensure the premises are safe and healthy for workers.

## Intellectual property registration

To get legal protection for any unique trademark, design or invention owned, you may be able to register the property with IP Australia (<www.ipaustralia.gov.au>).

Registration of intellectual property requires payment of a fee.

## Company registration

If you operate your business as a company, you must register the company. A company is created by registering it at the Australian Securities and Investments Commission (<www.asic.gov.au>) for a fee.

## Workplace agreement registration

Federal and state industrial relations legislation allows employers and employees to negotiate formal workplace agreements directly. There are different kinds of agreements under the legislation. Some agreements must be approved by the relevant federal or state industrial relations authority.

## Import/export requirements

Importers and exporters must comply with relevant legal requirements for their imports and exports. The Australian Customs Service (<www.customs.gov.au>) provides information about importing, exporting and customs duties applicable. The Australian Quarantine and Inspection Service (<www.daff.gov.au/aqis>) also has information about any import and export restrictions.

Table 2.8 summarises the main legal requirements to consider for the operation.

| **EXERCISE** | | |
| --- | --- | --- |
| 2.7 | Make a list of relevant legal requirements for your business to operate. Use the following headings: | |

| **Legal requirement** | **Relevant authority** | **Cost $** |
| --- | --- | --- |

## A.7 BUSINESS OBJECTIVES

The business profile section of the business plan should include a summary of the key business objectives for the operation (see Table 2.9).

Business objectives should be designed to achieve business goals (see Chapter 1). Business objectives are targets for the operation to work towards. They set a direction for your business to follow. Once your business objectives are defined, you will be able to plan strategies to achieve them.

**TABLE 2.8** Checklist for legal requirements

| Legal requirements | Relevant authority |
| --- | --- |
| Business licences | Local consumer protection authority or NOLA |
| Liquor licence—local | Liquor licensing authority |
| Business name registration | ASIC |
| Development approval | Local council |
| Building approval | Local council |
| Health clearance permit | Local council |
| External advertising sign permit | Local council |
| Streetside or stallholder permit | Local council |
| Waste permit | Local council, local water authority, local environmental protection authority |
| Equipment or dangerous goods permit | Local environmental protection authority or local work health and safety authority |
| Music-playing licence | APRA, PPCA |
| Tax file number registration | Australian Taxation Office |
| ABN registration | Australian Taxation Office |
| Factory registration | Local work health and safety authority |
| Intellectual property registration | IP Australia |
| Company registration | ASIC |
| Workplace agreement registration | Federal or state industrial relations authority |
| Import/export requirements | Australian Customs Service, Australian Quarantine and Inspection Service |

Objectives need to be set for each function of the operation. There should be annual objectives for each year of the plan period. The objectives need to be coordinated and consistent with each other.

To be an acceptable target, any business objective must satisfy the following criteria.

- *Be measurable.* A measurable business objective is expressed in terms that allow the success of results to be determined. For example, a sales objective expressed as 'to maximise sales' is not measurable, whereas a sales objective stated as '$200 000 p.a.' is measurable. A measurable objective does not necessarily have to be expressed in numeric terms, for example it might be a product range objective, as long as the success of the results can be evaluated.
- *Be clear and concise.* For a business objective to be understandable, it must be clearly stated and brief.

- *Be in writing.* Any worthwhile business objective must be written to be lasting and able to be referred to.
- *Be attainable.* A business objective must reflect a realistic expectation. It must be capable of achievement with the resources available (i.e. the target must be attainable). This requires a realistic assessment of the operating environment and operational capability.
- *Be challenging.* A business objective also needs to be sufficiently challenging to be beneficial. If the target is too easy to attain, there is no impetus for achieving full potential and getting the best results.
- *Be improving over time.* An acceptable business objective will be shown as improving over time, to indicate anticipated growth. If the sales objective for Year 1, for example, is $200 000 p.a., the sales objectives for the following years should be increased to reflect sales growth. Some targets, however, could decrease over time to reflect improvement—for example, debt levels and owner's hours worked.

Each specific objective in Table 2.9 will be examined in the following chapters.

| TABLE 2.9 Key business objectives | | | |
|---|---|---|---|
| | **Year 1** | **Year 2** | **Year 3** |
| **Marketing:** | | | |
| • sales | $_____ | $_____ | $_____ |
| **Production:** | | | |
| • output volume | _____units | _____units | _____units |
| **Purchasing:** | | | |
| • average gross profit margin | _____% | _____% | _____% |
| **Personnel:** | | | |
| • labour productivity ratio | _____% | _____% | _____% |
| • number of personnel (full-time equivalents) | _____ | _____ | _____ |
| **Financial:** | | | |
| • net profit | $_____ | $_____ | $_____ |
| • net cash flow | $_____ | $_____ | $_____ |
| • debt ratio | _____% | _____% | _____% |

## EXERCISE

**2.8**   The sales objectives for four different businesses are shown below. Each business is a similar size and operates in the same industry. The annual sales turnover of each business last year was $140 000.

### Sales objectives

|  | Year 1 | Year 3 |
|---|---|---|
| Gary's business | To maximise sales | To maximise sales |
| Liz's business | $150 000 p.a. | $130 000 p.a. |
| John's business | $30 000 p.a. | $140 000 p.a. |
| Mary's business | $145 000 p.a. | $800 000 p.a. |

Using the criteria for a worthwhile objective, evaluate the acceptability of the sales targets of each business. (Assume there will be no significant changes in resources used by each business during the period.)

## BUSINESS PROFILE EXAMPLE

### A. BUSINESS PROFILE

#### A.1 Business activity

The proposed business is a manufacturer and retailer of a variety of fresh bread products.

#### A.2 Ownership structure

The business will be operated as a small proprietary company by Hannah Baker, who will be the sole director and shareholder of the company. A company structure is chosen because personally owned assets are to be kept separate from the business assets owned by the company.

#### A.3 Business name

The company will trade under the business name of 'Hannah's Hot Bread Shop'.
   The business website is 'www.hannahsbreads.com.au'.

#### A.4 Business location

The operation will be located at shop premises at 101 Main Street, My-Town, which is also the registered address of the company. A commercial lease will be negotiated for an initial term of three years, with the option to renew the lease for a further five years. Under the lease, the rent is $1700 per calendar month for the first year, to be increased annually by 5%.
   The shop premises are centrally located in the main street of the shopping centre. The premises are at street level and have a floor space area of 80 m².

### A.5 Entry strategy

The business will be started up as a new operation. The reason for starting up as a new operation is because it is the cheapest way to establish the business. The proposed date of commencement of business is 1 July, Year 1.

### A.6 Legal requirements

The legal requirements to operate the business are:
- company registration with the Australian Securities and Investments Commission
- business name registration with the Australian Securities and Investments Commission
- development approval for using the premises from the local council
- health clearance permit (for food sellers) from the local council
- external advertising sign permit from the local council
- registration of factory premises with the state work health and safety authority
- ABN registration (for GST and PAYG tax) with the Australian Taxation Office.

Legal requirements will be met before business commences.

### A.7 Business objectives

The key objectives of the business for the next three years are summarised as follows:

|  | Year 1 | Year 2 | Year 3 |
|---|---|---|---|
| **Marketing:** | | | |
| • sales turnover | $240 000 | $264 000 | $290 000 |
| **Production:** | | | |
| • production capacity used | 70% | 70% | 70% |
| **Purchasing:** | | | |
| • average gross profit margin | 43% | 43% | 43% |
| **Personnel:** | | | |
| • labour productivity ratio (i.e. sales : labour costs) | $4.53 : $1 | $4.84 : $1 | $5.16 : $1 |
| • number of personnel (full-time equivalents) | 2 | 2 | 2 |
| **Financial:** | | | |
| • net profit | $1000 | $9000 | $17 000 |
| • net cash flow | $39 000 | $17 000 | $22 000 |

## EXERCISES

**2.9**   Identify someone you know who owns an existing small business. Interview the person to prepare a business profile for the person's business. The business profile format should be the same as that shown in Table 2.1.

**2.10**   Prepare a business profile for your own or proposed small business. Use the format shown in Table 2.1.

## QUICK QUIZ

Each of the following multiple-choice items has one correct answer. Select the letter that corresponds with the correct answer.

1.   A business that acquires trading stock to sell to resellers is classified as a:
A. service provider
B. wholesaler
C. retailer
D. manufacturer

2.   The easiest ownership structure to set up and operate under is the:
A. sole trader
B. partnership
C. small company
D. joint venture

3.   The maximum number of partners allowed in a general business partnership is:
A. 2
B. 10
C. 20
D. 100
E. none of the above

4.   The authority responsible for regulating companies is the:
A. Australian Securities and Investments Commission
B. Australian Competition and Consumer Commission
C. Australian Taxation Office
D. Federal Consumer Affairs Bureau

5.   The minimum number of shareholders required to operate a small proprietary company is:
A. 1
B. 2
C. 5
D. 50

6.   Which one of the following ownership structures is recognised by law as a separate legal entity?
A. sole trader
B. partnership
C. company
D. none of the above

7.   Which one of the following statements is correct?
A. A sole trader has limited liability for business debts.

B. A company has limited liability for business debts.

C. Partners have limited liability for partnership debts.

D. Shareholders have limited liability for company debts.

8. Julie Jenson and Mark Mitchell are in partnership together as business consultants. Which of the following proposed business names for the partnership have to be registered?
A. Julie Jenson & Mark Mitchell
B. J. Jenson & M. Mitchell
C. Jenson & Mitchell
D. Jenson, Mitchell & Co.
E. none of the above

9. Objectives are important in business planning because they:
A. determine business goals
B. prioritise business strategies
C. set a direction to follow
D. guarantee achievement of results

10. An objective stated as 'to do my best' is unacceptable because it is not:
A. clear and concise
B. measurable
C. attainable
D. challenging

# The marketing plan

**Objectives**

After studying this chapter, you should be able to:

- define the marketing objectives for an operation
- recognise that the marketing plan determines operational activities
- prepare a marketing plan for any operation
- design a control system to evaluate marketing success.

## REVIEWING THE EXISTING OPERATION

If there is an existing business, you need to know the state and capabilities of your present operation before beginning the marketing plan. This requires a review of your entire operation.

A review of your current operation establishes a starting point from which to develop your business plan logically. The purpose of the review is to:
- determine what resources you have to start with for planning realistic growth
- identify operating strengths and weaknesses for finding out what needs to be improved.

An operational review involves:
- reviewing the physical operation
- reviewing the financial performance of the operation.

### Physical operation review

A comprehensive review of the physical operation will consider all aspects of the business—for example, marketing, production, purchasing and personnel. For each operating function, you should:
- identify the type and quality of resources (e.g. personnel, equipment) in current use
- identify your current business strategies
- identify the current operating procedures in use
- determine the adequacy of existing record systems.

### Financial performance review

A review of financial performance requires you to obtain both past and current financial reports of the business. The three main financial reports on the performance of the operation are:
- the annual income statement (i.e. profit statement)
- the annual statement of cash flows
- the annual balance sheet (i.e. statement of financial position).

The information found in these financial reports should be compared over time and with industry averages to pinpoint strengths and weaknesses in your operation.

**EXERCISES**

3.1   What is the purpose of reviewing an existing operation for business planning?

3.2   What does an operational review mean?

**EXAMPLE**

You extract the following information from your financial reports for the last three years for comparison over time and with the industry average.

|  | Two years ago | Last year | Current year | Industry average |
|---|---|---|---|---|
| **Income statement:** | | | | |
| • sales turnover | $310 000 | $340 000 | $350 000 | $300 000 |
| • gross profit margin | 30% | 30% | 32% | 30% |
| (i.e. gross profit as % of sales) | | | | |
| • net profit | $18 600 | $13 600 | $10 500 | $18 000 |
| **Cash ☒ow statement:** | | | | |
| • net cash flow | $24 600 | $23 700 | $20 400 | $26 400 |
| • cash position—end of year | $8600 | $4200 | $3100 | $6700 |
| **Balance sheet:** | | | | |
| • debt ratio (i.e. debts as % of assets) | 59% | 62% | 65% | 59% |

**Operating strengths**

*Sales*

Sales are growing by an average of 6% each year and are better than the industry average. These results indicate that, overall, marketing strategies are effective.

*Gross profit margin*

The gross profit margin in selling prices has increased in the current year and is better than the industry average. This suggests an improvement in purchase supply terms and the maintenance of sound pricing policies for stock sales.

**Operating weaknesses**

*Net profit*

The net profit of the business has been decreasing each year and has been below the industry average for the last two years. This indicates that profit performance in the business is not being controlled properly. The main reason for the decline in net profit to an unacceptable level is the lack of control of rising operating costs.

*Net cash flows*

The net cash flows of the operation are declining each year and are consistently worse than the industry average. This is reflected in the reducing cash position of the business at the end of each year, which is also worse than the industry average. These problems are due to poor cash flow control systems. Specific reasons could include untimely debtor collections, slow stock turnover, payment of increased operating expenses or increases in owner's drawings.

*Debt ratio*

The level of debt used in the operation, as measured by the debt ratio, has been increasing each year. The present level of debt is significantly above the industry average. The business should not undertake any more borrowings because the existing debt level is excessive.

## SWOT ANALYSIS

Businesses exist in a dynamic environment that is changing continually. Due to the dynamic nature of the operating environment, you need to understand that environment. Information on the operating environment must be collected and analysed so that you can develop objectives and strategies for your operation.

From Figure 3.1, we can see that the operating environment for a business comprises:

- the general business environment (external)
- the specific industry environment (external)
- the existing operation, if applicable (internal).

You should do an analysis of the total operating environment for any business marketing plan. This analysis is sometimes referred to as a SWOT analysis—an analysis of business strengths, weaknesses, opportunities and threats.

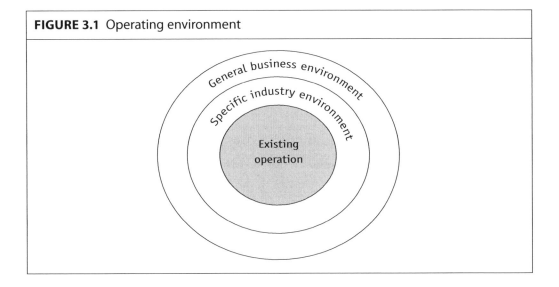

**FIGURE 3.1** Operating environment

The purpose of analysing the internal existing operation (if any) is to find out the strengths and weaknesses of the business. Examine all aspects of your existing business, including marketing, production, purchasing, personnel and finance. The external environment is analysed to identify opportunities and challenges (or threats) for the business. The general business environment includes economic, demographic, socio-cultural, technological, political and legal factors. The industry environment refers to demand and supply conditions.

A SWOT analysis provides a basis for developing your marketing plan. It is examined further later in the chapter.

## GATHERING ENVIRONMENTAL INFORMATION

### Research techniques

Research techniques are used to collect information about the external operating environment for business planning. The worth of any environmental information collected is dependent on it being:

- relevant
- current
- accurate.

Research methods are either primary (gathering information directly from the source) or secondary (collecting information already published). Personal surveys and direct observation are common primary research techniques. Secondary research often involves analysing published quantitative (e.g. statistical) information. It is sometimes called desktop research because the published information already collected only needs to be analysed.

The main research techniques are:

- personal surveys
- direct observation
- desktop research
- database analysis.

#### Personal surveys

Personal surveys (see Table 3.1) are used to collect information about people's attitudes—for example, their likes, dislikes, preferences, opinions and motives. A survey obtains direct responses from people to specific questions relating to your business. It can be conducted by telephone, face to face, via the internet or by mail.

Because it is impractical to survey everyone, samples of the population are randomly surveyed for their responses. A randomly selected sample of a reasonable number of people will give representative views of the entire population. However, convenience samples are easiest (e.g. survey people you know).

The results of a properly conducted survey will tell you what people with defined characteristics want from your kind of business. This information helps you to decide who your customers are and what your business will offer to them.

| **TABLE 3.1** Personal survey (based on a random sample of 100 people in the selected area) |
|---|
| **Respondent characteristics** |
| Sex:　50% male; 50% female<br>Age:　18 to 30 years<br>1.　Do you own a DVD player?<br>　　68%—yes; 32%—no<br>2.　How many DVDs do you hire each week?<br>　　38%—0; 14%—1; 23%—2; 19%—3; 6%—4 or more<br>3.　How much would you pay to hire a DVD?<br>　　31%—$3; 36%—$4; 29%—$5; 4%—$6 or more<br>4.　How far would you travel to a DVD shop?<br>　　76%—0 to 5 km; 16%—6 to 10 km; 8%—11 km or more<br>5.　What do you look for in a DVD hire shop?<br>　　39%—wide range of DVDs; 45%—current releases; 13%—convenient access;<br>　　2%—package deals; 1%—late opening hours<br>6.　What type of DVDs do you prefer?<br>　　45%—drama; 33%—comedy; 15%—horror/thriller; 7%—other |

## Direct observation

Direct observation is an essential research technique. It includes not only visual observation but also talking and listening to people.

Direct observation produces useful information for making marketing decisions on what your business will offer to customers. Information collected by direct observation includes:

- buyer characteristics
- what people are buying
- what competitors are doing
- competitors' strengths and weaknesses
- suitable business locations
- general economic conditions.

## Desktop research

Desktop research involves collecting and analysing published information on the environment. This information is usually statistical, but can also include non-statistical information such as published surveys and media reports. A lot of this information is now available online via the internet.

As with any information, if statistical information is to be useful, it must be relevant, current and accurate. A wide range of published statistical information is available to the business researcher.

### Database analysis

Analysis of any customer database maintained may help you determine future buying patterns of past customers. The information in a customer database is used to predict likely buyer behaviour based on previous purchases.

## Sources of statistics

### Australian Bureau of Statistics (ABS)

The ABS (<www.abs.gov.au>) is the main source of available published statistical information. It is the official statistical reporting agency of the Commonwealth government and collects statistics on business, the population (via periodic national census) and the economy Australia wide.

The types of statistical information relevant to a small business researcher that are available from the ABS include the following:

- *population statistics* for chosen areas showing:
  - population numbers
  - population projections
  - population characteristics such as gender, ethnic background, income level, education level, age and occupational status
- *industry statistics* for selected industries in chosen areas showing:
  - the number of competitors and suppliers
  - competitor and supplier characteristics such as number of employees, sales turnover, expense ratios and profit ratios
- *household expenditure statistics* for chosen areas showing:
  - household characteristics by sex, family size, employment status, income level, education level and occupancy status
  - household expenditure patterns
  - household expenditure components
- *housing statistics* for chosen areas showing:
  - rate of housing construction
  - housing types
  - housing costs
  - nature of occupancy
- *foreign trade statistics* showing:
  - values of different commodities exported to selected countries
  - values of different commodities imported from selected countries
- *economic performance indicators* that measure the performance of the general economy, including:
  - average weekly earnings
  - unemployment rates

- consumer price index (CPI—an inflation measure)
- levels of household expenditure
- number of new car registrations
- national accounts such as gross national product, gross national income and gross national expenditure.

The ABS has information consultancies in all state capitals to provide advice to users on the type of information available and how it can best be accessed.

The following examples show how statistical information can be used to obtain market information.

## EXAMPLE 1

You are hoping to establish a child-care centre somewhere in your city. The ABS can give you a report showing:
- the proportion of young children in particular areas selected
- which of these areas have the highest number of births
- population projections by age for each selected area
- housing construction activity for each selected area.

This information will enable you to make an informed decision on where to locate your business.

## EXAMPLE 2

You are a shoe retailer stocking a wide range of shoes for men, women and children. Recently, there has been an increase in the number of competitors in your area. You are considering selling imported leather shoes and handbags for women with medium to high incomes.

You need to determine whether there is a market for selling these products to customers within an 8 kilometre radius of your store. The ABS can give you a report showing:
- the population number in the chosen area
- the age, sex, incomes and occupations of the population in the chosen area
- projected population growth by number and characteristics for the chosen area
- values and sources of leather footwear and handbag imports.

This information will enable you to determine whether there are enough women with medium to high incomes in the region to change your product range.

### Private research organisations

Private research organisations, which are businesses themselves, can also provide useful statistical information. For example, RP Data provides free suburb demographic profiles at its website <www.myrp.com.au>.

### Industry associations

Industry associations often collect statistical and other business information for their business members, as well as giving management advice. There are industry associations for most types of small business activity. A list of various national industry associations is found at the Australian Chamber of Commerce and Industry website, <www.acci.asn.au>. You can also check the list of business and professional organisations for the relevant association in the *Yellow Pages* telephone directory (<www.yellowpages.com.au>). Alternatively, use an internet search engine like *Google* <www.google.com.au> to identify any association for your industry.

### Government agencies

Many government agencies, federal and state, produce statistical and other information useful for businesses, including the following:

- Austrade (<www.austrade.gov.au>) for overseas trade statistics
- Tourism Research Australia (<www.ret.gov.au>) for tourism statistics
- Australian Bureau of Agricultural and Resource Economics and Sciences (<www.daff.gov.au/abares>) for information and forecasts on commodities
- Australian Government Treasury (<www.treasury.gov.au>) for federal budget information and economic data
- Reserve Bank of Australia (<www.rba.gov.au>) for economic performance data
- Australian Customs Service (<www.customs.gov.au>) for information on importing, exporting and customs duties
- Australian Quarantine and Inspection Service (<www.daff.gov.au/aqis>) for import and export restrictions
- Bureau of Meteorology (<www.bom.gov.au>) for weather and climate statistics.

### Local councils

Local councils often publish demographic profiles and other statistical information relating to their local communities. Local community information may also be available on local council websites.

### Banks

The major banks publish statistics and forecasts related to interest rates or the performance of the economy using their own research. Some banks also release results of their own surveys of general economic confidence levels in the community. This information is available online by visiting a bank's website.

### Business publications

There are many good commercial publishers of magazines, journals and reference books, which contain useful current statistics and other business information.

### News media
The news media frequently report current statistics as well as other information of interest to business.

### Libraries
Many public libraries carry statistical publications and other business publications.

### Educational institutions
Educational bodies such as universities and colleges frequently research business conditions. Research findings are often published as statistics or survey results.

### Telephone directories
The *Yellow Pages* (<www.yellowpages.com.au>) directory has useful information on competitors and suppliers, as most businesses advertise in it. By checking under the relevant business industry heading, you can make a list of the competitors and suppliers to investigate further.

**EXERCISES**

| | |
|---|---|
| **3.4** | What are the three criteria used to judge the worth of any environmental information collected? |
| **3.5** | What is the difference between primary research and secondary research? |
| **3.6** | Briefly describe three research techniques used to collect information. |
| **3.7** | Refer to the personal survey in Table 3.1. Based on the information shown in the survey, what business decisions would you make about what to offer the customers surveyed? |
| **3.8** | If you are researching a particular area, what kinds of statistics can you get from the ABS for your chosen area? |
| **3.9** | List five sources of published statistical information. |
| **3.10** | Investigate five of the internet websites provided within this chapter. What specific information can be collected from each site that might be useful for preparing your business plan? |

## MARKETING OBJECTIVES
Marketing is about giving customers what they want in order to create sales. This requires the design of a business offer to satisfy targeted customers—the basis of any marketing plan.

The management aim for the marketing function of your operation should be to maximise sales. Therefore, your main marketing objective should be expressed as a measurable sales value (or volume or number of units sold) for each year of your plan. As for any business objective, your sales target is designed to achieve your business goal. The sales objective should also satisfy the criteria for an acceptable objective (see Chapter 2). Anticipated annual sales growth should at least equal the expected annual inflation rate. Generally, annual sales growth of 10% (or more) per annum is considered to be good growth.

You need to collect and analyse information on the operating environment, including your own operation, to define your sales objectives. Factors to consider when setting sales objectives that produce desired profit outcomes include:

- the business you are in
- the area and size of the total market (in kilometre and sales dollar terms)
- the extent of the competition (in sales dollar terms)
- the operating capability of your business (in sales dollar terms)
- the operating costs of your business.

Any business offer made to targeted customers should be intended to achieve your sales objectives.

The following example illustrates how to set a sales objective for your business.

## EXAMPLE

Assume that you intend starting up a hot bread shop in an area. You want to set an achievable sales objective for your operation. The following factors are considered in setting your sales target.

*Area and size of total market*

You define your market area as being within a 5 kilometre radius of the business location. ABS statistics obtained for the area show that there are 1600 households in the area. Statistics also highlight that the average annual consumption of bread per household is $912 p.a.

The total annual sales potential of the local market is therefore estimated to be:

1600 households × $912 p.a. = $1 459 200 p.a.

*Extent of competition*

You identify two direct competitors operating in the market area. No competitor has a particular location advantage. Competitor 1 has two full-time employees; Competitor 2 has five full-time employees.

Using current industry average statistics for hot bread shops, you estimate the annual sales turnover of each competitor, based on the number of full-time employees:

| Competitor | Industry average turnover |
|---|---|
| Competitor 1 | $160 000 (for two full-time employees) |
| Competitor 2 | $375 000 (for five full-time employees) |
| Competitor total sales | $535 000 p.a. |

With direct competitors' sales of $535 000 p.a. in a potential market size of $1 459 200 p.a., you conclude that there is room to operate in this market.

*Operating capability*
You intend to employ three full-time employees. Using the industry average statistics obtained of sales turnover based on the number of full-time employees, you estimate your annual sales turnover potential to be $240 000 p.a.

*Operating costs*
Current industry average statistics for a business with three full-time employees indicate that a net profit margin of 13% can be expected. The estimated profit return on the sales turnover expected is therefore:

$$240\ 000 \times 13\% = \$31\ 200 \text{ p.a.}$$

You conclude that this is an acceptable profit return.

*Sales objectives*
You decide to set a sales objective of $240 000 for Year 1. The target is achievable because it is less than the total sales potential of the market, it is within the business's operating capability and gives an acceptable profit return. You also set achievable sales targets for Years 2 and 3 by allowing for sales growth of 10% p.a. Your sales objectives are summarised as follows.

|  | **Year 1** | **Year 2** | **Year 3** |
|---|---|---|---|
| Sales objectives | $240 000 | $264 000 | $290 000 |

## MARKETING PLAN GUIDELINES

The marketing plan should be the first plan prepared because it determines the nature of your business activities.

The marketing plan describes relevant market information obtained, as well as your intended marketing strategies to achieve sales objectives for the period. An outline of the 'marketing plan' section of the business plan is shown in Table 3.2.

## B.1 ENVIRONMENTAL TRENDS

The purpose of analysing the general business environment is to identify favourable and unfavourable changes or trends occurring in the general environment that are relevant for your business. These environmental trends suggest opportunities and challenges (or threats) for the business, which in turn will influence the selection of marketing strategies.

A comprehensive examination of the general business environment is required—a process known as 'environmental scanning'. The factors to examine in the general business environment are discussed below.

| **TABLE 3.2** Marketing plan outline |
| --- |
| **Section B. Marketing plan** |
| **B.1 Environmental trends**<br>(List favourable and unfavourable trends identified in the general environment that could affect the business.) |
| **B.2 Industry conditions**<br>(Briefly describe existing (and likely) demand and supply conditions in the industry for your products or services.) |
| **B.3 Products/Services**<br>(Describe the range and expected contributions of products or services you are going to sell. Emphasise any unique or superior features of the product or service.) |
| **B.4 Competitors**<br>(Show details of likely competitors, including their strengths and weaknesses.) |
| **B.5 Target customers**<br>(Describe who your target customers are, what they want and where they will be found.) |
| **B.6 Marketing strategies**<br>(Briefly explain the marketing methods to be used to satisfy target customers and maintain competitiveness.) |
| **B.7 Marketing controls**<br>(Show how and when you will measure the effectiveness of your marketing methods.) |

## Economic factors

Most businesses are affected by the general level of economic or business activity, which fluctuates from booms to recessions (see Chapter 1).

You need to know the current level of general economic activity by knowing where the economy is and where it is heading in the business cycle. Economic activity is measured by economic performance indicators (see Table 1.3). Important economic indicators include the level of consumer and retail spending, interest rate levels, the consumer price index and the rate of growth in gross national product.

Most performance indicators, as well as future projections, are available from the ABS. Current indicators are also frequently published in the news media and business publications. You can also gauge existing and future levels of economic activity by listening and talking to people to determine their confidence levels and expectations for the future.

## Demographic factors

Demographic factors include population size and characteristics. Growth or projected growth in the total population number is a favourable trend because it means an increase in the number of potential customers for all businesses. Changes occurring in population characteristics such as age, gender, ethnic background, family size, income levels, occupations and education levels can also suggest business opportunities within particular customer groups.

A notable demographic trend occurring in Australia is the ageing of the population. Demographic figures indicate an increase in the proportion of the population aged over 65.

- 1901—4% of population was over 65 years
- 1981—10% of population was over 65 years
- 2024—20% of population expected to be over 65 years.

This trend presents business opportunities for the development of retirement villages and aged care centres, and for the provision of health-care services.

Demographic statistics for chosen areas are available from the ABS, local councils or private research organisations like RP Data.

## Sociocultural factors

An examination of sociocultural factors helps to understand the changes occurring in the attitudes, tastes, behaviour and preferences of the general population.

One cultural trend is an increasing interest in health and fitness. Because people are eating healthier foods due to better nutritional knowledge, there may be good business opportunities for fruit, vegetable and seafood retailers. Another cultural trend concerns people's attitudes to education. People are learning more and taking advantage of increasing education and training possibilities. This could mean more opportunities for computer and stationery sellers as well as for training businesses.

Other trends that reflect changes in people's attitudes include:

- higher divorce rates
- lower marriage rates and marriage at later ages
- a decline in religion
- growing environmental awareness
- earlier retirements
- changes in the roles of males and females.

Information on cultural trends can be collected by direct observation or by desktop research, such as analysing statistics or reading news media reports.

## Technological factors

Technology refers to the current state of knowledge and technical know-how used in business activities. Technological changes can affect businesses in different ways. The effects of technological change can include:

- improving product and service quality
- making products obsolete

- improving raw materials and production processes
- increasing business efficiency through time savings
- making the technology itself more affordable.

Rapid technological changes are currently occurring in communications and information processing. The growing use of the internet presents worldwide opportunities for many businesses that embrace online technology in their business dealings. On the other hand, the internet presents a major competitive challenge for those businesses that do not adopt the technology. Book retailers, for example, face challenges competing with online booksellers who can sell their products worldwide. Similarly, businesses such as travel agents face challenges keeping market share where customers can deal directly with suppliers via the internet.

Technological developments can be identified by direct observation and desktop research, such as reading current media reports and business publications.

## Political and legal factors

Knowing the attitudes and policies of political and government regulatory bodies could help you to determine where opportunities and challenges exist. For example, adverse attitudes and policies of public bodies towards an industry would probably deter you from starting a business in that industry.

You should also know what taxes and laws apply to businesses, and whether any changes are likely. For example, a challenge for many businesses is the goods and services tax (GST). Specific laws to investigate include consumer protection laws, environmental protection laws, industrial relations laws and industrial awards, as well as workplace safety laws. Too much regulation could diminish the value of an otherwise good business idea.

Information about relevant political and legal factors can be collected by desktop research (media reports and publications) and by getting expert advice.

## Natural factors

Primary production businesses, or businesses supplied from the primary sector, need to consider natural factors such as weather patterns, climatic changes and the availability of natural resources (e.g. water).

Good sources of information on the natural environment are government-run agricultural and meteorological agencies.

---

**EXERCISE**

3.11    After examining all factors in the general business environment, list six
environmental trends that suggest either an opportunity or a challenge for your
business.

## B.2 INDUSTRY CONDITIONS

After identifying general environmental trends, next examine the specific industry for your business. An examination of industry conditions means looking at existing (and likely) demand and supply conditions in your industry. Like general environmental trends, industry conditions influence the selection of your marketing strategies.

### Demand conditions

Demand conditions refer to market conditions. The factors affecting demand conditions in an industry are:

- the nature of buyers
- the market size
- the demand patterns occurring.

#### Nature of buyers

Find out what kinds of people are buying your goods or services in the market. Also identify any new kinds of customer likely to emerge in the future.

Buyers can be broadly characterised according to age, occupation and gender. Buyers identified, for example, could include:

- 25–40-year-old professionals
- 15–25-year-old females
- 55-year-old or over retirees.

The detailed categorisation of customers is examined under 'Target Customers' later in the chapter.

Information about which people are buyers is best obtained by direct observation or by random surveys of the total population.

#### Market size

Determine the full extent of the market area where potential buyers are to be found. The boundaries of the area could be defined by suburb, city, region, state or whatever.

Next, determine how many buyers there are in the defined area. Use ABS statistics to estimate how many people with the required characteristics (e.g. 25–40-year-old professionals) live in the chosen area. Statistical projections should also be considered.

#### Demand patterns

Also determine what demand patterns for the goods or services are occurring across the industry. Is demand increasing or decreasing?

Measures of demand include published annual statistics showing sales or consumption levels for the product or service. Specific statistics for your goods or services may be available from the ABS or your industry association.

**EXAMPLE**

The following industry statistics are obtained from the ABS measuring nationwide demand for a particular product.

| Demand measure | Last year | Current year | Next year (projected) |
|---|---|---|---|
| • Nationwide product sales | $400 million p.a. | $720 million p.a. | $790 million p.a. |
| • Nationwide product sales per head | $21 p.a. | $38 p.a. | $42 p.a. |
| • Nationwide consumption per head | 220 units p.a. | 395 units p.a. | 420 units p.a. |

These statistics indicate current and likely growth in nationwide demand for the product, although the rate of growth is expected to slow down next year.

## Supply conditions

The factors affecting supply conditions in an industry are:
- the extent of competition
- the availability of supplies
- the existence of entry barriers.

### Extent of competition

Determine the nature and extent of competition to ascertain whether there is room to operate in the industry. Find out how many competitors exist and who they are.

Competitors can be identified by direct observation and using directories like the *Yellow Pages*. The ABS also produces reports on the number of competitors in a chosen area. Indicators of industry profitability and sales turnover can be obtained from the ABS, private statistical organisations or the relevant industry association.

**EXAMPLE**

A study of competition could reveal:
- there are few competitors
- each competitor has been long established
- each competitor has a history of growth
- there are attractive profit margins and sales turnover in the industry.

This finding would indicate there is probably room to operate in the industry. The existence of long-established businesses with a history of growth is usually a good indicator of business viability.

### Availability of supplies

Evaluate the current and likely availability of any physical supplies required to operate a business in the industry. Shortages or inaccessibility of supplies can affect the ability of the business to compete successfully. Physical supplies could include raw materials, component parts, trading stock or job materials.

Use the *Yellow Pages* or internet to identify suppliers and contact them directly for information.

### Entry barriers

Identify the existence of any entry barriers to operate in the industry. Entry barriers determine the likelihood of new competitors entering the industry. An entry barrier observed could be an existing business that dominates the industry, making it difficult for a new business to compete successfully. Alternatively, there could be legal barriers (e.g. licensing requirements), high start-up costs or technical know-how requirements restricting the entry of new competitors. Information on legal barriers can be obtained from the relevant industry, association or consumer protection authority (see Table 2.6).

**EXERCISE**

3.12   Begin by identifying a single product or service you intend to sell. Prepare a profile of industry conditions for the product or service identified. Consider each of the following.

Demand conditions:
- Who are buyers?
- What is the market size?
- What demand patterns are occurring?

Supply conditions:
- What is the extent of competition?
- What is the availability of supplies?
- What entry barriers exist?

## B.3 PRODUCTS/SERVICES

Describe the main products or services your business is going to sell. Show the product or service range for each planned year as well as the expected contribution (percentage) of each product or service to the total sales forecast.

It is useful to construct a product/service mix table (see Table 3.3). A product/service mix table describes the intended product or service range and the expected contribution of each product to total sales for each planned annual period.

A fundamental issue to decide when planning what product or service range to offer for sale is whether to diversify or specialise—that is, whether to offer a wide product or service range or a concentrated range.

| **TABLE 3.3** Product/service mix table | | | |
|---|---|---|---|
| **Product/service range** | **Year 1**<br>**%** | **Year 2**<br>**%** | **Year 3**<br>**%** |
| Product A | 42 | 40 | 38 |
| Product B | 36 | 38 | 38 |
| Product C | 20 | 21 | 23 |
| Product D | 2 | 1 | 1 |
| **Totals** | **100** | **100** | **100** |

A wide product range of complementary or diverse products encourages custom-ers to buy. A wide product range is convenient for customers and caters to a wide range of tastes. For example, a retail florist decides to sell a wide range of complemen-tary products. These products could include toys, chocolates, gifts and cards as well as conventional floral lines. A wide product range, however, usually requires more business resources.

In contrast, a narrow product range may be advantageous in some circumstances. A specialised narrow product range may be justified if you intend selling to an untapped specialised segment of the total market—known as a niche market. Niche market customers are attracted to businesses that they perceive address their specialised needs, for example a clothing retailer specialising in selling casual menswear for larger men and boys. Specialised product ranges have restricted market appeal, however. They also present a business risk if demand suddenly falls: the business has no other products to sell.

Also explain any unique or superior features of your products or services to be sold.

## EXERCISES

3.13   Evaluate the relative merits of 'product diversification' and 'product specialisation'.

3.14   Construct a product/service mix table (see Table 3.3) showing the range and mix of products or services you intend offering for sale to customers in the first year of operation.

3.15   Explain any unique or superior features of the products or services you intend to offer for sale.

## B.4 COMPETITORS

Identify the main competitors to your business. Competitors can be identified by checking the *Yellow Pages* or by direct observation.

Next, gather details on each competitor by directly observing the competitor, visiting the competitor's website and asking around. Show in your marketing plan the following details for each major competitor:

- the name
- the address
- the size or scale of operation (in terms of the number of personnel)
- the age of the competitor
- the current strengths of the competitor
- the current weaknesses of the competitor.

The inclusion of strengths and weaknesses for each competitor helps you put together competitive strategies when designing your business offer. Knowing the weaknesses of your competitors will enable you to establish competitive advantages to attract customers away from the competition.

**EXERCISES**

3.16   Why should you find out about the strengths and weaknesses of your main competitors?

3.17   Identify two main competitors in your industry. What are the strengths and weaknesses of each competitor?

## B.5 TARGET CUSTOMERS

The first strategic decision in any marketing plan is to select customers to target with a business offer. This requires you first to allocate potential customers into distinct customer groups or segments. Next, target customer groups are selected from the various segments identified.

### Market segmentation

The process of market (or customer) segmentation is applied to analyse the potential customers in the market for your goods or services. Potential customers could be new ones or from an established base of existing customers. Market segmentation involves categorising potential customers into distinct customer groups or market segments. A detailed customer profile is constructed for each customer group identified. Each customer group will have its own distinct set of common characteristics and relevant wants.

The process of market segmentation is necessary because most industries have a diverse range of customers. Because of limited business resources, it is not possible to design a business offer that appeals to every different customer group. You need to target particular groups with your marketing.

Market segmentation or customer grouping involves the following steps.

*Step one*   Separate the total potential customers into distinct groups with their own sets of common characteristics.

Each customer group can be defined by the following characteristics.

**Personal characteristics:**

| | |
|---|---|
| geographic | suburban, regional, urban, country, town or rural dweller |
| demographic | age, gender, ethnic background, family unit, marital status |
| psychographic | lifestyle, tastes, personality, attitudes, values, motives, preferences |
| socioeconomic | social class, occupation, income level, education level |

**Likely responses to product:**

| | |
|---|---|
| volume of use | high, medium or low |
| loyalty | high, medium or low |

*Step two*   Give each group an identifying label.

*Step three*   Determine the relevant wants of each identified customer group.

Analyse each customer group to determine what it wants from businesses in your industry.

Information for customer grouping can be obtained by directly observing customers in your industry to identify their characteristics and relevant wants.

## Target segments

Choose target customer groups from the various customer groups identified in your market segmentation. There is no limit to how many customer groups you can choose to target, as long as your business resources are sufficient to reach each of them.

Use the following criteria to choose target customer groups from the customer groups you have identified.

- Can the customer group be reached—i.e. is the group accessible?
- Is the customer group viable—i.e. is the group large enough and potentially profitable?
- How does the customer group differ from other groups—i.e. are there any special features of the customer group that require a unique business offer or that may exclude other customer groups?
- Will you have sufficient business resources to reach the customer group?

You can choose target customers by directly observing customer groups that buy in your market. You simply apply the above criteria to choose desired customer groups to sell to. Alternatively, you can choose target customer groups by personally surveying different market segments. After applying the above criteria, you can choose as target groups those segments that returned the best survey results.

Construct a detailed profile showing distinguishing personal characteristics and relevant wants for each chosen target customer group. The more you know about your target customers, the better understanding you will have of what these customers will want from your business.

Also define the geographic area in which your customers will be found and their numbers. Market areas will depend on what business resources are available. Boundaries are limited to those areas you can reach with your business offer. Use population statistics from the ABS to find out the existing and projected numbers of target customers (with the required personal characteristics) in your chosen area.

Before designing the marketing strategies that comprise your business offer, you need to understand fully:

- who your target customers are
- what your target customers want
- where your target customers are located
- how many target customers there are.

A thorough understanding of target customers is necessary because they are the focus of your marketing strategies.

### EXAMPLE

Your proposed business is a fitness centre. After conducting random surveys and making direct observations, you identify as your customers the following customer groups (market segments) and their relevant wants.

**Target customer group 1: Good-time group**

- *Common characteristics*: local area dweller, aged 18–25 years, single, outgoing and fun-loving, active and energetic, impressionable, not practically minded, adventurous, students or working part time, low incomes.
- *Relevant wants*: a social atmosphere, a variety of group activities to participate in, a central location near public transport, cheap prices and late opening hours.

**Target customer group 2: Trendy group**

- *Common characteristics*: local area dweller, aged 25–40 years, single or couples, trendy lifestyle, well presented, fashionable, impressionable, professional types, well educated, middle to high incomes, live for the present.
- *Relevant wants*: to look good and be noticed, style and quality, convenience and safe parking, early opening hours.

**Target customer group 3: Business group**

- *Common characteristics*: local area dweller, aged 40–60 years, married with families, predominantly male, busy lifestyle, business executive types, well educated, conservative, high incomes.

- *Relevant wants*: to keep fit, comfort and amenities, privacy, convenience and flexible opening hours.

**Target customer group 4: Retiree group**
- *Common characteristics*: local area dweller, aged over 50 years, married or single, slow moving, independent, retired, moderate to medium incomes, old-fashioned, conservative.
- *Relevant wants*: to maintain mobility, ease of access, guidance and a pleasant atmosphere.

You obtain the following population statistics and projections from the ABS on the number of target customers in your chosen market area.

| Area—My area | | | | |
|---|---|---|---|---|
| | **Current year** | | **10 years ahead (projected)** | |
| **Customer group** | **No.** | **% of total** | **No.** | **% of total** |
| Good-time group (18–25) | 5 827 | 14 | 6 047 | 13 |
| Trendy group (25–40) | 7 341 | 18 | 8 842 | 19 |
| Business group (40–60) | 8 626 | 21 | 9 790 | 21 |
| Retiree group (over 50) | 6 243 | 15 | 7 459 | 16 |
| **Total population** | **41 622** | **100** | **46 617** | **100** |

## EXERCISES

**3.18**  What is market segmentation?

**3.19**  Why should a business choose target customers to market to?

**3.20**  Identify one likely target customer group for each of the following businesses:
- a takeaway food shop
- a sporting goods retailer
- an electrical goods wholesaler
- a domestic cleaning service
- a tent manufacturer.

Prepare a detailed profile for each target customer group identified, showing distinctive characteristics and relevant wants.

**3.21**  (a) Who will be your target customers?
(b) What do they want from businesses in your industry?
(c) Where are they located?
(d) What do you estimate their number to be in your chosen area?

## B.6 MARKETING STRATEGIES

Marketing strategies are the components of your business offer or business proposition. They are what your business intends to offer customers (see Figure 3.2). Target customers

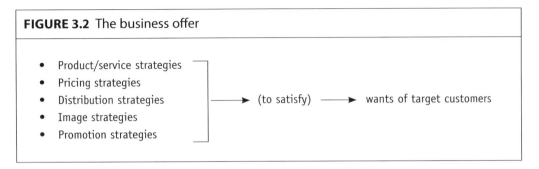

FIGURE 3.2 The business offer

- Product/service strategies
- Pricing strategies
- Distribution strategies
- Image strategies
- Promotion strategies

(to satisfy) → wants of target customers

are the focus of your marketing strategies. Marketing strategies are designed to give target customers what they want. If you give customers what they want, you will make sales as well as produce satisfied customers, who will return and tell others about the business.

To decide what your business will offer target customers, you must be both sensitive and responsive to what your customers want. That is, you must be customer-oriented when designing your marketing strategies.

Each marketing strategy should be designed in the following order:
- first, product/service strategies      [Products]
- second, pricing strategies      [Prices]
- third, distribution strategies      [Place]
- fourth, image strategies      [Personality]
- fifth, promotion strategies.      [Promotions].

The coordinated combination of the above strategies is sometimes known as the *marketing mix* of a business.

## Product/service strategies

### Products
Product decisions are intended to satisfy the wants of target customer groups. Relevant physical product decisions to consider could include:
- product range—what different types of product to offer
- product mix—how much of each product to offer
- product design/style—what particular product designs/styles to offer
- product quality—what quality of product to offer
- product brands—what product brand names to offer
- product returns—policies for returns, for example exchanges or refunds
- product packaging—what type of packaging and labelling to offer
- product warranties—what to do if defective products are returned
- product guarantees—what assurances of product quality to offer.

## Services

There are two aspects of service to consider when designing a business offer:

- service products—the services offered for sale to customers
- product services—the total servicing of customers—that is, customer service.

'Service products' refer to any services to be offered for sale to customers—for example, computer consulting. Such services are the products of the business. Service product decisions to be made by service-selling businesses include:

- service range—the different types of service to offer
- service mix—how much of each service to offer
- service quality—what quality of service to offer (see Table 3.4)
- service guarantees—what assurances of service quality to offer.

**TABLE 3.4** Service qualities

| Service quality | Specific factors to consider |
| --- | --- |
| Presentation | Grooming, cleanliness, attire |
| Expertise | Product knowledge, technical training, technical experience, record-keeping skills |
| Reliability | Punctuality, promptness, time management, scheduling |
| Accessibility | Telephone, face to face, mail, facsimile, internet, email |
| Communications | Interpersonal skills, listening skills, dispute resolution, customer relations skills, questioning skills |
| Attitudes | Care, concern, attentiveness, friendliness, helpfulness, courtesy, manners, self-confidence, calmness, eye contact |

'Product services', or customer service, is the other aspect of services to consider. Some form of customer service is offered by every business. Customer servicing occurs in every dealing a business has with its customers or potential customers. Types of customer service that could be offered by a business are as follows:

| Pre-sales service | After-sales service |
| --- | --- |
| • answering inquiries | • complimentary gift-wrapping |
| • providing information | • installations |
| • quotations | • deliveries |
| • order taking | • backup advice |
| • order acknowledgement | • ongoing advice |
| • pre-arrival courtesy calls | • billing |
| • responding to requests | • regular follow-up |

| Pre-sales service | After-sales service |
| --- | --- |
| • personal selling | • answering queries |
| • answering objections | • repairs |
| • replying to correspondence/calls | • handling complaints |
| • market surveys | • customer satisfaction surveys |
| • reminders | • acknowledgements—for example, birthday cards |

Good customer relations help sell the business. Design customer service strategies to foster the best possible customer relations. Begin by identifying what customer services are to be offered by your business. Next, determine what quality of service (see Table 3.4) to offer customers. Customer service strategies should be designed to give target customers what they want.

The internet also enables a business to deliver better customer service. By maintaining a website presence, your business is always open to existing and potential customers. People can visit your business website at any time to find out information about the operation. An informative website will satisfy many general business inquiries without having to commit staff for servicing. Similarly, customers can also make bookings or place orders online.

The provision of superior customer service is one effective way a small business can successfully compete with a larger one.

### Products/markets

To plan sales growth, existing businesses must consider product/market strategies. Four basic strategy options to consider to increase sales are:
- *market penetration*—increasing sales (by offering more products/services) to existing customers or finding new customers in the same market area
- *product development*—modifying existing products in some way, for example improving quality
- *market extension*—offering existing products to a wider market area
- *diversification*—offering a wider range of products to an existing market area.

## Pricing strategies

You can determine pricing strategies when you know what products or services are going to be sold to customers. Pricing decisions must appeal to target customers. When designing your pricing strategies, recognise that small businesses are rarely price leaders in an industry; they are more likely to be price followers.

There are five aspects to consider when planning pricing:
- base prices
- credit terms
- credit mix
- payment forms
- discount policies.

## Base prices

There are various factors to consider when setting base prices for your goods or services:

- marketing objectives
- operating costs
- market demand
- customer attitudes
- product uniqueness
- legal constraints
- competitors' prices
- competitors' reactions.

There are various pricing methods to choose from:

- stock costs plus mark-up pricing
- full cost recovery plus mark-up pricing
- going rate or competitive pricing
- suppliers' recommended pricing.

Pricing goods or services at competitive rates is generally recommended. Competitive prices should be high enough to return an acceptable profit margin and low enough to appeal to your target customers.

## Credit terms

Decide on any standard credit terms to offer approved customers. Credit terms should be based on what is normal practice in the industry—for example, fourteen or 30 days. For any long-term projects, the policy should be to seek progressive payments during the course of the work.

## Credit mix

If credit is offered, decide what proportion of sales will be credit. Excessive credit sales can expose the business to potential cash flow problems. Generally, credit sales should not exceed 30% of total sales for any period, and should be restricted during economic downturns.

## Payment forms

Decide on what are acceptable forms of payment from customers. Payment forms include cash, cheques, money orders, credit cards, debit cards, prepaid gift vouchers, e-cash systems, EFTPOS, BPay and direct electronic funds transfers. Be aware that different merchant charges and bank charges may be associated with various payment types.

### Discount policies

After setting base prices, determine what discount policies to adopt to reward buyers. Various kinds of discount to consider are:

- trade discounts—discounts to resellers
- quantity discounts—discounts to bulk buyers
- loyalty discounts—discounts to regular customers
- promotional discounts—discounts associated with promotional campaigns
- cash discounts—discounts for prompt payment of accounts, for example 2% if paid within seven days
- survey participation discounts—discounts provided as incentives for responses to customer satisfaction surveys.

Any discount rates adopted should ensure that profitable prices are maintained.

## Distribution strategies

Distribution decisions are necessary for determining how to get your products or services to customers. That is, distribution is concerned with how the products or services of the business will reach customers. Distribution relates to business availability as well as to delivering products or services to customers. Your distribution strategies must appeal to target customers.

There are four aspects to consider when planning distribution strategies:

- business location
- opening times
- deliveries
- channels of distribution.

### Business location

Unless an existing location is in use, select a suitable business location for access by customers. Any business location must be convenient for customers. Ideally, the location should be in the centre of the geographic area where your customers are. Position is a key decision for retailers who require exposed and accessible locations to attract customers. Any relevant legal requirements (e.g. local council approvals and permits) must be complied with for any location selected.

### Opening times

Determine when the business location will be available to customers. Decide:

- what days of the week to open
- what the daily hours of opening will be
- whether to open on public holidays.
  Scheduled opening times should appeal to target customers.

### Deliveries

Delivery decisions will be required where your goods or services are to be delivered direct to buyers. Delivery decisions to consider include:

- what mode of delivery to use (e.g. road transport, rail, air, mail, internet)
- whose vehicles are to be used (e.g. couriers, freighters, own vehicle)
- how deliveries are to be scheduled
- how often to deliver
- what to charge for deliveries.

### Channels of distribution

There are various channels to consider for distributing your goods or services to customers. There are direct distribution methods to customers as well as indirect ones through intermediaries (see Figure 3.3).

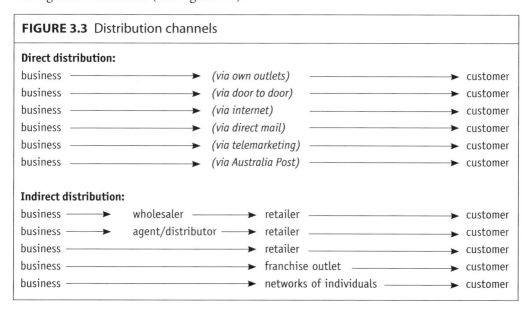

**FIGURE 3.3** Distribution channels

**Direct distribution:**

| business | → | (via own outlets) | → | customer |
| business | → | (via door to door) | → | customer |
| business | → | (via internet) | → | customer |
| business | → | (via direct mail) | → | customer |
| business | → | (via telemarketing) | → | customer |
| business | → | (via Australia Post) | → | customer |

**Indirect distribution:**

| business | → | wholesaler | → | retailer | → | customer |
| business | → | agent/distributor | → | retailer | → | customer |
| business | → | | | retailer | → | customer |
| business | → | | | franchise outlet | → | customer |
| business | → | | | networks of individuals | → | customer |

Your choice of channels of distribution will depend on factors such as the nature of the product, the market area and distribution costs.

Where multiple distribution methods are adopted, decisions have to be made about distribution intensity—that is, how much emphasis is to be placed on each channel.

The choice of intermediaries for indirect distribution will depend on factors such as geography and management ability.

## Image strategies

Decide how you want your business to look to customers. Personality or business image refers to the visual characteristics or appearance of your business. Business image creates an impression in the minds of your customers based on what they see of your business. Your business should project an image that attracts your target customers. For example, food sellers should present an image of cleanliness, and professional advisers should convey an image of success. Today, businesses that present an image of being 'green' and 'environmentally conscious' may also appeal to many customers.

Specific image themes to adopt to appeal to target customers include being upmarket, prestigious, professional, Australian, ethnic, nautical, trendy, healthy, discounters and so on. The following example illustrates what can be done to project a desired business image.

**EXAMPLE**

You operate a conventional retail menswear store. You decide to project the image of an outback clothing store. To convey the new image, you intend to do the following:

- trade under the registered name of 'The Outback Gear Store'
- adopt a registered logo showing an Australian symbol
- rearrange the appearance of the shopfront into an Australian colonial general store with a verandah
- redecorate the inside of the shop with Australiana pictures and displays, and paint the walls a sandy colour
- fit the shop out with old-style Australian colonial farm furniture and memorabilia
- offer a range of products associated with Australian bushwear such as moleskin pants, oilskin coats and elastic-sided boots
- use products with Australiana-style packaging
- dress personnel in neat outback gear
- train staff to use Australian mannerisms and words
- redesign stationery to use the new business name and logo
- design advertising that uses Australian-style expressions.

## Promotion strategies

You need to make your business offer known to customers to create sales. Choose promotional methods to communicate your business offer to target customers. The purpose of promotion is to inform customers of what your business has to offer. The most effective promotional methods will make contact with the largest number of target customers. The success of promotions must be regularly measured and evaluated.

The combination of promotion methods adopted by the business is known as the promotion mix.

The main ways to promote the business are as follows.

### *Advertising*

Advertising refers to any promotion that is paid for (see Table 3.5).

| **TABLE 3.5** Advertising forms | |
|---|---|
| • Window displays | • *Yellow Pages* |
| • Stock displays | • Sponsorships |
| • Newspapers (local and metropolitan) | • Local directories |
| • Trade publications (e.g. trade directories) | • Uniform badges |
| • Radio (commercial or community) | • Internet website |
| • Television (free-to-air or pay) | • Videos |
| • Outdoor signs (e.g. bus shelters, billboards, posters) | • Cinemas/drive-in theatres |
| • Outside and window signs | • Samples |
| • Brochures, pamphlets or fliers | • Giveaways (e.g. calendars) or gifts |
| • Direct mail | • Trade exhibits |
| • Stationery | • Information seminars |
| • Product labels | • Catalogues |
| • Packaging | • Motor vehicle signs |
| • Carry bags | • Transit signs (on buses, trams, taxis or ferries) |
| • Telephone | • Free products or services |

When choosing advertising forms (see Table 3.5), the factors to consider include:
- the cost of the advertising
- the market coverage of the advertising
- the durability of the advertising.

As a general guide, annual advertising costs budgeted for should be between 3 and 5% of forecast annual sales.

## *Publicity*

Publicity is using free exposure to promote your business.

You could get media coverage from your business by offering information to the local media that is of general interest to the community. For example, 'a seafood retailer informs us that eating fish is good for you'.

Another way of getting publicity is by having satisfied customers. Satisfied customers not only return, they tell others about your business.

Networking is an effective way to freely expose your business. It involves making networks of useful contacts with other people. These people may in turn recommend your business to potential customers. You could make contacts, for example, through knowing other business people or through membership of business and non-business organisations.

### Personal selling and customer service

Personal selling and customer servicing both involve direct contact with customers. Any form of customer dealing is an opportunity to inform customers or prospective customers about what your business has to offer them. Customer dealings could be face to face, by telephone or by email.

### Public relations

The aim of public relations promotions is to have the local community recognise your business as community-minded and responsible. Good public relations promotes the credibility and good name of your business in the general community. It is important because the general community is the source of your customers. Any public relations activities should be designed to appeal to your target customer groups. For example, a business that has targeted local young families as its customers will win much support from this customer group and the community if it is known that the business makes significant donations to the local children's hospital or school, or if the business provides free facilities, goods or voluntary services to help under-privileged families in the local area.

## Competitive advantages

Identify what competitive advantages to use in your business offer. Competitive advantage is any part of the total business offer that gives your business an edge over your competitors; it is a selling feature unique to your business that gives you an advantage in attracting target customers. The effect of a competitive advantage is that customers will see your business as being better than those of competitors.

You can only determine what your competitive advantages are after directly observing your competitors to see what they are offering.

Competitive advantages could include:

- offering a wider product or service range than competitors
- offering a better-quality product or service than competitors for the same price
- offering a unique product or service to customers
- presenting more attractive packaging than competitors
- providing better customer service than competitors
- providing a speedier service than competitors
- offering lower prices than competitors
- offering extended credit terms
- having a superior business location to competitors
- opening for longer hours than competitors

- providing a home delivery service where competitors do not deliver
- projecting a better business image than competitors
- using more effective advertising than competitors
- having better customer relations than competitors.

Small operations can often gain advantages over larger rivals by focusing on offering their customers 'convenience' and 'better quality products', including 'superior customer service'.

A competitive edge will only be beneficial if you can sustain it for a reasonable period. This will largely depend on your assessment of your competitors' likely reaction to your tactics. A competitive advantage will lose its effect if competitors quickly respond with countering tactics—for example, competitors cutting prices in response to your reduced prices.

Your competitive advantages must be consistent with the findings of your competitor analysis. Knowing your competitors' strengths and weaknesses will help you determine what competitive advantages you can use in your total business offer. Study them closely: emulate the strengths and avoid the weaknesses in your own business.

## EXERCISES

**3.22**  Explain the difference between 'service products' and 'product services' offered by a business.

**3.23**  Describe four strategy options for an existing business to achieve sales growth.

**3.24**  Provide five examples of pre-sales or after-sales customer service in a business.

**3.25**  How can online customer service benefit a business?

**3.26**  What factors determine service quality?

**3.27**  Give four valid reasons for offering discounts to customers.

**3.28**  What is the purpose of distribution strategies?

**3.29**  Where will you locate your business operation? What factors did you consider in making your choice?

**3.30**  At what times will you open your business each week?

**3.31**  What is meant by 'business image'?

**3.32**  What is the purpose of promotions?

**3.33**  (a) What factors should be considered for finding an effective way to advertise a business?
     (b) Identify five effective ways to advertise your business.

**3.34**  Why is 'networking' a useful way to promote a business?

**3.35**  In what ways can the internet be used to market your business?

**3.36**  In what ways can a small operation offer advantages over a larger one to customers?

**3.37**  Select a specific McDonald's fast-food outlet and explain why you think the business is successful. Examine each component of the total business offer.

**3.38** 'The growth of the 24-hour self-serve petrol station, complete with supermarket, has resulted in the decline of the small corner shop.' Consider this statement, and indicate what you think might be the reasons for this competitive dominance. Look at the competitive advantages involved in the business offer.

**3.39** (a) You operate a small café at an established location in a busy shopping mall. You find out that two different well-known nationwide coffee franchise chains intend to open retail outlets nearby. What marketing strategies could you adopt to maintain competitiveness with these large competitors?

(b) You operate a small suburban retail hardware shop. A large hardware retail warehouse has recently opened in the general area. What specific marketing strategies could you apply to effectively compete?

(c) You carry on a small hand carwash business. A large automated self-service carwash operation with seven separate wash bays is also running close by. What marketing strategies would you implement here?

## B.7 MARKETING CONTROLS

Because the operating environment of your business is continually changing, decide how and when you will evaluate the effectiveness of your marketing strategies. Evaluation methods could include the following.

### Sales performance analysis

Sales results should be analysed regularly. This requires the design of a summary record of sales results, which can conveniently be analysed. One such record is the sales register book/software program, where all sales transactions—cash and credit—are entered daily (as they occur) from sales invoices, sales receipts or cash register rolls. A sales register (see Figure 3.4) records details of daily sales results for each product or service line. An extra column can also be added to record where the customer found out about the business to measure the effectiveness of particular promotions. The information in the sales register is analysed regularly (e.g. monthly) and the results are compared with your targets.

Because sales performance is affected by changes in the external operating environment, you need to be aware of trends in your sales performance. Another method of analysing sales performance is to prepare a graph of monthly sales results for each year (see Figure 3.5). Your graph could also include corresponding sales forecasts for comparison purposes. From your graph, you can observe whether growing or declining trends are occurring in sales performance. A sustained declining trend in sales should alert you to investigate changes in your external operating environment that are adversely affecting your marketing strategies.

The graph in Figure 3.5 indicates that, although sales results for each month are better than the corresponding forecast, there is a steadily declining trend in sales performance that should be investigated.

**FIGURE 3.4**  Sales register

| Date—Thursday, 12 March, Year 1 | | | | | | | |
|---|---|---|---|---|---|---|---|
| Time | Type of sale | Product A $ | Product B $ | Product C $ | Product D $ | Total $ | Source of inquiry |
| 8.45 am | Cash | 42.15 | | | | 42.15 | Sign |
| 10.12 am | Cash | 32.40 | 18.20 | | | 50.60 | Local newspaper |
| 10.20 am | Credit | | | 126.00 | | 126.00 | Sign |
| 11.18 am | Cash | 12.50 | | | | 12.50 | Referral |
| 12.06 pm | Cash | | 8.15 | | | 8.15 | Sign |
| 3.12 pm | Credit | | | 246.00 | | 246.00 | Sign |
| 4.03 pm | Cash | | | | 22.60 | 22.60 | *Yellow Pages* |
| 4.34 pm | Cash | | | 86.60 | | 86.60 | *Yellow Pages* |
| 4.42 pm | Cash | 28.40 | | | | 28.40 | Sign |
| **Daily totals** | | **115.45** | **26.35** | **458.60** | **22.60** | **623.00** | |

**FIGURE 3.5**  Sales performance graph

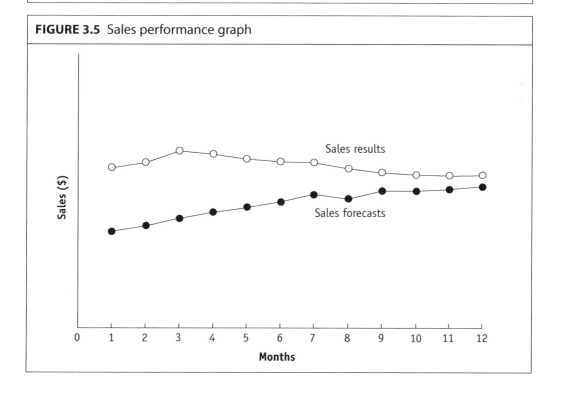

---

**FIGURE 3.6** Customer satisfaction survey

**Help us to help you**

In order to continue to improve our service, we'd like you to help us—by telling us a little about yourself and your needs.

As one of our valued customers, we are offering you 5% DISCOUNT on your next purchase.

All you need to do to take advantage of this offer is:

- fill in the information below; and
- give this survey to us when you visit us next time.

Thanks for your business.

**Let us know about you**

Please complete the following details:

Sex:   M ☐      F ☐

Age:   0–17 ☐   18–24 ☐   25–34 ☐   35–44 ☐   45–54 ☐   55+ ☐

How do you travel to do your shopping?

Car ☐          Rail ☐          Bus ☐          Other ☐

How far do you live from our shop?

Under 5 km ☐      6–10 km ☐      Over 10 km ☐

How do you normally pay for your purchase?

Credit card ☐      Cash ☐      Account ☐

When do you prefer to do your shopping?

Work days ☐      Before work ☐      After work ☐      Weekends ☐

How did you find out about our business?

Signs ☐          *Yellow Pages* ☐      Referral ☐      Other advertising* ☐

*Please specify _____

**What do you think about our business?**

|  | Poor | Average | Excellent |
|---|---|---|---|
| Location convenience | ☐ | ☐ | ☐ |
| Interior | ☐ | ☐ | ☐ |
| Exterior | ☐ | ☐ | ☐ |
| Product range and display | ☐ | ☐ | ☐ |
| Customer service | ☐ | ☐ | ☐ |

Is there anything you would like us to stock that we don't already have?

Please provide any other comments regarding how you rate our business.

Date and time of visit _____

## Customer satisfaction surveys

Regular (e.g. quarterly) customer satisfaction surveys can be conducted to evaluate the effectiveness of specific strategies. Surveys can be distributed either personally at the point of sale, by mail or email, or by leaving the survey at the counter to be completed and returned by the customer. An incentive, such as a discount or free offer, can be added to increase response rates. The type of information required in a survey is illustrated in Figure 3.6.

## Marketing program review

Also determine when you will regularly review your entire marketing program—that is, the selection of target customers and a business offer to satisfy them. Your marketing program should be reviewed at least annually. This will involve doing a comprehensive analysis of the operating environment, followed by the design of a new marketing program.

---

**EXERCISE**

3.40    Explain how you intend to evaluate the effectiveness of your marketing strategies during the period of your plan.

---

**MARKETING PLAN EXAMPLE**

**B. MARKETING**

**B.1 Environmental trends**

Research and analysis of the general business environment identifies the following opportunities and challenges for the business in the next three years.

*Opportunities:*
- General economic conditions are expected to improve.
- Steady increases in the general population are expected.
- People are working longer hours.
- Easing of regulatory red tape for small businesses is expected.

*Challenges:*
- rising levels of household debts
- a more litigious community
- greater public awareness of health and nutrition
- likely introduction of new business taxes.

    The conclusion reached from the environmental analysis is that there are opportunities for the business that will support the growth in sales forecasts. These environmental trends will influence the selection of marketing strategies for the business.

## B.2 Industry conditions

ABS statistics show that the national consumption of bread products per capita has been stable for the last three years. Consumption levels are expected to remain the same for the next three years. Direct observation and ABS statistics indicate that the number of hot bread shops has been growing steadily. The number of hot bread shops operating in the local area, however, is not expected to change in the foreseeable future.

The availability of grain and cereal supplies for breadmaking is likely to improve significantly in the short term. Growers are expected to yield record harvests due to good weather conditions.

## B.3 Products

The business will offer a variety of freshly made bread products comprising bread loaves, bread rolls and muffins. A limited range of freshly made cakes as well as soft drinks will also be offered as complementary products. Better-tasting bread products will be made according to a unique recipe belonging to the business owner.

The contribution of each product to annual sales turnover is expected to be as follows.

| Products | Year 1 | Year 2 | Year 3 |
|---|---|---|---|
| | % | % | % |
| Breads | 95 | 95 | 95 |
| Cakes | 4 | 4 | 4 |
| Soft drinks | 1 | 1 | 1 |
| **Totals** | **100** | **100** | **100** |

## B.4 Competitors

Through direct observation, two competitors have been identified that will compete directly with the business.

### Competitor 1

*Name:*        Harry's Bakery
*Location:*     My-Town
*Duration:*     eight years
*Personnel:*   five employees (full-time equivalents)

*Strengths:*
- wide range of bread products
- friendly staff
- loyal customers.

*Weaknesses:*
- poor location
- restricted opening hours
- unclean shop.

**Competitor 2**

*Name:*  Hong's Bread Shop
*Location:*  My-Town
*Duration:*  three years
*Personnel:*  two employees (full-time equivalents)

*Strengths:*
- quality products
- good location
- cheap prices.

*Weaknesses:*
- slow service
- unfriendly staff
- untidy shop.

It is not expected that there will be any change in the direct competition in the three-year period ahead. Competitor observations form the basis for designing competitive advantage strategies to follow.

## B.5 Target customers

The main customer groups that have been targeted by the business are shoppers and office workers. Target customer groups will remain the same during the period of the plan, unless changed in the annual marketing review.

**Target customer group 1: Shoppers**

*Personal characteristics:* 18–60 years old, predominantly female, homemakers, busy lifestyles, low to middle incomes.

*Relevant wants:* convenience, value for money, nutritious food products.

**Target customer group 2: Office workers**

*Personal characteristics:* 18–35 years old, work in local offices, modern tastes, busy lifestyles, energetic, low to middle incomes.

*Relevant wants:* tasty food, affordable prices, prompt service.

These target customers live within a 6 kilometre radius of the business location. Relevant demographic statistics obtained from the ABS show that the general population in the area has increased by 12% in the past ten years. Statistical projections indicate that these growth trends are likely to continue in the future.

## B.6 Marketing strategies

The business will adopt a customer-oriented approach in the marketing of its products. Any marketing strategy selected will focus on satisfying the relevant wants of the target customer groups.

*Products:*
- breads (loaves, rolls and muffins)
- cakes
- soft drinks.

*Services:*
- friendly and courteous customer service
- prompt attention given to customers.

*Prices:*
- products offered at affordable prices
- payment by cash
- discounts for quantity purchases.

*Distribution:*
- retail selling at business location
- business availability times for customers, Mondays to Saturdays (inclusive)—6 a.m. to 8 p.m.; also open on public holidays.

*Image:*
- clean and tidy presentation of staff and premises
- health-conscious attitudes to food handling and preparation
- friendly atmosphere for customers.

*Promotions:*
- counter and window displays
- signs outside the shop
- sponsorships of local sporting teams
- periodic circulation of advertising brochures
- developing a network of business contacts.

*Competitive advantages:*
- offering better-tasting fresh breads
- having a more exposed and accessible business location
- opening longer business hours than competitors
- projecting a healthier image than competitors
- providing friendlier and faster customer service than competitors.
  Competitive advantages are expected to be sustainable in the long term.

**B.7 Marketing controls**
Marketing strategies will be adaptable to change if business conditions change or new opportunities emerge.

A sales register will be maintained to record daily sales. Recorded sales results will be analysed quarterly by comparison with corresponding targets. Half-yearly customer satisfaction surveys will be conducted randomly to survey customers about their responses to marketing strategies.

The marketing program will be reviewed annually. This will involve a new analysis of the operating environment, followed by the choice of target customers and design of marketing strategies.

## EXERCISE

**3.41**   Prepare a marketing plan for your own business or someone else's. Your marketing plan format should be the same as that shown in Table 3.2.

## QUICK QUIZ

Each of the following multiple-choice items has one correct answer. Select the letter that corresponds with the correct answer.

1.   The first task to undertake when preparing a marketing plan is to:
   A. formulate marketing strategies
   B. design marketing controls
   C. analyse the operating environment
   D. define marketing objectives

2.   For an existing business, the purpose of reviewing the current operation in business planning is to:
   A. identify opportunities and challenges
   B. determine business resources available
   C. identify current operating procedures
   D. determine existing supply conditions

3.   An effective research technique for collecting information about people's attitudes is:
   A. database analysis
   B. direct observation
   C. personal survey
   D. desktop research

4.   Marketing is best defined as:
   A. selling goods or services to customers
   B. giving customers what they want
   C. promoting the business to customers
   D. identifying the size of the market

5.   The main marketing objective should be expressed in terms of:
   A. sales value
   B. market area
   C. market share
   D. customer numbers

6.   Good annual sales growth is generally considered to be at least:
   A. 3%       C. 10%
   B. 5%       D. 20%

7. A regulatory factor to consider when analysing the general business environment is:
   A. technological improvements
   B. climate change
   C. taxation increases
   D. none of the above

8. Which of the following indicates there might be room to operate in an industry?
   A. decreasing market demand
   B. large market area
   C. high set-up costs
   D. long-established competition

9. An example of an entry barrier in an industry is a:
   A. temporary supply shortage
   B. rise in inflation
   C. lack of demand
   D. dominant competitor

10. The focus of any marketing strategy should be:
    A. customers
    B. suppliers
    C. competitors
    D. management

11. When designing a business offer, the first marketing strategies considered should be:
    A. distribution strategies
    B. pricing strategies
    C. promotional strategies
    D. product strategies

12. Which of the following is *not* a determinant of service quality?
    A. packaging
    B. expertise
    C. reliability
    D. attitudes

13. 'Market penetration' is a business sales growth strategy that:
    A. changes the quality of existing products
    B. offers more products to existing customers
    C. widens the market area for customers
    D. diversifies the range of products

14. The pricing method generally recommended for any small business to be competitive is:
    A. stock cost plus mark-up pricing
    B. full cost recovery plus mark-up pricing
    C. going rate pricing
    D. suppliers' recommended pricing

15. Business image refers to:
    A. business reputation
    B. business goodwill
    C. business appearance
    D. business productivity

16. The purpose of any business promotion should be to:
    A. reach customers with a business offer
    B. inform customers of the business offer
    C. make contact with the most people
    D. persuade customers to buy

17. Which one of the following is *not* a promotional method?
    A. joining an organisation to establish useful contacts
    B. getting free coverage in the local media
    C. presenting the business on an internet website
    D. delivering sold goods or services direct to customers

18. A small business can compete effectively with a larger one by offering:
    A. more products
    B. fewer products
    C. better services
    D. quieter locations

19. Which one of the following is a marketing control method?
    A. employee job evaluation
    B. sales trend analysis
    C. supplier performance review
    D. existing operational review

20. The entire marketing program of the business should be reviewed at least:
    A. monthly
    B. quarterly
    C. annually
    D. three yearly

# The production plan

## Objectives

After studying this chapter, you should be able to:

- define production objectives
- prepare a production plan for a manufacturing operation
- design controls to ensure final product quality.

## PRODUCTION OBJECTIVES

A production function exists in every manufacturing operation. Production is the process of transforming raw materials into final products for sale.

The management aim for the production function of an operation should be to maximise output. The main production objective, therefore, should be expressed as a measurable quantity of output volume—that is, output units. Output targets should be consistent with your sales objectives for marketing.

The factors to consider in setting accurate output targets that will produce the desired profit target depend upon:

- sales targets
- production capacity.

The production plan you design is intended to achieve production objectives.

## PRODUCTION PLAN GUIDELINES

In manufacturing businesses, the production plan is prepared after the marketing plan. This is because the production plan must be coordinated with your marketing plan. The production plan describes your intended production activities to achieve output targets for the period. An outline of the 'Production plan' section of the business plan is shown in Table 4.1.

| **TABLE 4.1** Production plan outline |
| --- |
| **Section C. Production plan** |
| **C.1 Production capacity**<br>(Provide details of factory plant and equipment to be used in the manufacturing process.) |
| **C.2 Output levels**<br>(Prepare a schedule of monthly production output for each year of the plan.) |
| **C.3 Production method**<br>(Indicate what production method will be used, including planned production process times.) |
| **C.4 Production quality controls**<br>(Describe what methods will be adopted to ensure the desired final product quality is achieved.) |

## C.1 PRODUCTION CAPACITY

Production planning begins by determining the existing production capacity of the operation. Production capacity is established by factory plant and equipment.

Describe what factory plant and equipment is available to establish your production capacity (see Table 4.2).

**TABLE 4.2** Factory plant and equipment

| Item | Age years | Condition (Good/Fair/Poor) | Purpose | Output capacity (p.a.) |
|---|---|---|---|---|
| | | | | |
| | | | | |
| | | | | |
| | | | | |
| | | | | |
| | | | | |
| | | | | |
| | | | | |
| | | | | |
| | | | | |

There must be enough production capacity to achieve output targets. Any additional factory plant and equipment required to establish desired production capacity should also be included in Table 4.2.

Follow this by preparing a layout plan that shows the arrangement of plant and equipment in the production process. Figure 4.1 shows several production process layouts. The preparation of a production layout plan will enable you to:

- use available space effectively
- minimise process times, work flows and handling times
- plan for a safe work environment.

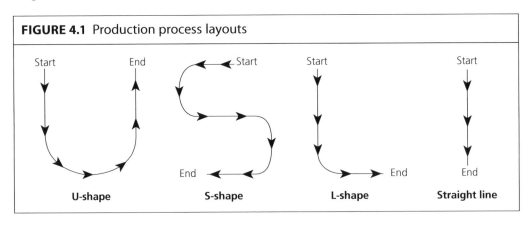

**FIGURE 4.1** Production process layouts

U-shape    S-shape    L-shape    Straight line

In any production process layout, raw materials should be stored close to their entry point in the production flow and completed product should be stockpiled close to the despatch point ready for quick delivery.

| **EXERCISES** |
|---|
| **4.1**    Make a list of the factory plant and equipment you will require to establish your production capacity. |
| **4.2**    Prepare a floor plan of your proposed production layout. |

## C.2 OUTPUT LEVELS

Plan production volume by setting output targets for the production of each product type. Prepare a schedule of monthly output for each year of the plan (see Table 4.3).

Output targets must be closely coordinated with marketing objectives. Planned monthly output should be consistent with varying seasonal demand. Increase production output before peak seasonal demand periods to ensure supply is available for the anticipated high demand. Conversely, reduce production output and operating costs for low-demand seasons.

**TABLE 4.3**  Production output schedule

**Year:**
**Product type:**

| Month | Output quantity | Average unit sales price | Sales value |
|---|---|---|---|
| 1 | _____ units | $ _____ per unit | $ _____ |
| 2 | _____ units | $ _____ per unit | $ _____ |
| 3 | _____ units | $ _____ per unit | $ _____ |
| 4 | _____ units | $ _____ per unit | $ _____ |
| 5 | _____ units | $ _____ per unit | $ _____ |
| 6 | _____ units | $ _____ per unit | $ _____ |
| 7 | _____ units | $ _____ per unit | $ _____ |
| 8 | _____ units | $ _____ per unit | $ _____ |
| 9 | _____ units | $ _____ per unit | $ _____ |
| 10 | _____ units | $ _____ per unit | $ _____ |
| 11 | _____ units | $ _____ per unit | $ _____ |
| 12 | _____ units | $ _____ per unit | $ _____ |
| **Total** | _____ **units p.a.** | | $ _____ **p.a.** |

When setting production output levels, keep your output between the points of production capacity (maximum possible output) and uneconomic idle capacity (minimum viable output).

Figure 4.2 illustrates this acceptable range for production levels. Production capacity is the maximum output that can be produced in the timeframe with the production resources available. The point of uneconomic idle capacity is the minimum output level below which production will be uneconomic because of excess idle (unused) capacity. At this point or below, production levels are not sufficient to recover fixed factory overhead costs.

**FIGURE 4.2** Production output levels

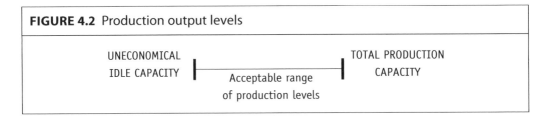

UNECONOMICAL
IDLE CAPACITY

Acceptable range
of production levels

TOTAL PRODUCTION
CAPACITY

**EXERCISE**

4.3　The annual targets for a single product manufacturing operation are shown as follows.

| Month | Forecast sales (units sold) | Forecast output (units made) |
| --- | --- | --- |
| Month 1 | 800 | 1600 |
| Month 2 | 1000 | 800 |
| Month 3 | 1200 | 800 |
| Month 4 | 1600 | 800 |
| Month 5 | 2200 | 800 |
| Month 6 | 2400 | 800 |
| Month 7 | 2000 | 1000 |
| Month 8 | 2000 | 1000 |
| Month 9 | 1800 | 1000 |
| Month 10 | 1400 | 1600 |
| Month 11 | 1200 | 2800 |
| Month 12 | 1000 | 1600 |

The maximum production capacity of the operation is 2400 units per month and the point of uneconomic idle capacity is 1000 units or below. Given that sales forecasts are correct, comment on the acceptability of the production output targets. Identify any problems that may occur.

## C.3 PRODUCTION METHOD

Choose what production method to use to manufacture the products. There are four production methods to choose from.

- *Continuous production* requires maintaining a continuous or repetitive production flow to make standardised final products; it usually involves producing large volumes. Continuous production methods are suitable when there is a high and consistent demand for a standardised product. There is always the risk with continuous production that large quantities of unsold output will build up due to insufficient demand. Another problem is that the factory equipment may be difficult to adapt to alternative products.

- *Batch production* involves making large quantities of different groups of identical products. Batch production is also suitable when there is a high and consistent demand for the groups of products. The problems with batch production are much the same as those for continuous production, although there may be more flexibility to adapt existing production facilities.

- *Job production* requires more flexibility for producing specific products to meet individual customer requirements. Output quantities will depend on orders received. With job production, raw materials are purchased only when there is a sales order. There is thus no risk of a build-up of finished goods. Job production is suitable in periods of irregular yet continual demand.

- *Project production* produces a single unique product. All production resources are usually devoted solely to the one project, which may take several weeks or months to complete.

The appropriate production method to use in any situation will depend on the nature of the product and the level of existing and likely demand. Job production is generally the safest production method for a small business with limited resources because output is already sold when produced.

Also determine what production process times, including daily production shifts, are required to achieve output targets. For example, you could decide on two daily production shifts for each weekday to produce the desired production volume for a given period. Scheduled daily production times could be 7 a.m. to 3 p.m. for the first shift and 3 p.m. to 11 p.m. for the second shift.

## EXERCISES

**4.4**   Refer to Exercise 4.3. What production method would you recommend in the circumstances to achieve the sales targets shown?

**4.5**   Which production method will you use in your small manufacturing business? Give reasons for your choice.

## C.4 PRODUCTION QUALITY CONTROLS

Decide what methods will be adopted to ensure the desired final product quality. Small manufacturers with limited resources should emphasise making a high-quality final product. A quality emphasis in production allows small operations to compete against larger ones, which tend to focus on volume. You need to design a total quality management (TQM) program for your production activities to ensure final product quality. Production quality controls to undertake include:

- regular inspections and scheduled maintenance for each item of factory plant and equipment—old equipment should be replaced at the end of its useful economic life
- regular checking for raw materials wastage
- supervising production employees and regularly evaluating their job performance
- providing ongoing training to line staff and regularly emphasising to them the need for quality
- adopting environmental protection safeguards in the production process
- regularly checking the quality of deliveries of raw materials and components to be used in the production process
- carrying out regular quality checks of raw materials at various stages of the production process
- using better-quality raw materials and components to get a better-quality final product
- regular random testing of final products and packaging for safety and quality
- conducting ongoing product research and development to improve product quality, carried out either in house or by contracts with outside services.

Any minimum legal standards relating to your manufactured products must be complied with. Minimum standards could apply for:

- product specifications
- product quality
- packaging specifications
- safety requirements
- labelling information.

Check with the Australian Competition and Consumer Commission (<www.accc.gov.au>) or your local consumer protection authority (see Table 2.6) for any relevant legal requirements.

**EXERCISES**

4.6     In what ways will you ensure the quality of manufactured products?

4.7     State any relevant legal requirements for your manufactured products.

## PRODUCTION PLAN EXAMPLE

### C. PRODUCTION

#### C.1 Production capacity
The following plant and equipment will be acquired at the start of Year 1 to establish production capacity.

| Plant and equipment ($) | Plant and equipment ($) | |
| --- | --- | --- |
| Scales | Trolley | |
| Cold-storage equipment | Proofing cabinet | |
| Shelving | Oven (2) | |
| Tools (knives, utensils, pots, pans) | Baking pans | |
| Containers | Thermometer | |
| Mixer | Bread slicer | |
| Blender | Dishwasher | |
| Stove | Microwave oven | |
| Tables | Racks | |
| Dough divider and rounder | | |
| Dough rollers | **Total cost** | **$90 000** |

The proposed arrangement of plant and equipment is shown in the production layout plan on the next page.

#### C.2 Output levels
Output volume will be coordinated with marketing objectives. It is anticipated that production capacity will be used as follows in the next three years.

| Year | Production capacity used |
| --- | --- |
| Year 1 | 70% |
| Year 2 | 70% |
| Year 3 | 70% |

#### C.3 Production method
The business will use a batch method of production. Standard batches of bread and cake products will be made daily. Daily production runs will be scheduled to meet expected continuous demand.

#### C.4 Production quality controls
Production quality controls will include:
- using proven recipes for making breads and cakes
- regularly checking for and replacing loose tools
- regularly maintaining machinery and equipment

- checking the quality of deliveries of ingredients
- regular random testing of batches of products made for quality
- providing thorough training to production staff
- closely supervising production staff and the bread- and cake-making processes
- adopting safe and healthy food-handling techniques.

Nutritional information will be shown on packaged bread products made. Nutritional information will also be displayed on signs at the business premises.

## Production layout plan

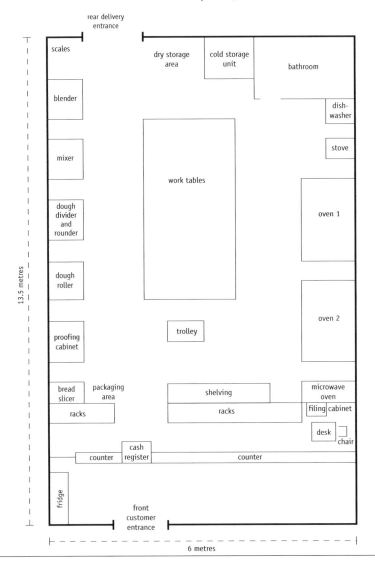

**EXERCISE**

**4.8**   Using the production plan outline shown in Table 4.1, prepare a production plan for your small business.

## QUICK QUIZ

Each of the following multiple-choice items has one correct answer. Select the letter that corresponds with the correct answer.

1.  Which one of the following kinds of operation has a production function?
    A. primary producer
    B. manufacturer
    C. wholesaler
    D. retailer
    E. service provider

2.  The main production objective should be expressed in terms of:
    A. process hours
    B. production staff
    C. output volume
    D. sales volume

3.  The production capacity of a manufacturing operation is determined by its:
    A. raw materials inventories
    B. plant and equipment
    C. management expertise
    D. potential customers

4.  Any production plan must be closely coordinated with the:
    A. marketing plan
    B. purchasing plan
    C. personnel plan
    D. financial plan

5.  The most suitable production method in periods of irregular demand is:
    A. continuous production
    B. batch production
    C. job production
    D. project production

6.  Which one of the following is a product quality control method?
    A. evaluating management performance
    B. conducting customer surveys
    C. maintenance of equipment
    D. analysing sales performance

## CHAPTER 5

# The purchasing plan

**Objectives**

After studying this chapter, you should be able to:

- define purchasing objectives for relevant operations
- prepare a purchasing plan for any relevant operation
- design controls to ensure purchasing is carried out effectively.

## PURCHASING OBJECTIVES

Purchasing is an operational function in any business requiring physical stock supplies. Purchasing activities involve sourcing and obtaining supplies, as well as paying for them. Many forms of business activity require some kind of stock supplies. Stock supplies required could include raw materials, component parts, trading stock or job materials.

The management aim for the purchasing function of the operation should be to obtain the best supply terms for the desired quality of supplies required. Because the major concern in negotiating supply terms is the cost of supplies, your main purchasing objective should be measured as the average gross profit margin. The gross profit margin is calculated as the percentage of gross profit made on the sale of a stock item. It measures how cheaply you purchase stock supplies. The more cheaply stock supplies are purchased, the higher the gross profit margin will be. The calculation of the gross profit margin for a stock unit sold is illustrated in the following example.

### EXAMPLE

You purchase stock costing $6 per unit from a supplier. You sell the stock for $10 per unit. The amount of gross profit you make on the sale of each stock unit is:

$$\$10 - \$6 = \$4 \text{ gross profit}$$

The gross profit margin on the sale of each unit is therefore calculated as:

$$\frac{\$4 \text{ gross profit}}{\$10 \text{ sales price}} \times 100 = 40\%$$

If you sell at competitive prices, a knowledge of the gross profit margin required will enable you to determine how much to purchase the stock for. Acceptable gross profit margin targets are usually industry average rates. Industry averages are available from the ABS, ATO (<www.ato.gov.au/businessbenchmarks>), private statistical organisations or the relevant industry association. Small businesses should use only current industry averages for small operations in the industry.

### EXAMPLE

You operate as a small hardware retailer who sells goods at competitive rates. The current industry average gross profit margin is, say, 33%. You adopt the industry average margin of 33% as your purchasing target when negotiating the cost of stock supplies. This means that you intend to buy your stock at a cost which ensures you earn a gross profit margin of 33% on resale (assuming you sell stock at competitive prices).

Suppose you have a stock item you intend selling for a competitive selling price of $100. To find the maximum cost to pay for it to achieve the 33% margin objective, the gross profit formula from the previous example is rearranged as follows:

| selling price | | gross profit | | cost price |
|---|---|---|---|---|
| $100 | – | (33% × $100) | = | $67 |

Therefore, the cost price to buy your stock for is $67 (or less) to achieve the gross profit margin objective.

## EXERCISES

**5.1**    Your business purchases the following stock items for the following costs:

Stock X                    cost $12 per unit
Stock Y                    cost $3 per unit
Stock Z                    cost $8 per unit

The competitive price you will sell each stock item for is as follows:

Stock X                    sales price $24 per unit
Stock Y                    sales price $10 per unit
Stock Z                    sales price $20 per unit

Calculate the gross profit margin for each stock item sold.

**5.2**    Your gross profit margin target is 40%, which is the current industry average for small businesses operating in the industry. Your business offers the following stock items for sale at the competitive prices shown.

| | Competitive selling price |
|---|---|
| Stock A | $20 |
| Stock B | $12 |
| Stock C | $5 |
| Stock D | $28 |
| Stock E | $60 |

What is the maximum purchase price to pay for each stock item to achieve the gross profit margin target of 40%?

## PURCHASING PLAN GUIDELINES

A purchasing plan is prepared for operations requiring supplies of physical stock. These operations include:

- manufacturers requiring raw materials and/or component parts
- wholesalers and retailers requiring trading stock for resale
- service sellers requiring job materials for stockpiling.

The purchasing plan must be coordinated with the marketing plan and any production plan completed. It is necessary to prepare the purchasing plan after these other two plans because purchasing decisions and policies depend on intended marketing and production activities.

The role of the purchasing plan is to explain how the requirements of the operation for stock supplies will be met. The plan describes intended purchasing activities for achieving defined objectives expressed as gross profit margin targets. The 'purchasing plan' section of the business plan is outlined in Table 5.1.

| |
|---|
| **TABLE 5.1** Purchasing plan outline |
| **Section D. Purchasing plan** |
| **D.1 Suppliers**<br>(Show details of the main proposed suppliers and supply terms available.)<br>**D.2 Purchasing policies**<br>(Describe stock level and other policies which affect purchasing procedures.)<br>**D.3 Purchasing controls**<br>(Describe what controls will be adopted to ensure purchasing is carried out efficiently and effectively.) |

## D.1 SUPPLIERS

Begin the plan by determining what types of stock supplies the operation requires. Next, identify who will be the business's main suppliers (see Table 5.2). Suppliers to investigate can be obtained from industry referrals, the *Yellow Pages* or other trade directories. Another way of sourcing supplies worldwide is via the internet.

For each supply requirement identified, decide whether to use one supplier, a few suppliers or a large number of suppliers. Using one supplier or only a few suppliers means that you will be buying in larger quantities from the supplier(s). This could result in quantity discounts, better service, faster deliveries and better credit terms. The supplier may also be more willing to help your business through any temporary problem periods. Spreading purchasing over a large number of suppliers gives you flexibility to shop around to find the cheapest deal. You also avoid being over-reliant on a single supplier, especially when supplies run out. It is generally prudent to establish relationships with two or three large suppliers to have secondary sources for quantity purchases.

To choose a particular supplier, look for the following features:

- an established, stable and large operation
- convenient availability times
- a convenient location
- reliable and prompt deliveries
- good customer service
- a wide range of relevant products
- large quantities of relevant products
- the cheapest supply source

**TABLE 5.2**  Summary of supply sources

| Type of stock supplies | Supplier 1 (name and address) | Supplier 2 (name and address) | Supplier 3 (name and address) |
|---|---|---|---|
| Raw materials: | | | |
| | | | |
| | | | |
| | | | |
| | | | |
| Component parts: | | | |
| | | | |
| | | | |
| | | | |
| | | | |
| Trading stock: | | | |
| | | | |
| | | | |
| | | | |
| | | | |
| Job materials: | | | |
| | | | |
| | | | |
| | | | |
| | | | |
| Other supplies: | | | |
| | | | |
| | | | |
| | | | |

- consistently good-quality stock
- acceptable trading terms (see below).

The most important considerations are whether the supplier can ensure reliable supplies and offer low enough prices to allow for the acceptable profit margin on resale.

Buying on the right terms is essential for maximising profits and cash flow surpluses. The following terms need to be negotiated:

- supply quantities
- supply prices
- discounts for quantity purchases and prompt payment
- credit terms (e.g. credit limits and credit periods)
- the possibility of consignment supplies
- product warranties (if applicable)
- the supplier's policy on returns (e.g. refunds, credit notes or exchange)
- delivery methods and times.

Most suppliers will require new customers to pay cash on delivery (COD) for stock supplies. In time, as you establish a satisfactory payment pattern, large suppliers will grant credit terms. Once a satisfactory relationship has been established, some large suppliers may be willing to provide stock supplies on consignment (where the stock is not paid for by the purchaser until it is sold).

It may be possible to enter into a distribution or selling agency agreement with some manufacturers directly. This could involve being granted exclusive selling territories, significant reseller discounts or attractive payment terms.

## EXERCISES

5.3   (a) What types of stock supplies are required for your operation?
      (b) How frequently do you expect to order each type of stock in your operation? For example, will it be daily, weekly, monthly or some other arrangement?

5.4   For each type of stock required, identify the names and addresses of your two main proposed suppliers.

5.5   For each supplier identified, determine:
- the supplier's length of time in business
- the size of the supplier (in terms of the number of employees)
- the availability times of the supplier.

5.6   For each supplier identified, determine the following trading terms available:
- supply prices
- discount policies
- credit terms (e.g. credit limit and credit period)
- the possibility of consignment supplies
- returns policies.

## D.2 PURCHASING POLICIES

Your marketing plan determines the nature of the business activities and what physical supplies are required for the operation. Purchasing must be coordinated with the marketing plan, as well as with any production plan, to ensure the stock is available when required by the operation. Purchasing policies are needed as guidelines for proposed purchasing activities.

### Stock levels

Purchasing frequency and quantities are influenced by decisions on what stock levels to carry. You could choose to purchase supplies when required to meet customer orders—a practice known as 'just-in-time' (JIT)—for example, buying stock supplies when required for use. This policy is suitable for periods of irregular demand where the requirements of each customer are different. For example, tradespeople in the building industry purchase job materials as required for each different job. By carrying little or no stock, however, you increase the risk of stockouts—running out of stock. Stockouts can result in dissatisfied customers not returning. Alternatively, you can choose to carry stock quantities to reduce the risk of stockouts occurring. Carrying stock quantities is most suitable for periods of steady customer demand where stock turnover rates are high. The carrying of stock requires funds to be tied up in the cost of stock and incurs carrying costs such as insurance, storage, rent for space used, stock shrinkage and interest on funds invested in the stock.

The factors to consider when choosing whether to carry maximum stock or minimum stock are as follows:

- lead time for purchases
- cost of stock
- resources available
- availability of supplies
- type of stock (e.g. perishable or durable)
- buying cycles (e.g. variations in seasonal demand)
- general economic conditions.

### Purchasing procedures

Design a standardised purchasing procedure to follow for acquiring any physical supplies for the operation. The use of signed purchase orders (see Figure 5.1) is central to any sound purchasing procedure. They provide written evidence of what was ordered for checking deliveries and billings by suppliers.

A standardised purchasing procedure to follow is described as follows:

- *Step 1:* Obtain supplier information (e.g. catalogues).
- *Step 2:* Issue signed purchase order to supplier.
- *Step 3:* File the purchase order copy.

**FIGURE 5.1** Purchase order

ORDER NO. 1

My Business
Main Street
My-Town 1234
Telephone 9876 5432

Date_____

To _____

_____

_____

Date required _____

Delivery instructions _____

| QUANTITY | STOCK DESCRIPTION | UNIT PRICE | TOTAL PRICE |
|---|---|---|---|
| | | | |
| | | | |
| | | | |
| | | | |
| | | | |
| | | | |
| | | | |
| | | | |
| | | | |
| | | TOTAL | |
| | | plus | |
| Authorised signature _____ | | TOTAL $ | |

- *Step 4:* Physically inspect deliveries.
- *Step 5:* Obtain a supplier's invoice.
- *Step 6:* Check and pay the invoice.

## Payments

Stock purchases are a major outgoing of any stock-carrying business. All payments for purchases should be by cheque or electronic funds transfer to ensure a banking record is kept of the outgoing payments. Payments should only be made after receiving the supplier's invoice—the supplier's written demand for payment. Invoices also provide evidence of the terms of the sale transaction.

You could decide to pay within any discount periods shown on an invoice to take advantage of any prompt payment discounts offered. Taking up discounts in this way can result in significant annual savings. Alternatively, you could decide to delay invoice payments as long as possible within any credit periods allowed to preserve cash flows. Under this policy, however, you run the risk of being overdue with payments, which could result in suppliers suspending future credit arrangements and insisting on payment by cash only.

### EXERCISES

**5.7**   What is meant by JIT purchasing?

**5.8**   Why are written purchase orders central to any sound purchasing procedure?

## D.3 PURCHASING CONTROLS

Decide what controls will be used to ensure purchasing activities are carried out efficiently and effectively. Purchasing controls could include:

- issuing purchase orders signed by authorised persons to suppliers
- issuing purchase orders in consecutive number sequence
- checking deliveries against purchase orders to ensure correct quantities and desired quality of supplies
- checking suppliers' invoices against purchase orders
- adopting an effective stock reordering system that determines how much and when stock should be reordered—for example, regular observation, periodic stock-counts or maintaining detailed stock records of stock movements
- analysing gross profit margins in periodic profit reports of the operation to determine the acceptability of supply prices
- regularly reviewing supply terms and supplier performance.

### EXERCISE

**5.9**   What methods will you use regularly to ensure that you get the best supply terms?

### PURCHASING PLAN EXAMPLE

#### D. PURCHASING

#### D.1 Suppliers

High-quality ingredients will be purchased to ensure a quality final product. The main suppliers will be as follows.

**Supplier 1**

| | |
|---|---|
| *Name:* | Mills |
| *Location:* | My-Town |
| *Duration:* | 60 years |
| *Supplies:* | all varieties of flour |
| *Supply terms:* | COD, quantity discounts |

**Supplier 2**

| | |
|---|---|
| *Name:* | South Star Food Supplies |
| *Location:* | My-Town |
| *Duration:* | 35 years |
| *Supplies:* | bread-making ingredients and additives |
| *Supply terms:* | COD |

**Supplier 3**

| | |
|---|---|
| *Name:* | Jim's Wholesalers |
| *Location:* | My-Town |
| *Duration:* | 15 years |
| *Supplies:* | soft drinks |
| *Supply terms:* | COD |

### D.2 Purchasing policies

Supplies will be purchased weekly according to needs. Purchases will be made by issuing signed purchase orders to suppliers. Purchases will be paid for when a supplier's invoice is received.

### D.3 Purchasing controls

The following purchasing controls will be maintained to ensure purchasing activities are carried out efficiently and effectively:

• checking purchase orders against deliveries and supplier invoices
• analysing gross profit margins in annual profit reports to determine the acceptability of supply prices
• reviewing supply terms and supplier performance annually.

**EXERCISE**

5.10    Prepare a purchasing plan for your operation. Use the format shown in Table 5.1 for your plan.

## QUICK QUIZ

Each of the following multiple-choice items has one correct answer. Select the letter that corresponds with the correct answer.

1. Which one of the following forms of business activity is least likely to have a purchasing function?
   A. manufacturing
   B. wholesaling
   C. retailing
   D. service selling

2. The main purchasing objective should be measured in terms of the:
   A. number of suppliers
   B. gross profit margin
   C. credit period
   D. discount rate

3. You purchase stock costing $20 to sell for $40. The gross profit margin when selling the stock is therefore:
   A. 25%
   B. 50%
   C. 100%
   D. 200%

4. You sell trading stock at competitive prices and require a gross profit margin of 40%. If you sell the stock for $12, the maximum price to pay for stock supplies is:
   A. $4.80
   B. $7.20
   C. $10.40
   D. $16.80

5. For any type of stock required, it is generally prudent to establish supply relations with a:
   A. single large supplier

   B. few large suppliers
   C. large number of suppliers
   D. single small supplier

6. The most important trading term to negotiate with a supplier is:
   A. supply price
   B. purchase discounts
   C. credit terms
   D. product returns

7. A stockout means:
   A. displaying stock outdoors
   B. consigning stock to customers
   C. stock moving outwards
   D. running out of stock

8. A cost of carrying stock is:
   A. office rent
   B. stock purchases
   C. stock insurance
   D. bad debts

9. A central business record in any sound purchasing system should be the:
   A. purchase order
   B. supplier invoice
   C. delivery docket
   D. supplier receipt

10. A supplier should be paid only after receipt of a:
    A. purchase order
    B. supplier invoice
    C. delivery docket
    D. supplier receipt

## CHAPTER 6

# The personnel plan

**Objectives**

After studying this chapter, you should be able to:

- define personnel objectives for an operation
- prepare a personnel plan for the operation
- design controls to measure labour performance in the operation.

## PERSONNEL OBJECTIVES

'Personnel' refers to the human resources to be used in the operation. The management aim for the personnel function of the operation is to maximise labour productivity in any given period. Labour productivity is the relationship between business output and labour input—for example, output volume and labour hours.

The main personnel objective should therefore be expressed as a summary measure of labour productivity. The easiest way to measure labour productivity is in financial terms as follows:

- labour costs as a percentage of sales for the period; or conversely
- the amount of sales generated by each dollar of labour cost for the period.

Both these financial measures of labour productivity describe the relationship of total personnel costs to revenues (sales) generated by the operation for a defined period.

### EXAMPLE

Annual sales are forecast to be $400 000 and forecast labour costs (comprising wages and wages on-costs) are $100 000 for the same year.

The labour productivity target of the operation for the year can therefore be measured as either:

- Labour cost to sales ratio

  i.e. $\dfrac{\$100\,000}{\$400\,000} \times 100 = 25\%$ labour cost for every $1 of sales

  or
- Sales to labour cost ratio

  i.e. $\dfrac{\$400\,000}{\$100\,000} = \$4$ of sales generated for every $1 of labour cost

Other personnel objectives to consider might include:

- the intended number of personnel (expressed in full-time equivalents at the end of each planned year)
- the business owner's intended hours worked weekly.

## PERSONNEL PLAN GUIDELINES

A personnel plan must be prepared for every operation because all businesses use human resources. The personnel plan must be coordinated with every other component plan of the business plan. The personnel plan is prepared after the marketing plan and any production and purchasing plans are completed. These other plans determine the human resource requirements of the operation.

The personnel plan describes your proposed personnel structure and staffing strategies for the operation. Personnel planning is intended to produce the most profitable outcomes for the business. These outcomes are measured in terms of labour productivity—that is, the relationship of business output (sales) to labour input (labour costs).

An outline of the 'Personnel plan' section of the business plan is shown in Table 6.1.

| **TABLE 6.1**  Personnel plan outline |
| --- |
| **Section E. Personnel plan** |
| **E.1 Management details**<br>(Show details of key management personnel, including owner's intended drawings.)<br>**E.2 Organisation structure**<br>(Describe the proposed organisation structure of the operation for the planning period. This shows the human resource requirements of the business for the period.)<br>**E.3 Staffing strategies**<br>(Describe what methods will be used to find suitable staff and keep them motivated and satisfied.)<br>**E.4 Professional advisers**<br>(List the professional advisers to be relied on by the business.)<br>**E.5 Personnel controls**<br>(Describe what methods will be used to monitor labour performance.) |

## E.1 MANAGEMENT DETAILS

Identify who the key management personnel of the operation will be and list their relevant skills, experience, training and qualifications. Evaluate the strengths and limitations of each person in management. From this analysis, design a training and development action plan to overcome any management weaknesses (see Figure 6.5 below).

Indicate what drawings or salary you expect to take from the business as owner/manager. You should also consider what hours you intend to work in your business. Your time commitment should be adequate to effectively run the operation and allow for sufficient free time.

If you are using the business plan to obtain borrowings, realise that lenders always look at the management's skills to ascertain their capacity to operate the business successfully.

## E.2 ORGANISATION STRUCTURE

There are three aspects to consider when planning an internal organisation structure of human resources for the operation:
- job needs—identifying job roles
- organisation structure—organising job roles
- job profiles—defining job roles.

## Job needs

Begin planning the organisation structure by identifying the job needs of the operation. This requires a detailed knowledge of the operation to determine exact human resource requirements. Analyse proposed activities in the marketing plan and any production and purchasing plans already prepared to determine what job tasks are necessary. Job roles and content are identified by doing an analysis of tasks required to be undertaken under these plans.

Also determine the extent of likely ongoing work flow for each job role identified. Employment alternatives to consider are full-time, part-time or casual. The choice of employment alternative will depend on the anticipated work flow. The use of part-time or casual employees is appropriate where there is irregular work flow or insufficient work for full-time employees.

Another issue for each job role identified is whether to use employees (full-time, part-time or casual) or independent contractors to do the work. It may be cheaper to use self-employed independent contractors for services such as payroll and couriers, as well as secretarial, bookkeeping or computing services. Although contractors' hourly labour rates are usually higher, you save paying wage on-costs (other costs, like superannuation and workers' compensation insurance, in addition to wage costs) and leave entitlements. You will also not have to maintain comprehensive wage records for contractors. Employers are also legally responsible for their employees' work. By having independent contractors instead of employees, you avoid the application of employee protection laws such as awards and unfair dismissal legislation. This gives you more flexibility to use your workforce. With self-employed contractors, however, you usually have no control over how they perform their assigned work tasks. You cannot expect contractors to be as loyal as employees; they will be less committed to the objectives of your enterprise.

The following example illustrates the relative costs of employees and independent contractors for the same work.

### EXAMPLE

You own a small retailing business. You analyse the job tasks required in your prepared marketing and purchasing plans. Job roles identified are for a salesperson (full-time), a secretary/receptionist (full-time) and a bookkeeper (part-time).

In relation to the bookkeeper, you determine that there are fifteen hours of ongoing work per week available. You consider whether to employ or contract the bookkeeper. You find out you can employ a bookkeeper part-time to work fifteen hours per week for $10 000 gross wages in a 48-week year. Wage on-costs such as superannuation and workers' compensation insurance are estimated to be 25% of gross wages. Alternatively, the contract rate for hiring a contractor to do the same work is $25 per hour.

You evaluate the cost of each alternative as follows:

- to employ:

  $10 000 p.a. + ($10 000 × 25%) = $12 500 p.a.

- to contract:

  (15 hrs p.w. × 48 weeks p.a.) × $25 per hour = $18 000 p.a.

In these circumstances, you conclude that it is cheaper to employ the bookkeeper part time.

The relative merits of labour alternatives are summarised in Table 6.2.

**TABLE 6.2**  Employee vs independent contractor

| **Employees** | |
|---|---|
| *Advantages:* | *Disadvantages:* |
| Greater loyalty and commitment is expected | Wage on-costs are incurred (e.g. leave entitlements, superannuation) |
| More management control over job performance | Increased payroll administration and taxation compliance |
| Flexible work options are possible (e.g. full-time, part-time, casual) | wider legislative protection exists |
| **Independent contractors** | |
| *Advantages:* | *Disadvantages:* |
| Savings on wage on-costs | Higher hourly rates |
| More flexibility to hire and fire | May require specific job training |
| Fewer legal restrictions apply | Less loyalty and commitment to enterprise |

The choice of labour alternatives will always depend on your particular business circumstances, including job needs, expected work flows and relative cost factors.

## Organisation structure

All job roles identified must be allocated within an organisation structure for the operation. An organisation structure must be designed that best meets the business's goals and objectives. The organisation structure chosen must be an effective and efficient organisation of human resources to be used in the operation. It must be capable of producing the planned profit outcomes for the business.

An organisation chart is prepared to show how human resources will be organised within the business. The organisation chart (see Figure 6.1) is a diagram showing the hierarchy of job roles in the operation. It specifies the number and types of job roles, as well as clearly defining the lines of authority between job roles.

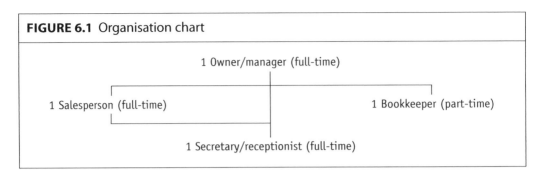

**FIGURE 6.1** Organisation chart

Design an organisation chart for each year of the plan to describe the proposed structure of the operation. Figure 6.1 shows a possible organisation chart for the job roles identified in the previous example.

The organisation chart in Figure 6.1 describes a simple organisation structure for a small operation employing four people, including the owner/manager. The person with the ultimate authority in the organisation will be the full-time owner/manager. Beneath the owner/manager are the full-time salesperson and the part-time bookkeeper, who are at similar levels of authority. The full-time secretary/receptionist is responsible to the salesperson and the owner/manager, with the ultimate authority being with the owner/manager.

## Job profiles

Complete the planning of your organisation structure by preparing a detailed profile of each job role identified. A detailed profile for each job role should consist of a:

- job description (statement of duties)
- job specification (statement of attributes)
- remuneration package (statement of rewards).

A job description for any job role is a statement of duties and who the job is accountable to. Figure 6.2 shows a possible job description for a secretary/receptionist.

A job specification is a statement of attributes required to perform a job role. It helps you to select the right person for the job.

You should be aware of both federal and state anti-discrimination legislation when designing job specifications. Anti-discrimination legislation prohibits discrimination in the workplace on grounds such as race, gender, religion, age and ethnic background.

A job specification for a secretary/receptionist is shown in Figure 6.3.

A remuneration package should also be designed for each job role. The remuneration package describes remuneration entitlements for the job role. A remuneration package designed for a secretary/receptionist is shown in Figure 6.4.

Employers need to be aware of the provisions of any relevant industrial awards. An industrial award is a binding order issued by a federal, state or territory industrial

---

**FIGURE 6.2** Job description

**Job title:**
Secretary/receptionist

**General nature of duties:**
Office and administrative duties

**Major job duties:**
- Receiving visitors
- Answering telephone enquiries
- Typing correspondences, reports and invoices
- Banking daily deposits
- Receiving and opening mail
- Filing

- Keeping petty cash
- Writing up the petty cash book and wages book
- Sending fax messages

**Minor job duties:**
- Arranging couriers
- Arranging business trips
- Arranging entertainment
- Maintaining staff amenities

**Responsible to:**
Owner/manager

---

**FIGURE 6.3** Job specification

**Job title:**
Secretary/receptionist

**Desired attributes:**

*Personality:*
Outgoing, pleasant, friendly

*Appearance and manner:*
Good grooming and dress presentation, polite and courteous

*Skills and training:*
Typing skills (70 words per minute), telephone and interpersonal communications skills, basic bookkeeping skills

*Education:*
Higher School Certificate from secondary school
Secretarial certificate from a business college

*Experience:*
Minimum of three years' relevant work experience as a secretary/receptionist in a small business

*Physical:*
None

---

tribunal. It prescribes legally enforceable minimum pay rates and employment conditions for a specific job classification. Employee remuneration and other entitlements must meet any award minimums for the job classification. Award information can be obtained from your federal or local industrial relations authority or the relevant industry association.

Alternatively, if you negotiate a formal, written workplace agreement with employees, it must still meet any minimum pay rates and other essential employment conditions and standards that apply under law. Some workplace agreements must be registered and approved by the relevant industrial relations authority.

---

**FIGURE 6.4** Remuneration package

**Job title:**
Secretary/receptionist

**Commencement date:**
1/7/Year 1

**Relevant award:**
None

**Employment basis:**
Full-time/part-time/casual/contractor

**Work hours (p.w.):**
35 hours p.w.

**Wage frequency:**
Fortnightly

**Gross wages:**
$30 000 p.a. (reviewable annually)

**Allowances:**
Nil p.a.

**Leave entitlements:**
Annual leave (28 days p.a.), sick leave (30 days p.a.), long-service leave (after qualifying period)

**Superannuation:**
12% of gross wages

**Incentives:**
Annual bonus based on sales turnover

---

 **EXERCISES**

6.1    What are the advantages and disadvantages of engaging self-employed contractors instead of full-time employees for job roles?

6.2    What is meant by 'wage on-costs'?

6.3    What is an award? Why must you know about them?

6.4    What is an organisation structure?

6.5    What information is found in an organisation chart?

6.6    Design an organisation chart for the first year of your proposed operation.

6.7    Develop a detailed job profile comprising a job description, job specification and remuneration package for each job role identified in your organisation chart.

## E.3 STAFFING STRATEGIES

Design staffing strategies to find the best personnel for job roles and to ensure that personnel are productive in their job roles. Any staffing strategy decision should be based on the principle of equal employment opportunity (EEO)—the merit principle in employment. There are various aspects to consider here.

### Recruitment and probation

Begin by deciding how you will find suitable personnel with the required attributes for job roles in the operation. The main ways of finding personnel are:

- newspaper/online job advertising
- referrals through the Commonwealth government job placement network

- referrals from private employment agencies
- advertising via online job recruitment sites (e.g.: <www.seek.com.au>)
- advertising at educational institutions
- advertising outside the workplace (e.g.: signs).

Also decide what probation periods apply for new employees. A probation period is an initial trial work period for evaluating job performance before a permanent position is offered. Employees can be terminated at any time during reasonable (and lawful) probation periods.

## Rewards and incentives

Determine what remuneration packages to offer for each job role (see Figure 6.4). Remuneration amounts and other entitlements must be at least equal to any legally enforceable award minimums that may apply. Remuneration should also be set at competitive rates to attract and maintain the right people. Compulsory superannuation contributions must also be paid by employers for most employees.

Employees must be kept motivated to work to maximise labour productivity. Additionally, employees should be kept satisfied (i.e. feel good about their work) to minimise absenteeism and job turnover.

Employers should establish a rewards and incentives system that maintains both employee motivation and job satisfaction. In doing so, you should understand that individual employees have their own unique needs and expectations that have to be addressed.

Strategies to consider to motivate and satisfy your employees include:

- Provide a variety of rewards (e.g. base pay, praise, compliments, promotion, leave).
- Be fair and equitable in the provision of rewards.
- Consult with staff individually to determine appropriate rewards.
- Link job performance to rewards (e.g. results-based cash bonuses, profit-sharing).
- Ensure individuals' objectives and measures of job performance are clearly understood.
- Provide effective feedback on job performance.
- Provide interesting and challenging work (very important).
- Provide ways for employees to improve and develop (see below).
- Provide good-quality supervision.
- Encourage staff involvement in decision-making through consultation or delegation of authority (see Figure 6.6 below).
- Create a pleasant physical work environment (e.g. comfortable work settings, adequate amenities, open and cooperative worker attitudes, teamwork).

## Training and development

Determine what initial period of induction training will be provided for new employees. Also conduct a skills audit of existing employees. A skills audit identifies current skills, competencies and qualifications of workers. It is a necessary starting point for determining what further training and development action is required for each person (see Figure 6.5).

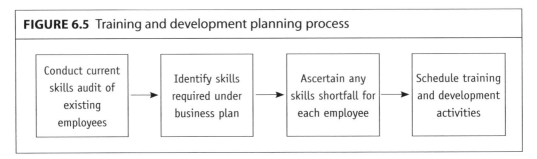

**FIGURE 6.5** Training and development planning process

The benefits of providing ongoing training and development to employees include:
- Better-trained staff perform their job tasks more effectively and efficiently.
- Training has a positive motivational effect on employees because they are acquiring and developing job skills.
- Training improves loyalty because staff feel that their long-term potential in the business is being recognised by their employer.
- Multiskilling means an employee can carry out a variety of job roles.
- Trained staff can take on greater responsibility and make more valuable contributions to management.

Training and development activities could include in-house training, full-day seminars or technical updates, short refresher courses or part-time tertiary education courses.

Particular skills areas to consider when planning training activities include:
- customer service
- personal selling and product knowledge
- interpersonal communications
- literacy and numeracy
- computer operation and applications
- record-keeping
- supervision and motivation
- specific technical services.

## Leadership

Choose a leadership style to adopt to direct and influence personnel for achieving your business goals. Two opposite styles of leadership are authoritarian and democratic leadership.

*Authoritarian leadership* is where operational decisions are centrally made by one person, who is task-driven to attain objectives. Under authoritarian leadership, one person exerts total control over employees. On the other hand, *democratic leadership* is where decisions and tasks are delegated to employees by a business manager who is people-oriented. A democratic leadership style encourages employee involvement in decision-making. In between these two leadership extremes are many variations to consider (see Figure 6.6). This range of leadership styles allows for varying degrees of employee input in decision-making.

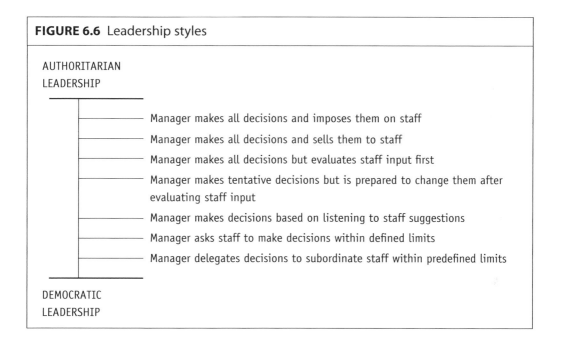

**FIGURE 6.6** Leadership styles

AUTHORITARIAN
LEADERSHIP

Manager makes all decisions and imposes them on staff

Manager makes all decisions and sells them to staff

Manager makes all decisions but evaluates staff input first

Manager makes tentative decisions but is prepared to change them after evaluating staff input

Manager makes decisions based on listening to staff suggestions

Manager asks staff to make decisions within defined limits

Manager delegates decisions to subordinate staff within predefined limits

DEMOCRATIC
LEADERSHIP

An effective leadership style to apply in any situation will depend on the circumstances. Factors that determine the choice of an effective leadership style include:

- the personality of the manager involved
- the personalities of the employees involved
- the urgency of the business situation.

Generally, authoritarian leadership can be effective in some crisis or pressure situations where deadlines have to be met. Authoritarianism, however, may be impractical in big organisations employing large numbers of employees. It may also be inappropriate in small, highly personalised workplaces. Democratic forms of leadership can often motivate staff and lead to greater job satisfaction among employees. Effective delegation can also relieve the pressure for business managers, particularly in some small businesses with limited resources.

## Work Health and Safety (WHS) compliance

Businesses must comply with WHS laws by taking reasonable care to ensure a safe and healthy workplace for workers and other visitors. Most states and territories have adopted national uniform laws requiring minimum standards for work health and safety. WHS policies to consider for your workplace include those listed in Table 6.3.

You should plan to conduct regular safety audits to identify workplace hazards—anything that has the potential to cause harm. Any workplace hazards identified should be eliminated or controlled by undertaking appropriate actions.

Businesses must maintain an injury/accident register for recording details of any workplace accidents.

Sources of advice for complying with WHS laws include your local WHS authority (see Table 2.7), insurance companies, insurance brokers and the relevant industry association.

| **TABLE 6.3** WHS policies |
| --- |
| • Train workers in health and safety techniques. |
| • Regularly evaluate health and safety awareness of workers. |
| • Regularly consult with workers about health and safety matters. |
| • Adequately supervise workers. |
| • Require workers to use appropriate safety wear. |
| • Restrict visitors' access to the workplace. |
| • Provide free access to and from the workplace. |
| • Maintain a clean and tidy workplace. |
| • Display warning signs and safety notices. |
| • Regularly test plant and equipment for safety. |
| • Regularly maintain plant and equipment. |
| • Design and follow safe work systems. |
| • Follow safety instructions on chemical labels. |
| • Eliminate excessive or unnecessary noise. |
| • Regularly monitor health and safety conditions. |
| • Provide adequate amenities and first aid resources. |

## EXERCISES

**6.8**    What are three ways to recruit suitable personnel for job roles in your operation?

**6.9**    What is the purpose of a probation period?

**6.10**    Suggest five possible strategies to motivate and satisfy workers.

**6.11**    Give three reasons why training and development of employees should be undertaken.

**6.12**    What is the difference between authoritarian and democratic leadership styles in an organisation?

**6.13**    Which leadership style will you adopt for staff in your own small business? Give reasons for your choice.

**6.14**    Why should a workplace safety audit be carried out?

# E.4 PROFESSIONAL ADVISERS

A personnel plan should identify what outside professional advisers will be used by the business. Outside professional advisers provide expert services and advice. Four essential advisers for any business are:

- qualified accountant (and registered tax agent)
- solicitor
- insurance agent/broker
- bank.

Table 6.4 shows the functions of various professional advisers.

There are several factors to consider when selecting a professional adviser. Any adviser chosen should be:

- appropriately qualified
- experienced in your industry
- accessible and convenient to the business location
- a good communicator
- reliable and punctual
- able to offer value and benefits for the fees charged
- friendly and likeable.

It is most important that you also feel comfortable with any professional adviser selected.

You can find a professional adviser by looking in the *Yellow Pages* (<www.yellow-pages.com.au>), searching on the internet, or by referral or direct observation.

Memberships of any relevant industry, business or professional bodies should also be maintained. These bodies usually provide useful business information, regular updates and contacts, as well as periodic training opportunities.

**TABLE 6.4** Professional adviser functions

| Professional adviser | Functions |
|---|---|
| Qualified accountant (and registered tax agent) | • Assessing fair purchase price of business<br>• Advising on record systems, taxation and finance<br>• Preparing financial reports, tax returns and financial forecasts<br>• Advising on general financial matters |
| Solicitor | • Representation in legal disputes<br>• Representation in contract negotiations<br>• Preparing contracts and legal documents<br>• Advising on general legal matters |
| Insurance agent/ insurance broker | • Checking business risks of operation<br>• Determining insurance needs<br>• Arranging insurance cover<br>• Processing insurance claims<br>• Advising on general insurance matters |
| Bank | • Providing account services<br>• Providing loan products<br>• Advice on financing<br>• Processing loan applications |

**EXERCISES**

6.15 Identify each of the following professional advisers for your business:
- qualified accountant (and registered tax agent)
- solicitor
- insurance agent/broker.

Why did you choose each one?

6.16 What is the name and address of your relevant industry, business or professional association?

## E.5 PERSONNEL CONTROLS

Decide how you will check and evaluate labour performance in the operation. The performance of personnel is a key factor in the success of any business. Measures should also be designed to prevent employee dishonesty in the operation.

### Labour productivity measures

Total labour productivity should be regularly measured (e.g. half-yearly) to identify any labour performance problems occurring in the operation. As previously shown, labour productivity can be measured in financial terms, by describing the relationship of sales to labour costs for a given period. The information required to do this is obtained from sales and wages records. If you identify unsatisfactory labour productivity, you would follow this with specific investigation of each employee and a review of the organisation structure.

---

**EXAMPLE**

Relevant financial results of your operation are summarised as follows:

|  | Last period | Current period |
| --- | --- | --- |
| Sales | $82 000 | $94 000 |
| Wages | $7 000 | $12 000 |

You financially measure labour productivity in your operation for each period as follows (industry averages are also shown).

|  | Last period | Current period | Industry average |
| --- | --- | --- | --- |
| Sales ($) : Labour costs ($) | $11.71 : $1 | $7.83 : $1 | $10.60 : $1 |
| Labour costs as percentage of sales | 8.5% | 12.8% | 9.4% |

Using either financial measure, labour productivity in the organisation is declining. The sales generated by each dollar of labour cost is declining between periods and is also currently below the industry average. Similarly, the cost of labour as a percentage of sales is rising and also is currently above the industry average.

This declining trend (measured in financial terms) should alert you to problems occurring in specific labour performance within your organisation. You should investigate individual job performance and also review your organisational structure of human resources.

---

## Job performance evaluation

The job performance of each employee should be evaluated regularly. New employees should be evaluated for permanent appointment at the end of a probationary period. All employees should be evaluated at regular intervals (e.g. half-yearly) to monitor job performance.

An evaluation of specific aspects of each employee's work performance (see Figure 6.7) helps you to identify individual strengths and weaknesses so that appropriate corrective actions can be undertaken. Individual job evaluation will also enable you to recognise and reward good job performance. Face-to-face job evaluations should be a two-way process. You should get employee feedback on any job dissatisfaction so that you can address any grievances.

## Employee dishonesty prevention

Implement measures to minimise the occurrence of employee dishonesty. Employee dishonesty could include theft and fraud, leaking of information, unjustified absences, making private telephone calls and time-wasting.

---

**FIGURE 6.7** Employee evaluation checklist

---

Employee name _____

Review period _____to _____(six months)

Date of evaluation _____ Evaluation by _____

---

**Rating scale**

| Job aspects | Unsatisfactory | Satisfactory | Excellent | Comments |
|---|---|---|---|---|
| • Work quality | _____ | _____ | _____ | _____ |
| • Job efficiency | _____ | _____ | _____ | _____ |
| • Safety consciousness | _____ | _____ | _____ | _____ |
| • Punctuality | _____ | _____ | _____ | _____ |
| • Absenteeism | _____ | _____ | _____ | _____ |
| • Personal presentation | _____ | _____ | _____ | _____ |
| • Attitudes | _____ | _____ | _____ | _____ |
| • Initiative taken | _____ | _____ | _____ | _____ |
| • Responsibility shown | _____ | _____ | _____ | _____ |

---

Skills/training acquired in period _____

_____

_____

---

Employee grievances/complaints _____

_____

_____

---

Suggested corrective actions _____

_____

_____

---

Favourable conditions for employee dishonesty are often created by lax management, where opportunities are provided for staff to abuse the system. Alert and diligent management can remove many temptations in the workplace. Specific measures to prevent staff dishonesty could include:

- direct and close supervision
- signing of a confidentiality agreement
- restricting the issue of keys
- providing generous remuneration
- carefully screening job applicants

- regular stock-counts
- restricting the handling of cash
- restricting signatories on cheques and purchase orders
- adopting proper internal controls for record-keeping
- installing surveillance cameras
- monitoring itemised telephone bills
- guidelines concerning non-work-related use of internet and telephone
- requiring medical certificates for absences.

## EXERCISES

6.17  What methods will you use to evaluate labour performance in your operation?
6.18  You own a small business. Your wage costs for the current year are $145 000 and sales totalled $525 000. In the previous year, total sales were $488 000 and wage costs were $120 000. From this information, is labour performance improving or declining?
6.19  List five aspects of work performance that any job evaluation should consider.
6.20  What is the best general management approach for minimising staff dishonesty in the workplace?
6.21  Describe three ways you could prevent the theft of cash in your business.

## PERSONNEL PLAN EXAMPLE

### E. PERSONNEL

#### E.1 Management details
The operation will be managed by Hannah Baker, whose relevant personal details are as follows.

*Relevant experience:*
- ten years' experience in bread-making
- four years' experience as bakery manager.

*Relevant training/qualifications:*
- bakery trade certificate
- pastry cook trade certificate.
In Year 1, Hannah Baker will complete a six-month (part-time) course in financial management and business law at the local TAFE college. Hannah will require wages of $2083 gross per calendar month. This amount of remuneration will be sufficient to meet her monthly personal expenses.

**E.2 Organisation structure**

The proposed staff organisation structure of the business for each of the next three years is as follows.

**Job profile: Director/manager**

Full-time—50 hours p.w.

*Job duties:*
- bread- and cake-making
- purchasing supplies
- selling
- banking takings
- paying bills and wages
- writing up record books

*Job attributes:*
- minimum ten years' relevant experience
- bakery trade qualifications

*Remuneration:* $25 000 gross p.a. start (plus bonuses)

**Job profile: Baker**

Part-time—10 hours p.w.

*Job duties:*
- bread- and cake-making.

*Job attributes:*
- minimum five years' relevant experience
- bakery trade qualifications

*Remuneration:* $10 000 gross p.a. start (plus bonuses)

**Job profile: General hand**

Full-time—50 hours p.w.

*Job duties:*
- general labouring
- picking up supplies
- selling to customers

*Job attributes:*
- enthusiastic and reliable

*Remuneration:* $18 000 p.a. start (plus bonuses)

### E.3 Staffing strategies

The staffing strategies that will be adopted to keep staff motivated and productive are as follows:

- local newspaper advertising to find suitable staff
- an initial three-month probation period for new employees
- remuneration at competitive, above-award rates
- remuneration increases by 3% p.a.
- an incentive scheme of bonus payments based on profit results
- adequate facilities and amenities for employees
- authoritarian leadership for directing employees
- induction training during probation periods and ongoing training and development activities for staff
- regular health and safety audits of the workplace.

### E.4 Professional advisers

The following business advisers will be used:

- Qualified accountant
  (and registered tax agent):   Penny Wise, My-Town
- Solicitor:   Justin Law, My-Town
- Insurance broker:   Donna Safeway, My-Town
- Bank:   Commercial Bank, My-Town

Annual membership of the Baking Industry Association will be maintained.

### E.5 Personnel controls

Total labour productivity will be measured half-yearly to identify any labour performance problems that may occur in the operation. For these purposes, labour productivity will be measured as the relationship between sales and labour costs in each relevant period.

Key aspects of individual job performance will also be evaluated after a three-month probation period for new employees and at three-monthly intervals for existing employees. Job evaluations will be conducted face to face to receive feedback.

The director/manager will directly supervise employees and the handling of cash, including banking takings, to prevent the occurrence of staff dishonesty.

---

## EXERCISE

**6.22**   Prepare a personnel plan for your operation. Use the format shown in Table 6.1 for your plan.

## QUICK QUIZ

Each of the following multiple-choice items has one correct answer. Select the letter that corresponds with the correct answer.

1. The main personnel objective should be expressed as a measure of:
   A. labour productivity
   B. personnel numbers
   C. labour hours
   D. wage costs

2. Labour productivity describes the relationship between:
   A. output volume and business costs
   B. business sales and business costs
   C. labour hours and labour costs
   D. labour costs and business sales

3. Wage on-costs include:
   A. commissions paid
   B. superannuation contributions
   C. fringe benefits
   D. bonuses paid

4. An advantage of using employees instead of independent contractors in job roles is:
   A. saved wage on-costs
   B. saved leave entitlements
   C. reduced wage records
   D. more job control

5. An organisation chart for an operation shows:
   A. the hierarchy of job roles
   B. the job duties for each job role
   C. the job attributes for each job role
   D. all of the above

6. A statement of job duties is called a:
   A. job specification
   B. job description
   C. remuneration package
   D. personnel policy

7. A benefit of providing training and development activities for employees is:
   A. job promotions
   B. higher motivation
   C. more customers
   D. job reductions

8. An essential professional adviser for any business is:
   A. a qualified accountant
   B. a computer consultant
   C. an advertising consultant
   D. a financial planner

9. A personnel control is the:
   A. analysis of sales results
   B. review of supplier performance
   C. analysis of wage costs
   D. evaluation of job performance

10. To reduce the risk of the theft of cash in your business, you should:
   A. conduct regular stocktaking
   B. monitor telephone bills
   C. directly supervise employees
   D. adopt record controls

# The financial plan

## Objectives

After studying this chapter, you should be able to:

- define profit objectives for an operation
- explain the significance of the financial plan
- prepare a financial plan for an operation
- design financial controls to monitor results.

## FINANCIAL OBJECTIVES

The financial function of the business operation involves measuring financial performance to reflect total operational performance. The aim in managing financial performance should be to maximise net profit and net cash flow surpluses of the operation. The two main financial performance measures, therefore, are net profit and net cash flow. Each indicator for any given period is calculated as follows:

total income – total expenses = net profit
total receipts – total payments = net cash flow surplus

Net profit is calculated as the excess of income over expenses of the operation for a given period. Income is the earnings of the operation; expenses are its running costs.

Net cash flow surplus is calculated as the excess of receipts over payments for a given period. Receipts are the cash inflows of the operation; payments are its cash outflows or outgoings.

---

**EXAMPLE**

For a given period, a business has income of $120 000 and receipts of $90 000. For the same period, the expenses of the operation are $70 000 and its payments are $50 000. The net profit of the business for the period is:

$120 000 – $70 000 = $50 000

The net cash flow surplus of the business for the same period is:

$90 000 – $50 000 = $40 000

---

The key financial performance measure to be shown as a business objective is net profit for the period. Other measures of financial performance, including net cash flow surplus, depend upon the profit measurement.

The annual profit target for each year in the plan period is arrived at by deducting forecast expenses from forecast income for the period. The bottom-line profit target must be acceptable as well as achievable. An achievable profit depends on the accuracy of income and expense forecasts. An acceptable profit target, however, should at least equal the minimum amount required for the operation to remain viable. This minimum profit amount required is sometimes referred to as the normal profit of the operation.

As a guide, an acceptable annual net profit should be sufficient to:

- remunerate a business owner for the time and effort put into the business
- provide an adequate return on the owner's funds invested in the business.

An adequate remuneration should at least equal what you could earn as an employee for the same time and effort put into your business. Alternatively, it could be based on what it would cost to pay someone to manage your business.

An adequate rate of return on your funds invested in the business should at least equal the current bank deposit rate for an equivalent amount plus an extra rate allowed for business risk. The required rate of return is calculated as follows:

| Required rate of return on owner's funds invested (%) | = | Risk-free rate of investment (current bank deposit rate %) | + | Allowance for business risk (%) |

The risk allowance is normally between 10 and 20%. The higher the perceived risk of your enterprise, the higher is the risk allowance rate.

---

**EXAMPLE**

You want to calculate the normal profit of your operation, which is the minimum amount of net profit you will accept for your operation to be viable. You obtain the following information:

- The total amount invested in your business is $25 000.
- The competitive wage payable for someone to manage your business is $40 000 p.a.
- If $25 000 was invested in the bank, it would earn 6% p.a.
- Industry sources indicate that the additional risk rate for your type of business is 12%.

With the above information, you calculate your normal profit as follows:

|  | **per annum** |
|---|---|
| Remuneration for time and effort | |
| (based on current market wages payable for a manager) | $40 000 |
| Return on owner's funds invested if desired rate of return is | |
| 6% + 12% = 18% | |
| then, | |
| $25 000 × 18% = | $4 500 |
| Normal profit | $44 500 |

The normal profit of $44 500 is the minimum amount of annual net profit that you will accept for the operation to be viable.

---

**EXERCISE**

**7.1**   You want to know what is an acceptable net profit for your business. You obtain the following information:

- You could earn $28 000 p.a. employed as a manager in a competitor's business.
- You currently have $40 000 invested in the business.
- The current bank deposit rate for a sum of $40 000 is 8% p.a.
- The acceptable risk allowance rate for businesses in your industry is 15% p.a.

Determine the minimum amount of annual net profit to accept for your business.

## BREAK‑EVEN ANALYSIS

A break-even analysis should be done before preparing financial plans for your operation. You should know the sales break-even point—that is, the level of sales necessary to meet total business running costs. You can also use break-even analysis to determine the level of sales required to achieve a desired profit target.

The steps for carrying out a break-even analysis for any period are as follows.

### Step 1: Estimate likely business costs

Business running costs (or expenses) can be identified for each operating function shown in your business plan. Some of the main running costs for each operating function are as follows.

*Marketing expenses:*

- advertising and promotions
- rent
- delivery costs (outwards)
- motor vehicle running costs (petrol, repairs, maintenance, depreciation, registration, insurance)
- packaging.

*Production expenses:*

- depreciation—factory plant and equipment
- repairs and maintenance—factory plant and equipment.

*Purchasing expenses:*

- trading stock purchases
- raw materials purchases
- job materials purchases
- delivery costs (inwards)
- duties and customs charges.

*Personnel expenses:*

- gross wages, including PAYG tax (excluding owner's drawings)
- wage on-costs (e.g. workers' compensation insurance, employee superannuation, training costs, staff amenities)
- gross contractors' fees, including any PAYG tax
- advisers' fees (e.g. accountant's fees).

*Financial and administrative expenses:*

- interest paid
- bank charges
- legal fees (e.g. licence/permit fees)
- stationery
- electricity
- telephone

- postage
- depreciation—office furniture and machines
- general business insurances
- ISP Fees
- other general expenses.

Expense estimates should reflect realistic expectations and be consistent with your proposed business strategies.

## Step 2: Categorise costs as fixed or variable

For break-even analysis purposes, business running costs identified are categorised as being either fixed or variable costs.

- *Fixed costs* (i.e. overheads) are constant. They do not change when sales volumes change provided the business does not change its operating capacity. Examples of fixed costs are rent, depreciation, wages and interest paid.
- *Variable costs* change proportionally to changes in volumes of business activity. When sales volumes change, these costs generally do so too. Examples of variable costs are stock purchases, raw materials purchases and job materials purchases.

## Step 3: Calculate the contribution margin

The sales income of the business must be enough to cover its variable costs and fixed costs as well as the required profit. The contribution margin is the excess of sales income over the variable costs of the business for the period. The contribution margin measures how much sales contribute towards meeting fixed costs and desired profit.

The contribution margin can also be expressed as a percentage. The contribution margin percentage measures how much in each sales dollar contributes towards meeting fixed costs and profit.

The contribution margin (%) is calculated as follows (for the period):

$$\text{Contribution margin on sales (\%)} = \frac{\text{Sales income (\$)} - \text{Variable costs (\$)}}{\text{Sales income (\$)}} \times 100$$

---

**EXAMPLE**

Your business's estimated sales income is \$316 000 for the year and its variable costs are expected to be \$194 000.

The contribution margin is:

$$\$316\,000 - \$194\,000 = \$122\,000$$

The contribution margin (%) on sales is:

$$\frac{\$316\,000 - \$194\,000}{\$316\,000} \times 100 = 38.6\%$$

This means that each \$1 of sales contributes 38.6 cents towards fixed costs and profit.

## Step 4: Calculate the break-even point

With a knowledge of the contribution margin (%), you can find the business's break-even point—the level of sales at which income equals expenses (costs) so that neither a profit nor a loss is made. The break-even level of sales is calculated as follows (for the period):

$$\text{Break-even point of sales (\$)} = \frac{\text{Fixed costs (\$)}}{\text{Contribution margin on sales (\%)}}$$

**EXAMPLE**

The following estimations are made for your business for the year:

| | |
|---|---|
| Sales | $380 000 |
| Fixed costs | $150 600 |
| Variable costs | $182 400 |
| Net profit (before tax) | $47 000 |

Variable costs ($182 400) as a percentage of sales ($380 000) are 48%. This means that 48 cents of every sales dollar is used to cover variable costs, while 52 cents must cover fixed costs and profit.

The contribution margin (%) is:

$$\frac{\$380\,000 - \$182\,400}{\$380\,000} \times 100 = 52\%$$

The break-even point of sales is therefore calculated as follows:

$$\frac{\$150\,600}{0.52} = \$289\,615$$

At this sales level, all costs are covered and there is no profit.

Annual break-even sales can be shown separately underneath forecast profit statements in your business plan.

You can also use break-even analysis to find the level of sales required to cover costs (both fixed and variable) to achieve any desired profit target. The desired sales level is calculated as follows (for the period):

$$\text{Required sales (\$)} = \frac{\text{Fixed costs (\$)} + \text{Desired profit (\$)}}{\text{Contribution margin on sales (\%)}}$$

**EXAMPLE**

The same estimates apply for your business as in the previous example. Additionally, your desired net profit target is $38 000. The required sales level is therefore calculated as follows:

$$\frac{\$150\,600 + \$38\,000}{0.52} = \$362\,692$$

At this sales level, total costs are recovered as well as the desired profit target of $38 000.

Any break-even analysis is based on the following assumptions:

- All costs can be separated into either fixed or variable costs.
- Fixed costs remain constant if the business is operating within its maximum capacity.
- Selling prices are constant.
- Labour productivity remains unchanged.
- Prices paid for inputs remain the same.
- The product mix is the same.
- Stock levels are steady.

---

### EXERCISES

7.2    Define each of the following:
       (a) fixed costs
       (b) variable costs
       (c) break-even point
       (d) contribution margin.

7.3    Your business has the following estimates for the year:

| | |
|---|---|
| Sales | $214 000 |
| Fixed costs | $132 000 |
| Variable costs | $64 000 |
| Profit (before tax) | $18 000 |

       (a) Calculate the sales break-even point for the business.
       (b) If the business has a desired profit target of $42 000, what level of sales is
           required?

---

## FINANCIAL PLAN GUIDELINES

The financial plan is always the last component plan attempted in the plan-building process for a business plan. It is prepared after completing the marketing and any production, purchasing and personnel plans for the operation. A financial plan is the financial expression of the objectives and strategies for all operational functions, such as marketing, production, purchasing and personnel. These objectives and strategies are shown in the other component plans.

The financial forecasts in the financial plan must be consistent with all the other aspects of the operational plan. Realistic and achievable financial forecasts will enable you to evaluate the viability of a proposed operation, as well as to set measurable targets to achieve. If you are seeking a loan, lenders will always examine the financial forecasts and look at how you intend to control the financial aspects of the business.

A comprehensive financial plan will include forecasts for the planned operation as well as controls to ensure financial targets are achieved. An outline of the 'Financial plan' section of the business plan is shown in Table 7.1.

**TABLE 7.1** Financial plan outline

**Section F. Financial plan**

**F.1 Personal financial position**
(Show the personal financial position of each business owner. Include a statement of personal net worth and a statement of monthly personal commitments for each owner.)

**F.2 Establishment costs**
(List the estimated establishment costs for the proposed business.)

**F.3 Borrowing requirements**
(Show here details of any proposed loans required.)

**F.4 Financial forecasts**
(Provide detailed financial estimates of business performance for each year of the plan. Include forecasts for profit, capital expenditure, cash flows and financial position for each year.)

**F.5 Financial records**
(Briefly describe the financial record system to be used to report financial results.)

**F.6 Business insurances**
(List proposed insurances to be arranged for the operation, including any compulsory insurances required under the law.)

**F.7 Financial controls**
(Describe what methods will be used to monitor and evaluate financial results of the operation.)

## F.1 PERSONAL FINANCIAL POSITION

To begin financial planning, assess the personal financial position of each business owner. This requires the preparation of two personal financial statements (see Figure 7.1).

To determine how much personal capital you have available to start the business, prepare a current statement of personal net worth. This will list all your assets (what you own) and liabilities (what you owe). The difference between your total personal assets and total personal liabilities is your personal net worth (which may be a surplus or a deficit). Lenders will require a statement of personal net worth to assess your history of financial success and whether your security is adequate. The format of a statement of personal net worth is shown in Figure 7.1. If you jointly own an asset or owe a liability, show only your share.

The second personal financial statement to prepare is a current statement of monthly personal expenses. Your statement of monthly personal expenditure could include the items shown in Figure 7.1.

**FIGURE 7.1**  Personal financial statements

STATEMENT OF PERSONAL NET WORTH AS AT _____

| | $ |
|---|---|
| PERSONAL ASSETS (current selling value) | |
| Real estate | _____ |
| Furniture and contents | _____ |
| Savings and investments | _____ |
| Collectables | _____ |
| Cash on hand | _____ |
| Motor vehicle | _____ |
| Other assets | _____ |
| *TOTAL PERSONAL ASSETS* | _____ |
| *less* PERSONAL LIABILITIES (current balance owing) | |
| Mortgage | _____ |
| Personal loans | _____ |
| Credit cards | _____ |
| Other liabilities | _____ |
| *TOTAL PERSONAL LIABILITIES* | _____ |
| **PERSONAL NET WORTH** | $_____ |

STATEMENT OF CURRENT MONTHLY PERSONAL EXPENSES

| | $ |
|---|---|
| EXPENSES | |
| Food | _____ |
| Household necessities | _____ |
| Clothing | _____ |
| Motor vehicle running costs (e.g. petrol, repairs, maintenance, registration, insurance) | _____ |
| Rent/mortgage | _____ |
| Rates | _____ |
| Electricity and telephone | _____ |
| Personal loans/credit cards | _____ |
| Entertainment | _____ |
| Medical | _____ |
| Superannuation/insurances | _____ |
| Other expenses | _____ |
| **TOTAL MONTHLY PERSONAL EXPENSES** | $_____ |

Convert all annual or quarterly outgoings to monthly equivalents. For example, annual car insurance for $600 would be $50 per month. Knowing your personal commitments will help you calculate the amount of cash drawings you will need to take from the business. Your business must be able to support and maintain your lifestyle.

**EXERCISES**

**7.4**    Prepare a current statement of your personal net worth.

**7.5**    Prepare a current statement of your monthly personal expenditure.

## F.2 ESTABLISHMENT COSTS

No matter what entry method you adopt, you will need an initial outlay of money to set up your operating structure and procure resources to commence the operation. Prepare a detailed list of estimated establishment costs (see Figure 7.2) to determine how much you will need. Cost items will depend on the entry method selected.

---

**FIGURE 7.2** Establishment costs

|  | Estimated cost |
|---|---|
| **Starting up a business** | **$** |
| Furniture and fittings<br>List the cost of items such as desks, chairs, filing cabinets, shelving, partitions | _____ |
| Plant and equipment<br>List the cost of items such as machinery, ovens, freezers, forklifts, staff amenities | _____ |
| Office machines<br>List the cost of items such as computers, photocopiers, facsimiles, telephone<br>systems, word processors, calculators | _____ |
| Motor vehicles<br>List the cost of motor vehicles to be used in the business | _____ |
| Repairs to premises<br>List the cost of any repairs needed to the business premises | _____ |
| Renovations to premises<br>List the cost of materials and labour for structural alterations, building<br>improvements or additions to the premises | _____ |
| Utilities<br>List the costs of connecting gas, electricity and telephones and any security<br>deposits to be paid on connection | _____ |
| Lease costs<br>If leasing the premises, list the costs of the lease such as advance rent,<br>security deposits, legal fees for lease preparation and stamp duty on the lease | _____ |
| Land and premises<br>If buying the premises, list the purchase price, legal fees for the purchase and<br>stamp duty on the purchase | _____ |
| Registrations, permits, licences and approvals<br>List the costs for various registrations, permits, licences and approvals required | |

to carry on the business (e.g. lodgement fee for development application to local council)   _____

Records and stationery
List the cost of items such as printed source documents, record books, business cards, letterheads, envelopes, writing aids, computer software   _____

Insurances
List the costs of all the various business insurances to be arranged   _____

Initial promotions
List the costs of initial advertising such as *Yellow Pages*, brochures, direct mail, window signs, outside signs, website design   _____

Trading stock
List the cost of initial stock or raw materials supplies   _____

Advisers' fees
List the cost of advisers' fees, such as accountants and solicitors   _____

Incorporation costs
If using a company structure, list the costs of incorporating the company   _____

First three months of operating expenses
When starting up a business, allow for the first three months of recurring operating expenses while sales are growing; these expense items include advertising, rent, wages, electricity, telephone; also include owner's drawings   _____

Borrowing costs
List the costs of any borrowings required, such as loan establishment fees, other lender charges and loan interest (for the first three months)   _____

**Total establishment costs**   $_____

| **Buying a business** | $ |
|---|---|

Purchase price
This is the price paid for the business: it consists of business assets and goodwill (include the stamp duty paid on the agreement)   _____

Trading stock
This is the agreed value paid for the trading stock or raw materials in the purchase of the business   _____

Additional business assets
List the cost of any additional business assets required for the business   _____

Additional trading stock
List the cost of additional trading stock or raw materials required for the business   _____

Lease costs
List the costs of the lease, such as advance rent, security deposits, legal fees for lease preparation and stamp duty on the lease   _____

Registrations, permits, licences and approvals
List the costs for various registrations, permits, licences and approvals (e.g. the lodgement fee for a DA with local council)   _____

Records and stationery
List the costs of all items of records and stationery required for the business    _____

Insurances
List the costs of all the various business insurances to be arranged    _____

Initial promotions
List the costs of all additional promotions required for the business
(these should be minimal for an existing business)    _____

Advisers' fees
List the cost of advisers' fees, such as accountants and solicitors    _____

Borrowing costs
List the costs of any borrowings required, such as loan establishment fees and
other upfront lender charges    _____

**Total establishment costs**    $_____

| | |
|---|---|
| **Obtaining a franchise** | $ |

Establishment cost items will be similar to those for starting up a business.
Also include additional amounts for the following:    _____

Franchise entry fee
Show any upfront fee paid to the franchisor    _____

Stamp duty
List the duty paid on the franchise agreement    _____

Extra operating expenses
List expenses in the first three months for franchise royalty fees and any
advertising levies (both based on a fixed percentage of sales) which are paid
to the franchisor    _____

**Total establishment costs**    $_____

### EXERCISE

**7.6**    For whichever entry method you adopt, estimate the total establishment costs to begin your operation.

## F.3 BORROWING REQUIREMENTS

When you have estimated your total establishment (or expansion) costs, you can estimate the amount to be borrowed. This is calculated by deducting your total cash capital from the estimated total establishment (or expansion) costs of the business:

Total establishment costs estimated    $_____

*less* Total available personal capital    $_____

Borrowing amount required    $_____

When deciding whether to borrow or to invest personal funds, be aware of the advantages and disadvantages of each alternative (see Table 7.2).

| **TABLE 7.2** Funding advantages/disadvantages | |
|---|---|
| **Borrowed funds** | **Owner's funds** |
| *Advantages:* | *Advantages:* |
| Generally cheaper than owner's funds | Easier to access than borrowed funds |
| No ownership rights given to lenders | Does not restrict future borrowing ability |
| Loan interest is tax deductible | No repayment obligations |
| *Disadvantages:* | *Disadvantages:* |
| Fixed loan obligations must be repaid | Owner's funds are usually limited |
| Lending criteria must be met | No taxation benefits |
| Lenders normally require security | Loss of control if outsiders involved |

As a general rule of thumb, any borrowing amount should not be more than 60% of the total estimated establishment costs. Too high a borrowing amount can over-burden the small business with loan repayments, especially in the early stages.

**EXAMPLE**

You estimate the total establishment costs to start your business to be $68 000. You have $15 000 cash available to put into the business as personal capital. Your borrowing requirement is determined as follows:

| | |
|---|---|
| Total establishment costs estimated | $68 000 |
| *less* Total available personal capital | $15 000 |
| Estimated amount to be borrowed | $53 000 |

Your borrowing percentage is calculated as:

$$\frac{\$53\ 000}{\$68\ 000} \times 100 = 78\%$$

This is more than the 60% recommended, which is not advisable.

Specify any borrowing requirements in the following terms:

- the type and amount of the loan
- the period of the loan
- the loan source
- the use of the loan
- the date the loan is required.

Be prepared to shop around to get the best financing deal—the commercial lending market is highly competitive. Generally, the major trading banks will offer the cheapest and widest range of financing options to small businesses. Some of the main commercial loan sources and the types of loans they offer are summarised in Table 7.3. Further information about each loan type can be obtained from the website of the particular lender.

Select the right type of loan (see Table 7.3) to minimise the costs of finance.

| **TABLE 7.3** Loan sources and types | |
|---|---|
| **Loan sources** | **Loan types offered** |
| Trade suppliers | Trade credit |
| Trading banks | Business overdraft, business term loan, credit card, finance lease, commercial bill, commercial hire purchase, equipment rental, debtor finance |
| Savings banks | Personal loan, home equity loan |
| Building societies | Business overdraft, business term loan, credit card, personal loan, home equity loan, finance lease |
| Credit unions | Personal loan, credit card, business overdraft, business term loan |
| Finance companies | Finance lease, credit card, personal loan, commercial hire purchase, equipment rental, factoring |

Short-term loans (for periods of up to one year) include supplier's trade credit, business overdrafts, credit cards, commercial bills, debtor finance and factoring. Short-term loans are best used for short-term applications such as trading stock purchases or to temporarily meet operating expenses—for example, wages and rent. Long-term loans (for periods beyond one year) include business term loans, finance leases, commercial hire purchase, equipment rental, personal loans and home equity loans. Capital expenditure for long-term assets (e.g. plant and equipment) is best financed with longer-term loans. The period of the loan should be similar to the period the business will benefit from using the asset. Matching loan periods with the estimated useful life of the asset keeps the costs of financing the asset to a minimum.

Fixed interest rate loans should be sought in periods when interest rates are low or are rising. Variable rate loans are more suitable in periods when interest rates are high or are dropping.

Business term loans, finance leases, commercial hire purchase and equipment rentals offer fixed rates; business term loans, business overdrafts, credit cards, commercial bills and debtor finance offer variable interest rates.

Any proposed borrowings should be included in your financial forecasts to follow.

## EXERCISES

**7.7** Determine the amount to be borrowed to establish your operation.

**7.8** Evaluate the acceptability of your borrowing amount.

**7.9** What lenders generally provide the cheapest and widest range of finance to small businesses?

**7.10** Detail the loan requirements you will seek for your borrowing amount. Specify:
- the type and amount of the loan
- the period of the loan
- the loan source
- the loan use
- the date the loan is required.

**7.11** You require a new motor vehicle for your business, costing $25,000 on 1 July. You intend to borrow the whole amount and use the vehicle for four years. Specify the best loan to seek. Refer to:
- the type and amount of the loan
- the period of the loan
- the loan source
- the loan use
- the date the loan is required.

## F.4 FINANCIAL FORECASTS

Financial forecasts are the detailed financial estimates of business performance for each financial year (1 July to next 30 June) of the operation. Financial forecasts are financial expressions of the operational plan. The financial forecasts must therefore be consistent with all parts of your operational plan.

Because financial forecasts are interdependent, prepare your business forecasts for the planning period in the following order:
- forecast monthly sales statements for each year
- forecast profit statements for each year
- forecast capital expenditure statements for each year
- forecast cash flow statements for each year
- forecast financial position statements at the end of each year.

Your financial forecasts should allow for any proposed borrowings and show any assumptions made in their preparation as a brief note underneath. You could also include a table of key financial ratios calculated (with industry averages) from the information shown in each year's financial forecasts. These ratios summarise the acceptability of your financial forecasts.

## EXERCISE

**7.12** Complete the following statement.
A financial year starts on the _____ and ends on the _____

## Forecast sales statements

Sales income forecasts should be the first forecasts made when planning profit. The sales forecast is of prime importance because it influences many of the cost forecasts for your operation.

Your sales forecasts must be consistent with the sales objectives for your marketing program. Sales should be increasing in successive years to reflect business growth and because business costs rise over time. As a general rule, satisfactory annual sales growth should be at least 10%.

Your sales forecasts must be achievable and reflect realistic expectations.

Forecast annual sales for each year of your plan. It may be easier to estimate the quantity to be sold (measured in product units or service hours) first, and then apply an average selling price to calculate forecast sales for the period (see Figure 7.3).

---

**FIGURE 7.3** Forecast sales quantities

Product/service type _____

|  | Product units/<br>service hours | Average sale price<br>(per unit/per hour) | Total sales (p.a.) |
|---|---|---|---|
| Year 1 | _____ units/hours | $_____ | $_____ p.a. |
| Year 2 | _____ units/hours | $_____ | $_____ p.a. |
| Year 3 | _____ units/hours | $_____ | $_____ p.a. |

---

You should prepare a separate statement of sales forecasts for each year. The statement should show annual sales at monthly intervals (see Figure 7.4). This allows you to consider monthly seasonal variations in annual sales.

Your total annual sales forecast should be the same as the sales objective for your marketing program. The seasonality factor is simply the percentage of total annual sales expected for each month.

## Forecast profit statements

Prepare a forecast profit statement showing the annual net profit target of the operation for each year. A forecast profit statement is also called a forecast income statement. Annual income and expense forecasts are arranged into the format of a forecast profit statement (see Figure 7.5). Income forecasts are the expected sales for the period (shown in the forecast sales statement). Expense forecasts are the expected running costs of inputs to be used in the operation to generate sales for the same period. Net profit is the excess of expected sales over expenses for the period.

---

**FIGURE 7.4** Forecast monthly sales statements

Product/service type _____

| Month | Seasonality factor (%) | Year 1 sales ($) | Year 2 sales ($) | Year 3 sales ($) |
|-------|------------------------|------------------|------------------|------------------|
| 1 | _____ | _____ | _____ | _____ |
| 2 | _____ | _____ | _____ | _____ |
| 3 | _____ | _____ | _____ | _____ |
| 4 | _____ | _____ | _____ | _____ |
| 5 | _____ | _____ | _____ | _____ |
| 6 | _____ | _____ | _____ | _____ |
| 7 | _____ | _____ | _____ | _____ |
| 8 | _____ | _____ | _____ | _____ |
| 9 | _____ | _____ | _____ | _____ |
| 10 | _____ | _____ | _____ | _____ |
| 11 | _____ | _____ | _____ | _____ |
| 12 | _____ | _____ | _____ | _____ |
| **Totals** | **100%** | $_____ | $_____ | $_____ |

---

Income and expense forecasts must reflect realistic expectations and be consistent with your business plan. They must be accurate financial expressions of your planned business activities.

The contents of a forecast profit statement (see Figure 7.5) are explained as follows.

## Income

Income is the forecast sales and/or service fees earned for the period.

## Cost of sales

If you sell stock, cost of sales is the estimated cost of stock sold in the period. Annual cost of sales can be calculated simply if you know both the forecast sales and the average gross profit margin you require (gross profit margin is explained later). The average gross profit margin can be based on the industry average—see Chapter 5. For example, if your forecast sales for Year 1 is $20 000 and the industry average gross profit margin is 30%, the cost of sales for Year 1 is calculated as follows.

| Year 1 | $ |
|--------|---|
| Sales | 200 000 |
| *less* Cost of sales | 140 000 |
| Gross profit (at 30%) | $60 000 |

**FIGURE 7.5** Forecast profit statements

|  | Year 1 $ | Year 2 $ | Year 3 $ |
|---|---|---|---|
| INCOME |  |  |  |
| Sales | ——— | ——— | ——— |
| *less* COST OF SALES | ——— | ——— | ——— |
| GROSS PROFIT (at ———%) | $____ | $____ | $____ |
| *less* OPERATING EXPENSES |  |  |  |
| Accounting fees | ——— | ——— | ——— |
| Advertising and promotions | ——— | ——— | ——— |
| Bank charges | ——— | ——— | ——— |
| Depreciation | ——— | ——— | ——— |
| Electricity | ——— | ——— | ——— |
| Insurances | ——— | ——— | ——— |
| Interest paid | ——— | ——— | ——— |
| Legal fees | ——— | ——— | ——— |
| Motor vehicle running costs | ——— | ——— | ——— |
| Rent | ——— | ——— | ——— |
| Stationery | ——— | ——— | ——— |
| Telephone | ——— | ——— | ——— |
| Wages (gross) | ——— | ——— | ——— |
| Wages on-costs | ——— | ——— | ——— |
| Other expenses | ——— | ——— | ——— |
| *Total operating expenses* | ——— | ——— | ——— |
| **NET PROFIT before tax** | $____ | $____ | $____ |

Assumptions

If you run a service business which does not sell stock, there will be no cost of sales forecast.

### Gross profit

If you sell stock, gross profit is calculated by deducting the cost of sales from sales for the period. If you run a service business which does not sell stock, there will be no gross profit calculation.

### Operating expenses

Operating expenses are the running costs of your operation. These costs are determined after analysing your planned operating activities. Expense forecasts should reflect realistic expectations and be consistent with your proposed business strategies. Cost forecasts will normally increase from year to year, as most costs rise over time. Unless costs are determinable, they should be increased by at least the rate of inflation from year to year. Annual movements in the consumer price index (CPI) published by the ABS can be used as a general measure of the yearly inflation rate.

Recognise that depreciation is included as an operating expense. Depreciation is an annual estimate of the rate of wear and tear on the long-term physical assets used in the operation, such as plant and equipment. Depreciation estimates are usually based on a percentage of the original cost of the asset—for example, 15% of $1000 = $150 p.a. (depreciation).

Note that the owner's drawings are not included as an operating expense in calculating profit. Owner's drawings are shown in your forecast cash flow statements, which are explained later. An exception to this is if you operate your business as a company. Because a company is a separate legal entity, owner's wages are a legitimate operating expense of the company.

Total operating expenses are also shown for each annual period.

### Net profit before tax

Net profit before tax is calculated by deducting your total operating expenses from gross profit (if applicable) or otherwise from income for the period. If expenses exceed the gross profit, the difference is a net loss.

Net profit is always calculated before income tax. This is because income tax is not included as a business expense to calculate profit. Anticipated income tax charged on business profit is included as a separate payment in the forecast cash flow statement.

### Assumptions

Any assumptions used to prepare your forecast profit statements should be briefly stated as a note underneath. Assumptions could include:
- annual inflation rate (%) used to increase non-determinable costs each year
- annual depreciation rates (%) used
- annual interest rates (%) used
- what percentage of wages are wages on-costs
- the components of any specific expenses such as wages on-costs or motor vehicle running costs
- stock levels are steady.

## Forecast capital expenditure statements

Prepare an annual capital expenditure forecast for each year. A forecast capital expenditure statement shows financial details of your proposed capital expenditure in the business plan.

Capital expenditure refers to outlays for long-term assets such as plant and equipment to be used in the operation. Each item of capital expenditure will normally involve a large cash outlay. It is likely that most of your proposed capital expenditure will be in the early stages to start your operation. Other reasons for capital expenditure could include replacing existing assets or expanding the business during the course of operations.

Annual forecast capital expenditure statements are shown in Figure 7.6. The format shows the date, type, amount and timing of proposed capital expenditure.

---

**FIGURE 7.6** Forecast capital expenditure statements

| Date and type of expenditure | Year 1 | Year 2 | Year 3 |
|---|---|---|---|
| _____ | $_____ | $_____ | $_____ |
| _____ | $_____ | $_____ | $_____ |
| _____ | $_____ | $_____ | $_____ |
| _____ | $_____ | $_____ | $_____ |
| Totals | $_____ | $_____ | $_____ |

---

Capital expenditure forecasts must be consistent with your other financial forecasts, as well as your business plan. Proposed capital expenditure must also be included in your cash flow forecasts and accounted for in your financial position forecasts.

**EXERCISE**

**7.13** Prepare a forecast capital expenditure statement for the next three years of your operation.

## Forecast cash flow statements

After you have prepared your forecast profit statements and capital expenditure statements, prepare forecast cash flow statements for each year of your business plan. Lenders will closely examine your cash flow forecasts to determine the ability of the business to meet loan repayments (see Chapter 8).

A cash flow statement shows the cash receipts and payments of the operation for a period, which enables the cash position to be calculated. A forecast cash flow statement shows the expected cash receipts and payments of the business, which enables future cash positions to be predicted. Cash receipt and payment forecasts must reflect realistic expectations.

Cash flow forecasts will largely depend on your income and expense (as well as capital expenditure) forecasts. However, you should recognise that income and expense items are not necessarily the same as cash receipts and payments items. These differences are observed by examining the illustrated formats of the forecast profit statement and forecast cash flow statement.

The format of a cash flow statement is arranged to be a continuous running account of the cash position of the business for the period. Each period begins with an opening cash position. Categories of cash receipts followed by cash payments are next shown for each period. The difference between total cash receipts and payments for the period is calculated as the net cash flow (which may be either positive or negative). The closing cash position at the end of the period is the opening cash position plus (or minus) the net cash flow for the period. The closing cash position also carries over to become the opening cash position of the next period.

The format of a forecast cash flow statement is shown in Figure 7.7.

**FIGURE 7.7** Forecast cash flow statements

|  | Year 1 $ | Year 2 $ | Year 3 $ |
|---|---|---|---|
| Cash position—start of year | $_____ | $_____ | $_____ |
| CASH RECEIPTS |  |  |  |
| Cash sales | _____ | _____ | _____ |
| Cash from sales debtors | _____ | _____ | _____ |
| Proceeds from long-term asset disposals | _____ | _____ | _____ |
| Capital contributions | _____ | _____ | _____ |
| Borrowings | _____ | _____ | _____ |
| Total cash receipts | _____ | _____ | _____ |
| less CASH PAYMENTS |  |  |  |
| Stock purchases | _____ | _____ | _____ |
| Operating expenses | _____ | _____ | _____ |
| Loan repayments | _____ | _____ | _____ |
| Capital expenditure | _____ | _____ | _____ |
| Owners drawings | _____ | _____ | _____ |
| Taxation | _____ | _____ | _____ |
| Total cash payments | _____ | _____ | _____ |
| **NET CASH FLOW** | $_____ | $_____ | $_____ |
| Cash position—end of year | $_____ | $_____ | $_____ |
| Assumptions |  |  |  |

The contents of the forecast cash flow statement are explained as follows.

## Cash position—start of year
For Year 1, the opening cash position is the expected cash balance at the beginning of the first year. This will be a positive amount or zero. If you have a pre-existing bank

overdraft at the start of planning, the cash position at the start of Year 1 will be a negative figure, representing the overdraft amount used.

For all years after Year 1, the cash position at the start of the year will equal the cash position at the end of the previous year (see below).

## Cash receipts

The main categories of cash receipts are shown in Figure 7.7.

Annual sales receipts will depend on your annual sales forecasts. Analyse the monthly sales forecasts to determine how much is in cash and how much is in credit. For the credit sales, you will need to make assumptions about when the cash will be received—for example, assume credit sales are collected in the following month. By analysing monthly sales in this way, you can determine annual sales receipts.

---

**EXAMPLE**

Say the sales estimate for Months 10, 11 and 12 of Year 1 are as follows:

|  | Month 10 | Month 11 | Month 12 |
|---|---|---|---|
| Sales | $4600 | $5200 | $5800 |

You make the following assumptions:

- 90% of monthly sales will be for cash
- 10% of monthly sales will be for credit
- credit sales will be collected in the following month
- sales for Month 9 were $4400.

The estimated sales receipts for each month would be:

|  |  | **Month 10** |
|---|---|---|
| Cash sales | $4140 | ($4600 × 90%) |
| Cash from sales debtors | $440 | ($4400 × 10%) |
| Total receipts | $4580 | |

|  |  | **Month 11** |
|---|---|---|
| Cash sales | $4680 | ($5200 × 90%) |
| Cash from sales debtors | $460 | ($4600 × 10%) |
| Total receipts | $5140 | |

|  |  | **Month 12** |
|---|---|---|
| Cash sales | $5220 | ($5800 × 90%) |
| Cash from sales debtors | $520 | ($5200 × 10%) |
| Total receipts | $5740 | |

Note that credit sales of $580 (i.e. $5800 × 10%) for Month 12 are expected to be collected in the first month of the next year.

---

Proceeds from asset sales are cash receipts from any disposal sale of long-term assets used in the business.

Capital contributions refer to any owners' cash put into the business.

Borrowings relate to any cash sums received from lenders. They do not include bank overdrafts. A bank overdraft is a line of credit granted by a bank, allowing a bank account to be overdrawn up to a limit.

After you have forecast your annual cash receipts, show a total.

## Cash payments

The main categories of cash payments shown in the forecast cash flow statement are self-explanatory (see Figure 7.7). Payments for major operating expenses could be shown separately—for example, materials purchases, rent, wages and wages on-costs.

Note that cash payments are not necessarily the same as operating expenses included in the forecast profit statement. Not all cash payment items are shown as operating expenses in the forecast profit statement. Both owner's drawings and capital expenditure are cash payments but are not included as operating expenses in the forecast profit statement. Conversely, depreciation is shown as an operating expense but is not a cash payment. With loan repayments, only the interest paid is recognised as an operating expense; the full amount of the loan repayment is shown as a cash payment. Any anticipated income tax on business profit is also shown as a separate payment, not as an operating expense.

Cash payments for stock purchases and capital expenditure are likely to be abnormally high in the first year of operation to account for set-up costs.

After you have forecast your annual cash payments, show a total.

## Net cash flow

Net cash flow is calculated by deducting estimated total cash payments from the estimated total cash receipts for the year. The net cash flow may be either positive or negative.

## Cash position—end of year

The closing cash position at the end of each year is calculated as the estimated opening cash position at the start of the year (positive or negative) plus (or minus) the calculated net cash flow estimate for the year. A positive end-of-year cash position indicates an anticipated cash surplus, while a negative end-of-year cash position represents a cash shortage or deficit. A negative end-of-year cash position will be acceptable as long as any overdraft limit is not exceeded.

The end-of-year cash position is carried over to become the opening cash position at the start of the next year.

## Assumptions

Any assumptions used to prepare your forecast cash flow statements should be stated briefly as a note underneath. Assumptions could include:
- the relative proportion of cash sales and credit sales in annual sales
- the average collection period for credit sales
- interest rates (%) used

- the average payment period for credit expenses
- the timing of taxation payments.

## Forecast financial position statements

Forecast financial position statements should be the last financial forecasts prepared, because they depend on your earlier forecasts. If you are already in business, prepare a current financial position statement of the business. Next, prepare forecast financial position statements for the end of each year of your planning period. Forecast financial position statements are condensed balance sheets, without the balancing aspects.

A financial position statement shows the assets and liabilities of the business as at the last day of the financial period. In the statement, assets and liabilities are categorised as being either short term or long term.

The format of a financial position statement is presented so that:

Total assets – Total liabilities = Net assets (= Proprietor's funds invested in the business)

Net assets represent the value of your investment in the business.

Make sure that your financial position forecasts are consistent with your other statements of financial forecasts.

The format of a forecast financial position statement is shown in Figure 7.8 and the contents are explained below.

### Assets

'Assets' is the first major heading. Assets are further classified as either 'short-term assets' or 'long-term assets' (see below).

### Short-term assets

Short-term or current assets are assets owned by the business at 30 June that will be converted into cash within twelve months. The three main types of short-term assets are cash, stock-on-hand and trade debtors. If you show cash as a short-term asset, make sure your cash amount is consistent with the cash surplus in your closing cash position shown in the cash flow forecast for the same period. Any debtors shown should also be consistent with the assumptions in your cash flow forecast for debtor collections.

A total should be shown for short-term assets.

### Long-term assets

Long-term or non-current assets represent the cost of physical assets owned by the business at 30 June that are expected to be used for more than twelve months. The main types of long-term assets are: plant and equipment, furniture and fittings, office machines and motor vehicles. The amount of accumulated depreciation for each asset should also be separately shown as a deduction underneath the asset. Accumulated depreciation is the cumulative amount of depreciation expense (found in the forecast

**FIGURE 7.8** Forecast financial position statements

|  | Year 1 | Year 2 | Year 3 |
|---|---|---|---|
|  | $ | $ | $ |
| ASSETS |  |  |  |
| *Short-term assets* |  |  |  |
| Cash | _____ | _____ | _____ |
| Stock (at cost) | _____ | _____ | _____ |
| Debtors | _____ | _____ | _____ |
| *Subtotal* | _____ | _____ | _____ |
| *Long-term assets* |  |  |  |
| Plant and equipment (at cost) | _____ | _____ | _____ |
| *less* Accumulated depreciation | _____ | _____ | _____ |
| Furniture and fittings (at cost) | _____ | _____ | _____ |
| *less* Accumulated depreciation | _____ | _____ | _____ |
| Office machines (at cost) | _____ | _____ | _____ |
| *less* Accumulated depreciation | _____ | _____ | _____ |
| *Subtotal* | _____ | _____ | _____ |
| TOTAL ASSETS | $_____ | $_____ | $_____ |
| *less* LIABILITIES |  |  |  |
| *Short-term liabilities* |  |  |  |
| Overdraft | _____ | _____ | _____ |
| Creditors | _____ | _____ | _____ |
| *Subtotal* | _____ | _____ | _____ |
| *Long-term liabilities* |  |  |  |
| Term loan | _____ | _____ | _____ |
| *Subtotal* | _____ | _____ | _____ |
| TOTAL LIABILITIES | $_____ | $_____ | $_____ |
| **NET ASSETS** | $_____ | $_____ | $_____ |

Assumptions

profit statement) for each asset. For example, if the depreciation expense for plant is $600 in each annual profit forecast, the accumulated depreciation for plant will be $600 in Year 1, $1200 in Year 2 and $1800 in Year 3.

A total should be shown for long-term assets.

## Total assets
Total assets are calculated after adding total short-term assets to total long-term assets.

## Liabilities
Liabilities is the second major heading used. Liabilities are further classified into either short-term liabilities or long-term liabilities (see overleaf).

### Short-term liabilities

Short-term or current liabilities are the value of short-term obligations owed by the business at 30 June that are expected to be repaid within twelve months. Two possible short-term liabilities could be the bank overdraft and trade creditors. Any bank overdraft amount should be consistent with any cash deficiency in your closing cash position shown in the cash flow forecast for the same period.

A total should be shown for short-term liabilities.

### Long-term liabilities

Long-term or non-current liabilities are the value of any long-term obligations owed by the business at 30 June which are expected to be repaid in more than twelve months. An example of a long-term liability is a term loan for a period of more than one year.

A total should be shown for long-term liabilities.

### Total liabilities

Total liabilities are calculated by adding total short-term liabilities to total long-term liabilities.

### Net assets

Net assets are calculated by deducting total liabilities from total assets. This amount also represents the business owner's level of investment in the business.

### Assumptions

Any assumptions used to prepare your forecast financial position statements should be briefly stated as a note underneath. Assumptions could include:

- the rate of stock turnover
- the value shown for assets (e.g. at original cost price).

## Financial ratios

You could also supplement your forecast financial statements with a table of financial ratios (see Table 7.4).

Financial ratios measure relationships between the financial information shown in these statements. The calculation of financial ratios provides a useful summary of the acceptability of forecasts. They can be used to identify strengths and weaknesses in planned operating activities.

Ratios are compared with standard benchmarks such as industry averages for acceptability. Ratios should also be improving over time. The identification of any unacceptable ratios should cause you to review and adjust relevant sections of the operational plan to produce satisfactory forecasts.

Each financial ratio shown in Table 7.4 is now explained briefly.

**TABLE 7.4** Table of financial ratios

|  | Year 1 | Year 2 | Year 3 | Industry average |
|---|---|---|---|---|
| **Financial performance ratios**: | | | | |
| • *gross profit margin* | _____% | _____% | _____% | _____% |
| i.e. $\dfrac{\text{gross profit}}{\text{sales}} \times 100 = x\%$ | | | | |
| • *operating expenses ratio* | _____% | _____% | _____% | _____% |
| i.e. $\dfrac{\text{operating expenses}}{\text{sales}} \times 100 = x\%$ | | | | |
| • *net profit margin* | _____% | _____% | _____% | _____% |
| i.e. $\dfrac{\text{net profit}}{\text{sales}} \times 100 = x\%$ | | | | |
| **Financial position ratios**: | | | | |
| • *short-term solvency ratio* | \$_____ : \$1 | \$_____ : \$1 | \$_____ : \$1 | \$_____ : \$1 |
| i.e. $\dfrac{\text{short-term assets}}{\text{short-term liabilities}} = \$x : \$1$ | | | | |
| • *debt ratio* | _____% | _____% | _____% | _____% |
| i.e. $\dfrac{\text{total liabilities}}{\text{total assets}} \times 100 = x\%$ | | | | |

## Gross profit margin (for stock-selling businesses)

This ratio indicates what percentage of each sales dollar is gross profit. This is the gross profit margin in the sales dollar. The higher the ratio, the better.

The ratio helps to determine the acceptability of purchase costs for stock sold (assuming stock is sold at competitive prices). If the gross profit margin is too low, then stock supplies will have to be purchased more cheaply.

## Operating expense ratio

This ratio indicates what percentage of the sales dollar is absorbed by total operating expenses. The lower the ratio, the better.

If the ratio is too high, this should warn you that the costs of running the operation are excessive. In response, you should change planned operating strategies to reduce operating costs and/or change marketing strategies to increase sales. Specific ratios can also be calculated for individual major expense items such as advertising, rent and wages. Each specific expense is expressed as a percentage of sales. If specific expense ratios are too high, you can pinpoint which operational strategies need to be changed to reduce relevant costs.

## Net profit margin

This ratio indicates what percentage of each sales dollar is net profit. This is the net profit margin in the sales dollar. The higher the ratio, the better.

An unacceptable net profit margin suggests that the profitability of the total operation is unsatisfactory. You should revise all operational strategies so as to increase sales and/or reduce business costs.

### Short-term solvency ratio

This ratio is an indicator of the debt-paying ability of the business in the short term. It measures the availability of short-term assets to meet short-term liabilities, for example the amount of short-term assets there are for every $1 of short-term liability. The higher the ratio, the better.

This ratio tells you the level of short-term assets you own in relation to the level of short-term liabilities you owe. If the ratio is too low, you will have to change your strategies so as to increase short-term assets and/or decrease short-term liabilities.

### Debt ratio

The debt ratio is an important financial position ratio. It tells you the extent to which the business relies on outside borrowings to finance its assets. The lower the ratio, the better.

If the ratio is too high, then the debt level to be used in the operation is excessive. You will need to change your operating strategies to reduce debt levels and revise your financing needs.

### Benchmarks

Each financial ratio calculated must be interpreted for acceptability. This requires each ratio calculated to be compared with a similar ratio benchmark. Appropriate benchmarks could include past-period ratios and current industry averages for similar-sized businesses. A website showing industry averages is <www.ato.gov.au/businessbenchmarks>. There are also generally accepted standard benchmarks for some ratios. For example, the solvency ratio should be $2 : $1 (or better) and the debt ratio should be 60% (or less).

In addition, ratios based on forecasts should also be compared over time to indicate improving or declining trends.

**EXAMPLE**

Your profit statement forecasts for the next three years are summarised as follows.

|  | Year 1 $ | Year 2 $ | Year 3 $ |
|---|---|---|---|
| Sales income | $180 000 | $200 000 | $240 000 |
| *less* Cost of sales | $122 400 | $140 000 | $170 400 |
| Gross profit | $57 600 | $60 000 | $69 600 |
| *less* Operating expenses | $41 400 | $52 000 | $64 800 |
| **NET PROFIT before tax** | **$16 200** | **$8 000** | **$4 800** |

Your financial position statement forecasts for the next three years are summarised as follows:

|  | Year 1 | Year 2 | Year 3 |
|---|---|---|---|
|  | $ | $ | $ |
| Short-term assets | $120 000 | $130 000 | $140 000 |
| Long-term assets | $70 000 | $60 000 | $55 000 |
| Total assets | $190 000 | $190 000 | $195 000 |
| Short-term liabilities | $70 000 | $90 000 | $105 000 |
| Long-term liabilities | $40 000 | $35 000 | $30 000 |
| Total liabilities | $110 000 | $125 000 | $135 000 |
| **NET ASSETS** | **$80 000** | **$65 000** | **$60 000** |

You calculate the following financial ratios for each year using the forecasts above. You also include industry average ratios obtained from your industry association and any generally accepted standard ratios to use as benchmarks for comparison.

|  | Year 1 | Year 2 | Year 3 | Industry average | General standard |
|---|---|---|---|---|---|
| Gross profit margin | 32% | 30% | 29% | 34% | – |
| Operating expense ratio | 23% | 26% | 27% | 22% | – |
| Net profit margin | 9% | 4% | 2% | 14% | – |
| Short-term solvency ratio | $1.71 : $1 | $1.44 : $1 | $1.33 : $1 | $1.78 : $1 | $2 : $1 |
| Debt ratio | 58% | 66% | 69% | 54% | 60% |

Each ratio is analysed as follows:
- *Gross profit margin*. The gross profit margin is decreasing each year and is worse than the industry average for each year. This ratio is unacceptable.

  For each year, you will need to revise your purchasing strategies to obtain cheaper stock supplies (assuming you are selling stock at competitive prices).
- *Operating expense ratio*. The operating expense ratio is increasing each year and is worse than the industry average for each year. This ratio is unacceptable.

  This ratio alerts you to the fact that there are excessive operating costs in running the operation. You will need to revise all your operating strategies to trim back operating costs for each year.
- *Net profit margin*. The net profit margin is decreasing each year and is worse than the industry average for each year. This ratio is unacceptable.

  You should revise all operating strategies so as to increase sales and/or reduce operating costs in each year.
- *Solvency ratio*. The short-term solvency ratio is decreasing each year and is worse than both the industry average and general standard for each year. This ratio is unacceptable.

For each year, you will need to change your operating strategies to increase short-term assets (e.g. cash, stock, debtors) and/or decrease short-term liabilities (e.g. bank overdraft, creditors).

- *Debt ratio.* The debt ratio is increasing each year and is worse in Years 2 and 3 than both the industry average and general standard for each year. This ratio is unacceptable.

    This ratio alerts you to the fact that there is excessive debt used to finance the assets of the operation. You will need to revise your operating strategies to reduce debt levels in the operation.

### EXERCISE

**7.14**   You prepare profit statement forecasts for the next three years, which are summarised as follows.

|  | Year 1<br>$ | Year 2<br>$ | Year 3<br>$ |
|---|---|---|---|
| Sales income | $450 000 | $460 000 | $480 000 |
| *less* Cost of sales | $297 000 | $303 600 | $336 000 |
| Gross profit | $153 000 | $156 400 | $144 000 |
| *less* Operating expenses | $99 000 | $110 400 | $72 000 |
| **NET PROFIT before tax** | **$54 000** | **$46 000** | **$72 000** |

You also prepare financial position statement forecasts for the next three years, which are summarised as follows.

|  | Year 1<br>$ | Year 2<br>$ | Year 3<br>$ |
|---|---|---|---|
| Short-term assets | $75 000 | $80 000 | $85 000 |
| Long-term assets | $35 000 | $30 000 | $25 000 |
| Total assets | $110 000 | $110 000 | $110 000 |
| Short-term liabilities | $50 000 | $60 000 | $70 000 |
| Long-term liabilities | $20 000 | $20 000 | $20 000 |
| Total liabilities | $70 000 | $80 000 | $90 000 |
| **NET ASSETS** | **$40 000** | **$30 000** | **$20 000** |

(a) Complete the following table by calculating each ratio. (The relevant industry average and the generally accepted standard are also shown.)

| | Year 1 | Year 2 | Year 3 | Industry average | General standard |
|---|---|---|---|---|---|
| Gross profit margin | _____% | _____% | _____% | 32% | – |
| Operating expense ratio | _____% | _____% | _____% | 20% | – |
| Net profit margin | _____% | _____% | _____% | 12% | – |
| Short-term solvency ratio | _____ : $1 | _____ : $1 | _____ : $1 | $1.60 : $1 | $2 : $1 |
| Debt ratio | _____% | _____% | _____% | 66% | 60% |

(b) Interpret each ratio for acceptability.

(c) What should you do in your business planning for each unacceptable ratio identified?

## F.5 FINANCIAL RECORDS

You will need to design a comprehensive record system that records the financial transactions of the business. Financial records are necessary for the financial control of the operation. Records of financial transactions enable accurate reports to be prepared for monitoring the financial results of the operation. Financial results are compared with corresponding targets to identify any unsatisfactory performance so that follow-up action can be taken.

Every small business should establish and operate a business bank account for record-keeping purposes. If all receipts and payments are processed through the bank account, these transactions will be shown on completed bank records. The account should also facilitate online banking.

The components of a simple manualised cash recording system for a business are described in Figure 7.9.

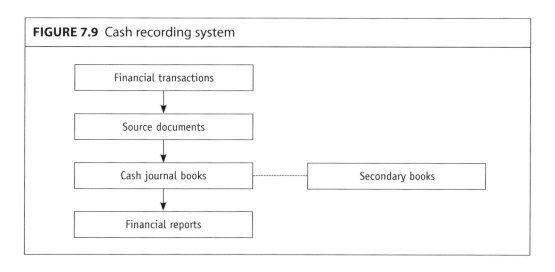

**FIGURE 7.9** Cash recording system

- *Financial transactions.* These are dealings by the business with outsiders which involve either a receipt or a payment.
- *Source documents.* Source documents provide evidence of a transaction occurring. Examples include invoices, receipts, purchase orders, cash register rolls, deposit slips, cheque butts and bank statements.
- *Cash journal books.* Cash journal books are chronological summaries of the cash transactions detailed on source documents. Examples include cash receipts journals, cash payments journals and petty cash books.
- *Secondary books.* Secondary books provide further details of transactions shown in the cash journals. A major secondary book is the time and wages book, which shows details of wages paid to employees.

Today, computerised record systems are often the norm as they reduce administrative time. This requires the selection of suitable software that will report the information you require on your operation. There is a wide range of specialised accounting software to choose from. Software can be custom designed or purchased as an off-the-rack package. Specialised accounting software will produce computerised financial records and accounting reports of financial performance, as well as perform financial analysis of these reports.

In addition to your financial records, you will also need to consider what internal controls you will use in your record system. Record controls are safeguard measures designed to protect the accuracy of your financial records. Major internal controls for records include:

- using standardised pre-numbered source documents in consecutive number sequence
- issuing source documents in triplicate form, where the original goes to the outsider, the duplicate goes to the relevant file and the triplicate remains in the book as a central record
- having only authorised persons sign cheques and purchase orders
- checking purchase orders against suppliers' invoices to ensure correct billing
- crossing cheques and marking them 'not negotiable'
- adopting a standardised payment system of only paying by cheque on suppliers' invoices received
- banking your takings daily
- preparing monthly bank reconciliations to check cashbook totals with bank statement balances
- adopting a petty cash imprest system to monitor minor cash disbursements
- maintaining records in secure storage facilities
- using a password code for entry into the computer system
- keeping a current copy of computer records off-site in case of fire or theft.

**TABLE 7.5** Various insurances

| Insurance type | Risks covered |
| --- | --- |
| • Fire (or building) | Damage to building caused by fire, water and other hazards |
| • Contents | Damage to business contents caused by fire, water and other hazards |
| • Loss of profits | Extra cover for loss of income caused by fire or other hazards insured (or business interruption) against |
| • Public liability/public risk | Being sued for careless maintenance of business premises |
| • Product liability | Being sued for faulty or defective products sold |
| • Professional indemnity (*compulsory for some professionals*) | Being sued for the careless performance of services |
| • Workers' compensation (*compulsory for employers*) | Claims for sickness or accidents to employees occurring in the workplace or during work journeys |
| • Burglary | Losses caused by burglary |
| • Fidelity/employee dishonesty | Losses caused by employee dishonesty |
| • Cash in transit | Theft of cash in transit |
| • Comprehensive motor vehicle | Theft and accident damage to motor vehicle, accident damage caused by motor vehicle |
| • Compulsory third party (*compulsory for vehicle owners*) | Injury to passengers or pedestrians caused by motor vehicle |
| • Third-party property | Accident damage to property caused by motor vehicle |
| • Marine | Loss or damage of goods in transit |
| • Plate glass | Glass breakage |
| • Whole of life | Death of business owner |
| • Personal sickness/accident or income protection | Income losses caused by sickness or accident to business owner |

## F.6 BUSINESS INSURANCES

Plan what types of insurance to arrange for the business. Comprehensive insurance cover should be arranged and maintained for your operation to minimise exposure to daily risks that cause financial losses. Table 7.5 summarises the various types of insurance to consider.

Some types of business insurance are compulsory under law. Compulsory insurance includes workers' compensation insurance for employers and compulsory third-party insurance for motor vehicle owners. Other types of insurance may be compulsory under the rules of the relevant professional body—for example, professional indemnity insurance for professional persons. In addition, public risk insurance is highly recommended for occupiers of business premises.

Schedule an annual risk check of your operation to determine your insurance needs. A risk check will also enable you to design risk-prevention measures in your operation to minimise risks. An insurance agent or broker can advise you on any aspect of insurance.

## EXERCISES

**7.15** What is the purpose of business insurance?
**7.16** Identify two types of compulsory insurance under law.
**7.17** What types of specific insurance cover will you arrange for your operation?

## F.7 FINANCIAL CONTROLS

After you have designed your financial record system, decide what financial controls to adopt for your operation. Financial controls are the methods or techniques you will use to monitor and evaluate the financial results of your operation. Key financial results to control are profit, cash flow and financial position.

### Profit controls

*Profit reports*
Decide how frequently income statements showing profit results will be prepared. Regular detailed profit reports (e.g. monthly or quarterly) will allow for early detection of unfavourable profit performance.

*Variance analysis*
One technique used to analyse profit results is variance analysis. Variance analysis involves comparing each income and expense result in your actual financial performance statement with its corresponding forecast for the same period. Any unfavourable variances are identified and their causes are investigated, so that appropriate follow-up action can be undertaken to correct them.

*Financial ratio analysis*
Financial ratio analysis is another technique that can be used to analyse your detailed profit results. Profitability ratios such as gross profit margin, specific expense ratios and the operating expenses ratio can be calculated to pinpoint strengths and weaknesses in your operating results. When these calculated ratios are compared with benchmarks (e.g. past-period ratios, industry averages) they can be evaluated for acceptability.

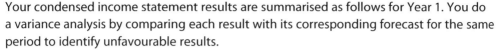

**EXAMPLE**

Your condensed income statement results are summarised as follows for Year 1. You do a variance analysis by comparing each result with its corresponding forecast for the same period to identify unfavourable results.

|  | Year 1 actual $ | Year 1 forecast $ | Variance (+ or –) $ |
|---|---|---|---|
| Sales | 86 600 | 85 400 | +1200 |
| *less* Cost of sales | 56 500 | 56 364 | –136 |
| Gross profit | 30 100 | 29 036 | +1064 |
| *less* Operating expenses | 24 200 | 23 900 | –300 |
| **NET PROFIT BEFORE TAX** | **$5 900** | **$5 136** | **+$764** |

Each variance calculated above is the difference between the actual and forecast figures for each item. A negative variance indicates an unfavourable result where the result is worse than the corresponding forecast. In contrast, a positive variance indicates a favourable result where the result is better than the forecast expected.

## Cash flow controls

*Cash flow reports*

Decide how frequently reports of cash flow results will be prepared. Effective cash flow control requires you to monitor the cash flows (receipts and payments) of your operation closely and continually. Ideally, cash flow reports should be prepared at least monthly. This will enable unfavourable cash flow results to be identified and rectified by taking appropriate follow-up action before serious cash shortages occur.

*Debtor control system*

If you will have sales debtors, design an effective debtor control system to ensure the prompt collection of debtor accounts for timely receipts. There are three aspects to consider when designing a comprehensive debtor control system: debtor selection, debtor monitoring and debtor collection.

- *Debtor selection.* A comprehensive debtor control system begins by issuing credit applications and granting standard credit terms only to approved applicants.
- *Debtor monitoring.* Individual debtor accounts need to be regularly monitored (preferably weekly) by preparing aged debtor schedules. An aged debtors schedule lists the ages of amounts due by each debtor at a point in time. Individual debtor positions in the schedule should be analysed to identify overdue or otherwise unsatisfactory accounts.
- *Debtor collection.* Develop a standardised collection procedure for overdue accounts.

## Stock control

If you carry stock in any form, you will need to have a stock control system to monitor stock levels. Stock monitoring enables you to determine stock turnover and stock condition and decide when and how much to reorder.

There are three stock control systems to consider.

- *Stock records.* If it is practical, a perpetual stock record system should be maintained. The maintenance of accurate stock records for each product line will enable you to monitor physical stock movements on a daily basis.
- *Visual observation.* As an alternative to maintaining daily stock records, it may be more practical, in some situations, to monitor stock levels by regular observation. Regular observation is suitable in high stock turnover situations where the values of stock items are low. In these situations, stock levels are observed regularly (e.g. weekly) to determine stock depletion in order to make re-order decisions.
- *Periodic stocktakes.* Periodic stocktakes are an essential stock-control task in any stock-carrying business. However, because stocktakes are costly and time consuming, they should only be undertaken at periodic intervals—say at the end of each quarter.

## Financial position controls

### Financial position reports

Plan to review the financial position of your operation at the end of each financial year. The purpose of reviewing your actual financial position is to monitor the type and amount of outside debt used to finance your operation, so that it remains appropriate and at an affordable level. This is done by preparing an actual statement of financial position at the end of each financial year.

### Financial ratio analysis

Apart from examining the information shown on your financial position report, financial ratio analysis is the main technique used to analyse your financial position information. Financial ratios such as the solvency ratio and debt ratio can be calculated to determine the acceptability of debt levels. As with all calculated ratios, ratios are compared with benchmarks such as industry averages to be interpreted for acceptability.

## EXERCISES

**7.18**    What are the three key financial results that need to be controlled?

**7.19**    What is the purpose of financial controls?

**7.20**    Complete the following variance analysis by calculating each variance.

| | Year 1 actual $ | Year 1 forecast $ | Variance (+ or −) $ |
|---|---|---|---|
| Sales | 62 800 | 64 600 | _____ |
| *less* Cost of sales | 37 680 | 38 660 | _____ |
| Gross profit | 25 120 | 25 940 | _____ |
| *less* Operating expenses | 17 980 | 18 120 | _____ |
| **NET PROFIT BEFORE TAX** | **7 140** | **7 820** | _____ |

## FINANCIAL PLAN EXAMPLE

### F. FINANCIAL

#### F.1 Personal financial position
The current personal financial position of Hannah Baker is shown as follows.

### Statement of Personal Net Worth at Start of Year 1

| | $ |
|---|---|
| **Personal assets** (current selling value) | |
| Real estate | 220 000 |
| Motor vehicle | 18 000 |
| Furniture and contents | 16 000 |
| Investments | 99 000 |
| | 353 000 |
| *less* **Personal liabilities** (current balance owing) | |
| Mortgage | 18 000 |
| Credit card | 2 000 |
| | 20 000 |
| **PERSONAL NET WORTH** | **$333 000** |

### Statement of Current Monthly Personal Expenses

| **Expenses** | $ |
|---|---|
| Mortgage payment | 200 |
| Credit card payment | 100 |
| Food | 300 |
| Household consumables | 15 |
| Clothing | 30 |
| Motor vehicle running costs | 500 |
| Rates | 100 |
| Electricity and telephone | 100 |
| Health insurance | 70 |

| | |
|---|---:|
| Entertainment | 100 |
| Other living expenses | 50 |
| **TOTAL MONTHLY PERSONAL EXPENSES** | **$1 565** |

### F.2 Establishment costs

| | Estimated cost |
|---|---:|
| | $ |
| Plant and equipment | 80 000 |
| Drink refrigerator | 1 500 |
| Display counters (2) | 1 000 |
| Cash register | 500 |
| Desk, chair and filing cabinet | 500 |
| Repairs to premises | 500 |
| Utilities | 500 |
| Lease costs | 500 |
| Registrations, permits and approvals | 600 |
| Records and stationery | 300 |
| Insurances | 1 800 |
| Advisers' fees | 200 |
| Incorporation costs | 700 |
| Borrowing costs | 800 |
| First three months of operating expenses | 24 000 |
| **TOTAL ESTABLISHMENT COSTS** | **$113 400** |

### F.3 Borrowing requirements

The borrowing amount required is calculated as follows.

| | |
|---|---:|
| Total establishment costs | $113 400 |
| *less* Personal capital | $98 400 |
| Borrowing amount required | $15 000 |

Details of the loan sought are:

| | |
|---|---|
| Date required: | start of Year 1 |
| Loan type: | business term loan |
| Loan amount: | $15 000 |
| Loan period: | 5 years |
| Repayment method: | monthly, by interest only |
| Interest rate basis: | fixed interest |
| Loan purpose: | to buy plant and equipment |

## F.4 Financial forecasts

### Forecast Monthly Sales Statements
Products—breads, cakes and drinks

| Month | Seasonality factor % | Year 1 $ | Year 2 $ | Year 3 $ |
|---|---|---|---|---|
| July | 10 | 24 000 | 26 400 | 29 000 |
| August | 10 | 24 000 | 26 400 | 29 000 |
| September | 6 | 14 400 | 15 840 | 17 400 |
| October | 9 | 21 600 | 23 760 | 26 100 |
| November | 9 | 21 600 | 23 760 | 26 100 |
| December | 6 | 14 400 | 15 840 | 17 400 |
| January | 5 | 12 000 | 13 200 | 14 500 |
| February | 9 | 21 600 | 23 760 | 26 100 |
| March | 10 | 24 000 | 26 400 | 29 000 |
| April | 6 | 14 400 | 15 840 | 17 400 |
| May | 10 | 24 000 | 26 400 | 29 000 |
| June | 10 | 24 000 | 26 400 | 29 000 |
| **TOTALS** | **100%** | **$240 000** | **$264 000** | **$290 000** |

### Forecast Profit Statements

| | Year 1 $ | Year 2 $ | Year 3 $ |
|---|---|---|---|
| INCOME | | | |
| Sales | 240 000 | 264 000 | 290 000 |
| *less* Purchases | 136 800 | 150 480 | 165 300 |
| GROSS PROFIT (at 43%) | 103 200 | 113 520 | 124 700 |
| *less* OPERATING EXPENSES | | | |
| Advertising and promotions | 500 | 515 | 530 |
| Advisers' fees | 200 | 206 | 212 |
| Bank charges | 800 | 309 | 318 |
| Depreciation | 8 350 | 8 350 | 8 350 |
| Electricity | 1 800 | 1 854 | 1 910 |
| Gas | 1 200 | 1 236 | 1 273 |
| Insurances | 1 800 | 1 854 | 1 910 |
| Interest paid | 1 200 | 1 200 | 1 200 |
| Legal fees | 500 | 150 | 155 |
| Packaging and wrapping | 300 | 309 | 318 |
| Rent | 20 400 | 21 420 | 22 491 |
| Repairs and maintenance | 700 | 500 | 525 |
| Stationery | 300 | 309 | 318 |
| Telephone | 800 | 824 | 849 |

| | | | |
|---|--:|--:|--:|
| Wages (gross) | 53 000 | 54 590 | 56 228 |
| Wages on-costs | 10 600 | 10 918 | 11 246 |
| Other expenses | 500 | 515 | 530 |
| *Total operating expenses* | *102 950* | *105 059* | *108 363* |
| **NET PROFIT before tax** | **$250** | **$8 461** | **$16 337** |

**Assumptions:**
- No allowance is made for GST.
- Ingredients and drink supplies are at constant levels.
- Depreciation is 10% p.a. of the original cost of long-term assets.
- Interest is at 8% p.a.
- 'Wages on-costs' comprise superannuation, workers' compensation insurance and staff amenities for employees.
- 'Wages on-costs' are 25% of wages.
- Unless determinable, each cost is increased by 3% p.a.

### Break-even sales

| | Year 1 | Year 2 | Year 3 |
|---|--:|--:|--:|
| | $ | $ | $ |
| Estimated sales | 240 000 | 264 000 | 290 000 |
| Variable costs | 136 800 | 150 480 | 165 300 |
| Fixed costs | 102 950 | 105 059 | 108 363 |
| **Break-even point for sales** | **$239 419** | **$244 323** | **$252 007** |

**Assumptions:**
- Purchases are variable costs.
- All operating costs are fixed costs.

*[See text pages 126 to 129 for how to calculate break-even sales]*

### Forecast Capital Expenditure Statements

| | | Year 1 |
|---|---|--:|
| **Date and type of expenditure** | | **$** |
| 1/7/Year 1—plant and equipment | | 80 000 |
| 1/7/Year 1—furniture and fittings | | 3 500 |
| | **Year 1 total** | **83 500** |
| | | **Year 2** |
| | | **$** |
| | **Year 2 total** | – |
| | | **Year 3** |
| | | **$** |
| | **Year 3 total** | – |

## Forecast Cash Flow Statements

|  | Year 1 $ | Year 2 $ | Year 3 $ |
|---|---|---|---|
| Cash position—start of year | 0 | 38 500 | 55 221 |
| **CASH RECEIPTS** | | | |
| Cash sales | 240 000 | 264 000 | 290 000 |
| Cash from debtors | – | – | – |
| Capital contributions | 98 400 | – | – |
| Borrowings | 15 000 | – | – |
| Total cash receipts | 353 400 | 264 000 | 290 000 |
| *less* **CASH PAYMENTS** | | | |
| Purchases | 136 800 | 150 480 | 165 300 |
| Operating expenses | 93 400 | 95 509 | 98 813 |
| Loan repayments | 1 200 | 1 200 | 1 200 |
| Capital expenditure | 83 500 | – | – |
| Taxation | – | 90 | 3 046 |
| Total cash payments | 314 900 | 247 279 | 268 359 |
| **NET CASH FLOW** | **$38 500** | **$16 721** | **$21 641** |
| Cash position—end of year | $38 500 | $55 221 | $76 862 |

**Assumptions:**
- 100% of annual sales are cash sales.
- Purchases and operating expenses are paid for in cash.
- Operating expenses paid exclude depreciation and interest.
- Loan repayments include interest only.
- Taxation on annual net profit is paid in the following year.

## Forecast Financial Position Statements

|  | Year 1 $ | Year 2 $ | Year 3 $ |
|---|---|---|---|
| **ASSETS** | | | |
| **Short-term assets** | | | |
| Cash | 38 500 | 55 221 | 76 862 |
| Stock (at cost) | – | – | – |
| Debtors | – | – | – |
| *Subtotal* | *38 500* | *55 221* | *76 862* |
| **Long-term assets** | | | |
| Plant and equipment | 80 000 | 80 000 | 80 000 |
| *less* Accumulated depreciation | (8000) | (16 000) | (24 000) |
| Furniture and fittings | 3 500 | 3 500 | 3 500 |
| *less* Accumulated depreciation | (350) | (700) | (1 050) |

|  | | | |
|---|---|---|---|
| *Subtotal* | *75 150* | *66 800* | *58 450* |
| TOTAL ASSETS | 113 650 | 122 021 | 135 312 |
| *less* Liabilities | | | |
| Short-term liabilities | | | |
|    Overdraft | – | – | – |
|    Creditors | – | – | – |
|    *Subtotal* | – | – | – |
| Long-term liabilities | | | |
|    Term loan | 15 000 | 15 000 | 15 000 |
|    *Subtotal* | *15 000* | *15 000* | *15 000* |
| TOTAL LIABILITIES | 15 000 | 15 000 | 15 000 |
| **NET ASSETS** | **$98 650** | **$107 021** | **$120 312** |

**Assumptions:**
- Long-term assets are shown at original cost.
- The term loan is an interest-only loan.

### Key Financial Ratios

| | Year 1 | Year 2 | Year 3 | Industry average |
|---|---|---|---|---|
| **Profitability ratios:** | | | | |
| Gross profit margin | 43% | 43% | 43% | 43% |
| Wage costs to sales ratio | 22% | 21% | 19% | 22% |
| Rent to sales ratio | 9% | 8% | 8% | 10% |
| Operating expenses to sales ratio | 43% | 40% | 37% | 47% |
| Net profit margin | – | 3% | 6% | 3% |
| **Financial position ratio:** | | | | |
| Debt ratio | 13% | 12% | 11% | – |

### F.5 Financial records

A business bank account will be operated at the Commercial Bank, My-Town. All receipts and payments will be processed through the account.

A manual system of financial records will be established and maintained. These records include:
- *source documents:* cash register rolls, deposit slips, cheque butts and bank statements
- *cash journal books:* cash receipts journal, cash payments journal and petty cash book
- *secondary books:* sales register, time and wages book.

Internal controls will be adopted to ensure the accuracy of financial records. These include:
- having only the manager sign cheques
- crossing cheques drawn with 'not negotiable'
- banking takings daily
- paying suppliers' invoices by cheques

- preparing monthly bank reconciliations to check cashbook totals with bank statement balances.

### F.6 Business insurances

The following insurances will be maintained by the business:
- workers' compensation insurance (compulsory under law)
- public liability insurance
- business contents insurance.

An annual check of operating risks will be conducted to design risk-prevention measures and determine insurance needs.

### F.7 Financial controls

The following financial controls will be used to monitor and evaluate the financial performance of the operation.
- *Profit control.* Detailed profit results will be reported annually. Profit results will be compared with corresponding forecasts by applying variance analysis. Any unsatisfactory variances identified will be corrected by appropriate follow-up actions.
- *Cash flow control.* Cash flows of the operation will be monitored closely by the preparation of monthly cash flow reports. Unsatisfactory cash flow results identified will be rectified by taking appropriate corrective action.
- *Financial position control.* The total debt of the business will be reviewed annually by preparing an annual report of the financial position.

---

### EXERCISE

7.21   After you have prepared your other component plans (e.g. marketing, production, purchasing and personnel plans) for the operation, prepare a three-year financial plan for your operation. Use the format shown in Table 7.1 for your financial plan.

---

## QUICK QUIZ

Each of the following multiple-choice items has one correct answer. Select the letter that corresponds with the correct answer.

1. The main financial objective should be expressed as:
   A. net cash flow
   B. net profit
   C. net assets
   D. owner's drawings

2. For a given period, forecast sales are $45 000, forecast cost of sales are $27 000 and forecast operating expenses are $12 000. What is the forecast net profit for the period?
   A. $18 000

B. $33 000
C. $3000
D. none of the above

3. When business forecasting, the first financial forecast to prepare is the:
A. forecast profit statement
B. forecast capital expenditure statement
C. forecast sales statement
D. forecast cash flow statement

4. A forecast profit statement shows estimated:
A. income and expenses
B. receipts and payments
C. capital outlays
D. assets and liabilities

5. Forecast sales for the period are $30 000 and the required gross profit margin is 20%. What is the forecast cost of sales for the period?
A. $6000
B. $24 000
C. $36 000
D. none of the above

6. To improve an unacceptable gross profit margin, you will need to:
A. increase sales volume
B. reduce sales prices
C. buy cheaper stock
D. reduce operating expenses
E. reduce debt levels

7. Capital expenditure refers to:
A. expenditure of owner's capital
B. outlays for long-term assets

C. incurring daily running costs
D. repayments of debts

8. Forecast owner's drawings are shown in the:
A. forecast profit statement
B. forecast cash flow statement
C. forecast capital expenditure statement
D. forecast sales statement

9. Which one of the following is shown in the forecast cash flow statement?
A. depreciation
B. debtors
C. asset outlays
D. net profit

10. The cash position at the beginning of a period is estimated to be $800. Expected receipts and payments for the period are $8000 and $8400 respectively. What is the net cash flow for the period?
A. ($400) deficit
B. $400 surplus
C. ($1200) deficit
D. $1200 surplus
E. none of the above

11. Using the information in Question 10, what is the predicted cash position at the end of the period?
A. ($400) deficit
B. $400 surplus
C. ($1200) deficit
D. $1200 surplus
E. none of the above

12. In a statement of financial position:
    A. net assets = total liabilities – total assets
    B. net assets = total assets – total liabilities
    C. net assets = total liabilities
    D. net assets = total assets

13. The extract from a forecast profit statement for a period is as follows:

    | | |
    |---|---|
    | Sales | $100 000 |
    | *less* Cost of sales | $60 000 |
    | Gross profit | $40 000 |
    | *less* Operating expenses | $10 000 |
    | Net profit | $30 000 |

    The operating expense ratio is:
    A. 10%
    B. 30%
    C. 40%
    D. 70%

14. Forecasts from a forecast statement of financial position show total assets of $80 000, total liabilities of $60 000 and net assets of $20 000. What is the debt ratio?
    A. 25%
    B. 33%
    C. 75%
    D. 300%

15. The most suitable type of loan to finance the purchase of a new motor vehicle for the business would be:
    A. an overdraft
    B. a commercial bill
    C. use of a credit card
    D. a term loan

16. The purpose of internal controls in record-keeping is to:
    A. preserve cash in the business
    B. maximise profit in the business
    C. provide guides to record-keeping
    D. ensure accuracy of the records

17. A type of insurance compulsory for a business under law is:
    A. public liability insurance
    B. professional indemnity insurance
    C. workers' compensation insurance
    D. fire insurance

18. A type of insurance that protects occupiers of premises from being sued by visitors for careless maintenance of the premises is:
    A. product liability
    B. business contents
    C. public liability
    D. income protection

19. Which one of the following is *not* a stock-control system?
    A. periodic stocktakes
    B. purchase orders
    C. visual observation
    D. stock records

20. Which one of the following is a financial control technique?
    A. variance analysis of profit results
    B. evaluation of employee job performance
    C. maintenance of factory equipment
    D. conduct of customer satisfaction surveys

# The completed business plan

### Objectives

After studying this chapter, you should be able to:

- combine component plans prepared to construct a complete business plan
- evaluate any written business plan for soundness
- implement a business plan
- prepare a contingency plan.

## PRESENTING THE PLAN

A completed business plan contains the business profile, objectives to work towards business success and strategies to follow for the business. The plan also tells you what resources are required by the operation.

The business plan is created by preparing a series of coordinated component plans for each relevant function of the operation. Each component plan is prepared in the following order:

1. marketing plan—see Chapter 3
2. production plan—see Chapter 4
3. purchasing plan—see Chapter 5
4. personnel plan—see Chapter 6
5. financial plan—see Chapter 7.

The above component plans for each relevant function of the operation are combined to construct the business plan. The format of the complete business plan was shown in Table 1.2. It is reproduced in Table 8.1. Samples of complete business plans are shown in Part 2.

The structured format in Table 8.1 is recommended for your business plan. It provides comprehensive coverage and a logical sequence of all the relevant aspects to consider for planning. Each major heading and subheading should be numbered as shown. If applicable, omit any irrelevant sections (for example, Production) and adjust this format appropriately. Start each major heading on a new page. Wherever possible, list the contents of each subheading in point form under its heading, and use tables and illustrations to enhance the presentation. The plan should be typed on one side of A4 size paper, with each page numbered for easy referencing. The plan should also be presented in an attractive and durable folder.

There should be a title page (see Figure 8.1) as the cover sheet of the business plan .

List the contents of the business plan on the page following the title page. Show the headings in Table 8.1 with a page number reference for each one (every page of the plan should be numbered). Show the business goal statement (see Chapter 1) on a separate page after the table of contents.

If the business plan is to be used for a loan application, attach relevant supporting documents as part of the plan. Documents could include:

- detailed résumés of the business owners
- legal documents—for example, leases, distributor/agency agreements, sale of business agreements, franchise agreements, partnership agreements
- statistical information
- personal survey results
- press clippings
- design plans or engineering specifications for a new product

**TABLE 8.1** Business plan format

| | |
|---|---|
| TITLE PAGE | C.3 Production method |
| LIST OF CONTENTS | C.4 Production quality controls |
| BUSINESS GOAL STATEMENT | |
| | **D. Purchasing** |
| **A. Business profile** | D.1 Suppliers |
| A.1 Business activity | D.2 Purchasing policies |
| A.2 Ownership structure | D.3 Purchasing controls |
| A.3 Business name | |
| A.4 Business location | **E. Personnel** |
| A.5 Business history/entry strategy | E.1 Management details |
| A.6 Legal requirements | E.2 Organisation structure |
| A.7 Business objectives | E.3 Staffing strategies |
| | E.4 Professional advisers |
| **B. Marketing** | E.5 Personnel controls |
| B.1 Environmental trends | |
| B.2 Industry conditions | **F. Financial** |
| B.3 Products/services | F.1 Personal financial position |
| B.4 Competitors | F.2 Establishment costs |
| B.5 Target customers | F.3 Borrowing requirements |
| B.6 Marketing strategies | F.4 Financial forecasts |
| B.7 Marketing controls | F.5 Financial records |
| | F.6 Business insurances |
| **C. Production** | F.7 Financial controls |
| C.1 Production capacity | |
| C.2 Output levels | SUPPORTING DOCUMENTS |

**FIGURE 8.1** Title page

[show any business logo]

'Private and Confidential'

**BUSINESS PLAN**

**OF**

[State the name of the business]

**FOR**

**YEAR 1, YEAR 2 AND YEAR 3**

Prepared by : .................

Completion date : .................

Email address : .................

- past annual financial reports of the business
- a detailed inventory list
- a detailed list of long-term assets.

**EXERCISE**

**8.1**    Why should a structured format be used in the presentation of a business plan?

## EVALUATING THE PLAN

When you have prepared your business plan, check it for soundness. Also get an independent expert to examine it and to offer constructive comments.

The quality of your business plan will depend on how well it meets three basic criteria—a business plan must be *informative*, *presentable* and *viable*. Any completed business plan can be evaluated using the following criteria.

- *information quality* criteria:
  - information is relevant
  - information is accurate
  - information is current.
- *presentation quality* criteria:
  - presentation is clear and understandable
  - presentation format is structured and comprehensive
  - sections are consistent and coordinated.
- *viability quality* criteria:
  - business objectives are acceptable
  - business growth is anticipated
  - analysis is sound.

**EXERCISE**

**8.2**    Explain the criteria used to evaluate a business plan.

## APPROACHING LENDERS

Apart from being a vital management tool to use in your business operation, your business plan is also an essential selling tool to use for seeking a loan. Commercial lenders such as banks will require a detailed business plan (and other information) from any business borrower applying for a loan.

You should always submit a detailed business plan to the lender when applying for a business loan. Your business plan must be both informative and persuasive to a lender. That is, it must provide details of a sound business proposition. Remember, lenders are businesses themselves. They make returns by lending their funds to viable undertakings. A viable loan proposition will be one that indicates there is a good chance of future success and the ability to meet loan repayments. In particular, most lenders are well aware of the high failure rates of small businesses and are cautious about lending to new enterprises.

When submitting your business plan to a lender, your plan should be professionally presented and include relevant supporting documents as attachments.

When assessing your business plan, the lender will focus on several key sections:
- financial forecasts (especially cash flows)
- financial controls
- evidence of management ability
- debt levels
- adequacy of security.

The financial forecasts in your plan are of vital importance. To a lender, your detailed financial forecasts need to be realistic, suggest viability and reflect growth occurring over time. They should also include anticipated borrowings. Lenders closely examine your financial forecasts—especially cash flow forecasts—to assess your ability to repay the loan. Using the information in your financial forecasts, lenders will apply financial ratio analysis as a means of focusing on the strengths and weaknesses of your proposal. Because of the importance of financial forecasts, you should get a qualified accountant to check them. Financial controls are also important to lenders, who are interested in how you will effectively control the financial functions of your operation.

Another key aspect of your plan about which lenders are vitally concerned is the ability of management to run the business successfully. If the business is an existing operation, reports of past financial results will provide evidence of management success. The inclusion of detailed profiles of the qualifications and experience of key management staff will also indicate evidence of management ability.

Lenders also scrutinise the debt level in your business to ensure you are not over-borrowing.

Even with a sound business plan, you will have to provide adequate security to the lender for almost any loan. In most cases, the preferred security required will be real estate.

Before submitting your business plan to a lender, always get an independent expert to assess it and suggest possible improvements.

## IMPLEMENTING THE PLAN

Your completed business plan prescribes a course of action to take to achieve stated business objectives. Any deviation, delays or omission of follow-up action could undermine the effectiveness of the entire operational plan.

Figure 8.2 summarises the sequence of actions to take for implementing your business plan.

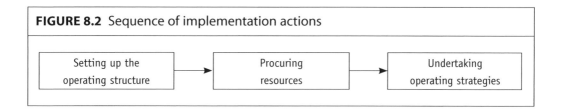

**FIGURE 8.2** Sequence of implementation actions

| Setting up the operating structure | → | Procuring resources | → | Undertaking operating strategies |

The ultimate responsibility for implementing the business plan lies with the business owner. However, the responsibility for implementing some actions may be delegated to competent staff. You should make staff aware of what is expected under the plan so that everyone is heading in the one direction, by working towards the same business goals. This also has a positive effect on employee motivation and morale.

## Setting up the operating structure

The first implementation action for your plan is to set up the basic operating structure. The operating structure is the systematic organisation of a basic operating framework through which business can be carried out. At the start of your planning period, you need to establish an operating structure capable of achieving your business objectives so as to produce the intended outcomes set out in your plan.

The extent of your setting-up actions will depend upon the entry strategy you have selected. Essential actions for setting up an operating structure are described in the action plan in Table 8.2.

## Procuring resources

After your operating structure is set up, business resources will be required for the operation. Business resources are the physical inputs to be used in operating activities for generating income.

Your business plan will determine what resources you require for your operation. Business resources will be required for all functions of your operation. There are six main categories of resources to consider.

- *Natural resources.* These are the land and other natural resources such as water, livestock, crops, fodder and timber required for the operation. These resources will relate mainly to primary producers.
- *Physical materials resources.* These resources are the recurring physical materials supplies acquired for short-term use in the operation. Physical materials resources could include raw materials, component parts, job materials or trading stock.
- *Human resources.* Human resources are the labour requirements of the operation. These include employees, contractors, consultants and professional advisers.

**TABLE 8.2** Action plan for setting up

| Action | Person responsible | Completion date | Cost ($) |
|---|---|---|---|
| Establish ownership structure | _____ | _____ | _____ |
| Select premises | _____ | _____ | _____ |
| Obtain permits and approvals for premises | _____ | _____ | _____ |
| Negotiate lease for premises | _____ | _____ | _____ |
| Obtain business licences and compulsory registrations | _____ | _____ | _____ |
| Design layout plan | _____ | _____ | _____ |
| Prepare premises | _____ | _____ | _____ |
| Design organisation structure | _____ | _____ | _____ |
| Arrange insurances | _____ | _____ | _____ |
| Open business bank account | _____ | _____ | _____ |
| Design records and stationery | _____ | _____ | _____ |
| Arrange initial promotions | _____ | _____ | _____ |
| Select professional advisers | _____ | _____ | _____ |
| | | **Total cost:  $** | _____ |

- *Long-term asset resources.* These are the physical assets required for long-term use in the operation. They include:
  - factory plant and equipment
  - furniture and fittings
  - office machines
  - motor vehicles
  - buildings.

- *Management resources.* These are the management skills and knowledge and technical know-how required to run the operation successfully.
- *Financial resources.* These refer to the amount of money required to establish and continue the operation. The source of these funds will be either external (borrowings) or internal (owner's capital).

You will need to gather relevant information on each resource required before procuring it. The steps to follow for gathering information on any business resource are as follows.

**Step 1:** *Define resource requirement.* Begin by fully defining your resource requirements. For any resource required, there are four aspects to consider:

- the type of resource
- the quantity of the resource
- the quality of the resource
- the timing of the resource.

**Step 2:** *Evaluate resource sources.* When you have defined your resource requirements, the next step is to evaluate possible sources for the resource. This involves:

- identifying relevant sources of the resource
- determining the availability of supplies from each source
- ascertaining the cost of resources from each source.

**Step 3:** *Procure resources.* After you have identified each necessary resource and selected its source, you are ready to procure your resources. This requires the preparation of an action plan for the procurement of resources (see Table 8.3). Your action plan must be consistent with your business plan. Design a separate action plan for each function of your operation.

## Undertaking operating strategies

The final category of actions to be implemented is the undertaking of prescribed operating strategies according to your business plan. Operating strategies are planned business activities intended to achieve your objectives.

Operating strategies cannot be undertaken until you have set up your operating structure and procured the necessary resources. Your operation must have the physical operating capability to achieve them.

The implementation of your business plan strategies should be approached in the following order:

1. marketing strategies
2. production strategies
3. purchasing strategies
4. personnel strategies.

The reasons for this were explained in earlier chapters.

**TABLE 8.3** Action plan for procuring resources

**Operational function: Marketing/Production/Purchasing/Personnel/Financial**

| Resource required | Quantity | Source | Date required | Person responsible | Cost $ |
|---|---|---|---|---|---|
| Natural resources: | | | | | |
| _____ | _____ | _____ | _____ | _____ | _____ |
| _____ | _____ | _____ | _____ | _____ | _____ |
| _____ | _____ | _____ | _____ | _____ | _____ |
| _____ | _____ | _____ | _____ | _____ | _____ |
| Physical materials resources: | | | | | |
| _____ | _____ | _____ | _____ | _____ | _____ |
| _____ | _____ | _____ | _____ | _____ | _____ |
| _____ | _____ | _____ | _____ | _____ | _____ |
| _____ | _____ | _____ | _____ | _____ | _____ |
| Human resources: | | | | | |
| _____ | _____ | _____ | _____ | _____ | _____ |
| _____ | _____ | _____ | _____ | _____ | _____ |
| _____ | _____ | _____ | _____ | _____ | _____ |
| _____ | _____ | _____ | _____ | _____ | _____ |
| Long-term asset resources: | | | | | |
| _____ | _____ | _____ | _____ | _____ | _____ |
| _____ | _____ | _____ | _____ | _____ | _____ |
| _____ | _____ | _____ | _____ | _____ | _____ |
| _____ | _____ | _____ | _____ | _____ | _____ |
| Management resources: | | | | | |
| _____ | _____ | _____ | _____ | _____ | _____ |
| _____ | _____ | _____ | _____ | _____ | _____ |
| _____ | _____ | _____ | _____ | _____ | _____ |
| _____ | _____ | _____ | _____ | _____ | _____ |
| Financial resources: | | | | | |
| _____ | _____ | _____ | _____ | _____ | _____ |
| _____ | _____ | _____ | _____ | _____ | _____ |
| _____ | _____ | _____ | _____ | _____ | _____ |
| _____ | _____ | _____ | _____ | **Total cost:** | $_____ |

**EXERCISES**

**8.3**   Briefly describe the sequence of actions required to implement your business plan.

**8.4**   What is the sequence of actions you will undertake to set up your operating structure to commence your business plan?

**8.5**   List the types of resources you will require to implement your business plan.

**8.6**   What factors do you need to consider in determining your requirements for a particular resource?

**8.7**   What factors do you consider relevant for selecting a suitable source of a resource?

## OPERATIONAL REVIEW

Operational performance must be monitored regularly to determine whether plan targets are being met. Prompt corrective actions will need to be undertaken for any unfavourable business results identified during the plan period.

Prepare an operational review schedule (see Table 8.4) showing when business controls will be used to evaluate results for each function of the operation. Business controls refer to actions taken to evaluate results. The business controls to include are outlined in the main operational plan.

An operational review schedule could be included with the business plan.

**EXERCISES**

**8.8**   What is a business control?

**8.9**   What is the purpose of an operational review schedule?

## THE CONTINGENCY PLAN

Recognise that business planning is a dynamic process. It occurs in an operating environment that is uncertain and continually changing.

A business plan must be adaptable to environmental changes. Your operational plan, as well as your attitudes to planning, must be flexible enough to deal with contingencies occurring in the operating environment, during the period of your plan. In this context, 'contingencies' refers to significant changes that can occur in the external operating environment, which adversely affect your planned operational performance. Significant changes which are beyond your control that can occur in the external operating environment include:

- shifts in demand patterns
- the entry of new competitors
- changes in competitors' policies
- the unavailability or shortage of business resources (e.g. stock or labour)
- sudden downturns in general economic activity
- new legal restrictions or taxes

**TABLE 8.4** Operational review schedule

Years: _____

| Control action | Frequency | Review date | Person responsible |
|---|---|---|---|
| **Marketing controls:** | | | |
| • Analyse sales performance | Monthly | _____ | _____ |
| • Conduct customer satisfaction surveys | Monthly | _____ | _____ |
| • Review marketing program | Annually | _____ | _____ |
| **Production controls:** | | | |
| • Check quality of raw materials | Daily | _____ | _____ |
| • Check final product and packaging quality | Daily | _____ | _____ |
| • Supervise production process | Daily | _____ | _____ |
| • Check factory plant and equipment | Monthly | _____ | _____ |
| • Monitor production output levels | Monthly | _____ | _____ |
| **Purchasing controls:** | | | |
| • Check deliveries against purchase orders | Daily | _____ | _____ |
| • Check stock levels for re-ordering | Daily | _____ | _____ |
| • Review supply terms and supplier performance | Half-yearly | _____ | _____ |
| • Analyse gross profit margins | Half-yearly | _____ | _____ |
| **Personnel controls:** | | | |
| • Supervise employees | Daily | _____ | _____ |
| • Evaluate individual job performance | Half-yearly | _____ | _____ |
| • Analyse overall staff productivity | Half-yearly | _____ | _____ |
| **Financial controls:** | | | |
| • Check credit applications | Daily | _____ | _____ |
| • Analyse debtor positions | Weekly | _____ | _____ |
| • Evaluate profit results | Quarterly | _____ | _____ |
| • Evaluate cash flow results | Quarterly | _____ | _____ |
| • Conduct stocktakes | Quarterly | _____ | _____ |
| • Review financial position | Annually | _____ | _____ |
| • Check business risks | Annually | _____ | _____ |

● increases in the cost of business resources (e.g. interest rate, wage or stock price increases).

Be prepared to change parts of your plan if changes in the operating environment cause adverse business results. If there are major changes in the operating environment, your entire operational plan of objectives and strategies may have to be changed. If this happens, you will have to begin your business planning process again.

Many environmental contingencies can be planned for without having to change your entire business plan. This requires you to develop a contingency plan of possible responses to unsatisfactory results. A contingency plan (see Table 8.5) outlines what

| TABLE 8.5 Contingency plan of responsive actions to unsatisfactory performance | |
|---|---|
| **Unsatisfactory performance function** | **Possible responsive action** |
| **Marketing** | Change marketing strategies (for example, vary promotions)<br>Increase target customers and change marketing strategies<br>Change target customers and change marketing strategies<br>Change market area<br>Begin a new marketing program |
| **Production** | Increase process time<br>Change production method<br>Replace inefficient factory plant and equipment<br>Introduce new production technology |
| **Purchasing** | Increase selling prices<br>Renegotiate new supply terms<br>Change suppliers<br>Change stock supplies |
| **Personnel** | Increase labour productivity<br>Redesign organisation structure<br>Redeploy staff<br>Dismiss staff<br>Train staff<br>Use employment alternatives (e.g. casuals, contractors) |
| **Financial**<br>Profit | Increase sales or prices<br>Reduce operating costs<br>Buy stock more cheaply |
| Cash flow | Mark down prices to increase stock turnover<br>Shorten debtor collection times<br>Restrict credit offered<br>Increase prices<br>Defer paying creditors<br>Increase borrowings<br>Contribute more capital<br>Reduce owner's drawings<br>Decrease or defer capital expenditure<br>Sell surplus long-term assets<br>Extend supplier's credit terms<br>Negotiate instalment payments with creditors<br>Reduce operating costs |
| Financial position | Reduce external debt |

actions you will take to deal with any unsatisfactory performance where results are significantly less than the objective set.

If you have a contingency plan, you can follow a standardised course of corrective actions to deal with any unsatisfactory operating performance identified. These actions are described in Figure 8.3.

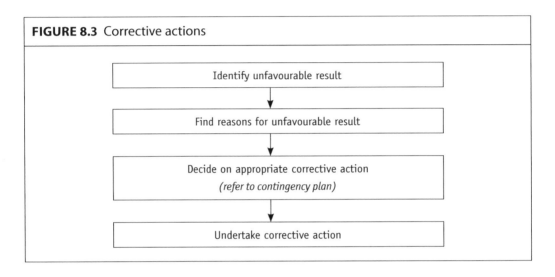

**FIGURE 8.3** Corrective actions

**EXAMPLE**

The process of taking corrective action according to your contingency plan is illustrated in the following example.

Step 1:    Identify unfavourable result.
           After analysing your operating results, you find that your gross profit margin on stock sales for the period was 26%. This is an unsatisfactory result when compared with your planned gross profit margin of 35%, which is also consistent with the industry average.

Step 2:    Find reasons for unfavourable result.
           You investigate the reasons for this unfavourable result and find that your supplier has increased prices during the period while you have maintained the same competitive selling prices. This has caused a decrease in your gross profit margin in the price of stock sold.

Step 3:    Decide on appropriate corrective action.
           After referring to your contingency plan of possible responses to unsatisfactory performance (see Table 8.5), you decide to renegotiate for better supply terms with the supplier. You also decide to look around for new suppliers of the same stock at cheaper prices.

*Step 4:*    Undertake corrective action.

You carry out your decisions made in Step 3. You negotiate extended credit periods and higher quantity discount rates with the existing supplier. You also find new suppliers who will supply the same stock at cheaper prices.

---

**EXERCISE**

**8.10**    What is the purpose of a contingency plan?

---

## QUICK QUIZ

Each of the following multiple-choice items has one correct answer. Select the letter that corresponds with the correct answer.

1. The first action for implementing a business plan should be to:
   A. establish an operating structure
   B. procure business resources
   C. undertake operating strategies
   D. review business operating results

2. A key section of your business plan focused on by lenders is:
   A. marketing strategies
   B. purchasing activities
   C. cash flow forecasts
   D. production capacity

3. An operating structure refers to a/an:
   A. systematic organisation of business resources
   B. framework through which operating activities are carried out

   C. business operation which is active and trading
   D. systematic organisation of human resources
   E. ownership structure to run the business under

4. Which one of the following is *not* recognised as a business resource?
   A. contract labour
   B. trading stock
   C. technical know-how
   D. business licence
   E. loan funds

5. Which one of the following is *not* a relevant consideration for defining a resource requirement?
   A. the type of resource
   B. the quantity of the resource
   C. the timing of the resource

D. the quality of the resource

E. the price of the resource

6. The reason for preparing an operational review schedule is to:

   A. determine responses to unfavourable results

   B. detect unfavourable business results

   C. determine what resources are required

   D. set times for reviewing business results

7. Business controls are used in business planning to:

   A. check results

   B. change targets

   C. procure resources

   D. schedule actions

8. Which one of the following is *not* an environmental contingency?

   A. an award wage increase

   B. the entry of new competitors

C. a downturn in economic activity

D. a decline in employee performance

E. a reduction in competitors' prices

9. A contingency plan will enable you to:

   A. identify unsatisfactory results

   B. set performance standards

   C. select appropriate corrective actions

   D. find reasons for unsatisfactory results

10. Which one of the following possible responses would be most appropriate for an unsatisfactory cash flow result?

    A. increase credit sales

    B. reduce operating expenses

    C. buy more stock

    D. increase labour productivity

# 2
# Sample Business Plans

## INTRODUCTION

The three sample business plans in this section apply to different business circumstances. Choose a sample plan for guidance that best reflects your own business situation.

A summary of the different circumstances applying to each sample plan is shown in the grid below to help you select an appropriate plan.

## SUMMARY OF DIFFERENT BUSINESS CIRCUMSTANCES FOR SAMPLE PLANS

|  | Ownership structure | Entry strategy | Business location | Sales type | Industry |
|---|---|---|---|---|---|
| **PLAN 1** |  |  |  |  |  |
| Carla's Café | Sole trader | Buying existing business | Shop premises | Goods | Food hospitality |
| **PLAN 2** |  |  |  |  |  |
| Kate's Bush Tours | Sole trader | Start-up | Home-based and Australia-wide | Services | Tourism |
| **PLAN 3** |  |  |  |  |  |
| Mike's Building Co. Pty Ltd | Private company | Existing business | Home-based and various job sites | Services | Building trades |

**PRIVATE AND CONFIDENTIAL**

# Business Plan of Carla's Café

## for Year 1, Year 2 and Year 3

Prepared by: Tina Coffey

Completion date: 1/7/Yr1

Email address: tcoffey@mymail.com

# CONTENTS

|  |  | Page number |
|---|---|---|
| **BUSINESS GOAL STATEMENT** |  | **3** |
| **A. BUSINESS PROFILE** |  | **4** |
| A.1 | Business activity | 4 |
| A.2 | Ownership structure | 4 |
| A.3 | Business name | 4 |
| A.4 | Business location | 4 |
| A.5 | Entry strategy | 5 |
| A.6 | Legal requirements | 5 |
| A.7 | Business objectives | 5 |
| **B. MARKETING** |  | **6** |
| B.1 | Environmental trends | 6 |
| B.2 | Industry conditions | 6 |
| B.3 | Products | 7 |
| B.4 | Competitors | 7 |
| B.5 | Target customers | 8 |
| B.6 | Marketing strategies | 8 |
| B.7 | Marketing controls | 9 |
| **C. PURCHASING** |  | **11** |
| C.1 | Suppliers | 11 |
| C.2 | Purchasing policies | 11 |
| C.3 | Purchasing controls | 11 |
| **D. PERSONNEL** |  | **12** |
| D.1 | Management details | 12 |
| D.2 | Organisation structure | 12 |
| D.3 | Staffing strategies | 13 |
| D.4 | Professional advisers | 13 |
| D.5 | Personnel controls | 13 |
| **E. FINANCIAL** |  | **14** |
| E.1 | Personal financial position | 14 |
| E.2 | Establishment costs | 15 |
| E.3 | Borrowing requirements | 15 |
| E.4 | Financial forecasts | 16 |
| E.5 | Financial records | 20 |
| E.6 | Business insurances | 20 |
| E.7 | Financial controls | 21 |
| **F. OPERATIONAL REVIEW** |  | **22** |
| **SUPPORTING DOCUMENTS** |  |  |

# BUSINESS GOAL STATEMENT

My business goal is to achieve a minimum annual sales turnover of $240 000 and a minimum annual net profit of $50 000 by the end of Year 3.

# A. BUSINESS PROFILE

## A.1 Business activity
The existing business is a café that sells a wide range of coffee drinks, non-alcoholic beverage drinks and light snacks.

## A.2 Ownership structure
The business will be operated by Tina Coffey as a sole trader. The proprietor has chosen to operate as a sole trader to have total control over her business.

## A.3 Business name
The business will trade under the registered name of 'Carla's Café'.

The business website is <www.carlascafe.com.au>.

## A.4 Business location
The operation is located at 10 Chatter Street, My-Suburb. The existing commercial lease will be renegotiated for an initial term of five years with the option to renew for a further five years. Under the lease, the rent is $500 per week for the first year, to be increased annually by 4%.

The existing premises are in a highly visible and accessible position to passing pedestrian traffic. The location is a street-level shop premises of 48 m². The premises are opposite the railway station in a busy shopping centre within a growing region. The premises are also at the entrance to an arcade, which provides a thoroughfare for shoppers and rail commuters to a large parking area at the rear.

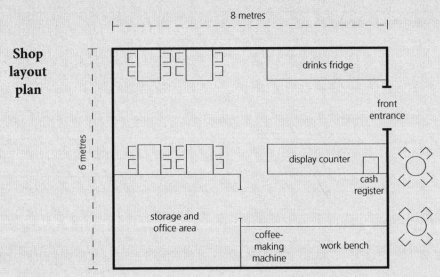

## A.5 Entry strategy

The business will be purchased as a going concern on a walk-in, walk-out basis. Pre-existing debtors or creditors of the business will be the responsibility of the previous owner. The reason for buying an existing business is because there is no set-up time required and the opportunity was offered to the proprietor.

The purchase of the business is expected to be completed by 1 July, Year 1.

The business started twelve years ago and its growth history for the past five years is summarised by the following results.

| Year | Annual sales turnover | Annual net profit | Number of personnel |
|---|---|---|---|
| 5 years ago | $202 716 | $33 944 | 1 |
| 4 years ago | $204 819 | $34 116 | 1 |
| 3 years ago | $212 420 | $40 398 | 2 |
| 2 years ago | $226 717 | $48 420 | 2 |
| 1 year ago | $230 016 | $50 600 | 2 |

## A.6 Legal requirements

The legal requirements to operate the business are:
- business name registration with the Australian Securities and Investments Commission
- development approval for using the premises from the local council
- health clearance permit (for food sellers) from the local council
- external advertising sign permit from the local council
- outdoor use permit (for tables and chairs) from the local council
- ABN registration (for GST and PAYG tax) with the Australian Taxation Office.
  Legal requirements will be met before the business purchase is completed.

## A.7 Business objectives

The key objectives of the business for the next three years are summarised as follows:

| | Year 1 | Year 2 | Year 3 |
|---|---|---|---|
| **Marketing:** | | | |
| Sales turnover | $233 000 | $238 000 | $244 000 |
| **Purchasing:** | | | |
| Average gross profit margin | 60% | 60% | 60% |
| **Personnel:** | | | |
| Labour productivity ratio (i.e. sales : labour cost) | $4.84 : $1 | $4.76 : $1 | $4.69 : $1 |
| Number of personnel (full-time equivalents) | 3 | 3 | 3 |

|  | Year 1 | Year 2 | Year 3 |
|---|---|---|---|
| **Financial:** | | | |
| Net profit | $50 000 | $51 000 | $52 000 |
| Net cash flow | $26 000 | $6 000 | $6 000 |
| Debt ratio | 39% | 30% | 21% |

## B. MARKETING

### B.1 Environmental trends

Research and analysis of the general business environment identifies the following opportunities and challenges for the business in the next three years.

*Opportunities:*
- General economic conditions are expected to improve.
- A steady increase in the general population is expected.
- There is increasing desire for leisure time.
- People are working longer hours.
- Easing of regulatory red tape for small business is likely.
- Reductions in import duties are likely.

*Challenges:*
- rising levels of household debts
- increased consumer protection laws
- more legal regulation of the workplace
- a more litigious community
- greater public awareness of health and nutrition
- likely introduction of new business taxes.

The conclusion reached from the environmental analysis is that there are opportunities for the business that will support the growth in sales forecasts. These environmental trends will influence the selection of marketing strategies for the business.

### B.2 Industry conditions

Direct observation shows that the number of cafés and other kinds of business (e.g. car washes, bookshops) combining café facilities with their main business activity is growing. The number of coffee shops operating in the local area is not expected to change in the near future, however.

ABS statistics show that the national consumption of coffee per capita has been increasing by an average of 3% p.a. for the last three years. This trend is expected to continue for the foreseeable future.

## B.3 Products

The business will offer coffee and non-alcoholic beverages in informal surroundings or as takeaways. The coffee has a unique and delicious taste and is made from an imported blend of coffee.

The contribution of each product to annual sales turnover is expected to be as follows.

| Products | Year 1 | Year 2 | Year 3 |
|----------|--------|--------|--------|
|          | %      | %      | %      |
| Coffee drinks | 42 | 43 | 44 |
| Other drinks | 14 | 14 | 15 |
| Sweets | 22 | 21 | 18 |
| Light snacks | 22 | 22 | 23 |
| **Totals** | **100%** | **100%** | **100%** |

## B.4 Competitors

Through direct observation, two competitors have been identified that will compete directly with the business.

### Competitor 1

| | |
|---|---|
| Name: | The Corner Café |
| Location: | local area |
| Duration: | six years |
| Personnel: | four employees (full-time equivalents) |

*Strengths:*
- prominent corner position
- wide range of beverages
- delicious-tasting coffee drinks.

*Weaknesses:*
- restricted opening hours
- unfriendly service
- inconsistent food quality.

### Competitor 2

| | |
|---|---|
| Name: | George & Sophie's Café |
| Location: | local area |
| Duration: | four years |
| Personnel: | two employees (full-time equivalents) |

*Strengths:*
- high-quality food
- courteous service
- loyal customers.

*Weaknesses:*
- slow service
- price information not displayed
- high prices.

It is not expected that there will be any change in this direct competition in the three-year period ahead. Competitor observations form the basis for designing competitive advantage strategies to follow.

## B.5 Target customers

The main customer groups that have been targeted by the business are shoppers and office workers. Target customer groups will remain the same during the period of the plan unless changed in the annual marketing review.

### Target customer group 1: Shoppers

*Personal characteristics:*
- 18–60 years old, predominantly female, homemakers, busy lifestyles, low to middle incomes.

*Relevant wants:*
- convenience, a short relaxing shopping break, a delicious drink.

### Target customer group 2: Office workers

*Personal characteristics:*
- 18–35 years old, work in local offices, modern tastes, busy lifestyles, low to middle incomes.

*Relevant wants:*
- to relax and chat, a delicious drink, affordable prices, prompt service, takeaways.

These target customers live within a 5 kilometre radius of the business location. Relevant demographic statistics obtained from the ABS show that the general population in the area has increased by 28% over the last ten years. Statistical projections indicate that these growth trends are likely to continue in the future.

## B.6 Marketing strategies

The business will adopt a customer-oriented approach in the marketing of its products. Any marketing strategy selected will focus on satisfying the relevant wants of the target customer groups.

### Products:
- coffee drinks
- other drinks
- sweets
- light snacks.

### Services:
- friendly, courteous and prompt customer service.

### Prices:
- products offered at competitive prices
- price information displayed on sign and menus
- payment by cash
- loyalty discount for regular customers.

### Distribution:
- retail selling from café location
- business opening times, Mondays to Saturdays (inclusive)—8 a.m. to 8 p.m.
- products available for consumption at premises or as takeaways.

### Image:
- clean and tidy staff and premises presentation
- health-conscious attitudes to food handling (e.g. wearing gloves)
- friendly, relaxed and informal atmosphere for customers.

### Promotions:
- window displays and outside signs.

### Competitive advantages:
- having a more exposed and accessible business location
- opening longer business hours than competitors
- projecting a healthier image than competitors
- using a uniquely blended coffee to make a more delicious coffee drink than competitors
- providing friendlier and faster customer service than competitors
- offering a more relaxed and informal atmosphere than competitors.
  Competitive advantages are expected to be sustainable in the long term.

## B.7 Marketing controls
Marketing strategies will be adaptable to change if business conditions change or new opportunities emerge.

A sales register will be maintained to record daily sales. Recorded sales results will be analysed quarterly by comparison with corresponding targets. Half-yearly customer satisfaction surveys will be conducted to survey customers for their responses to marketing strategies.

The marketing program will be reviewed annually. This will involve a new analysis of the operating environment followed by the design of a new marketing program.

# C. PURCHASING

## C.1 Suppliers

Supply relationships will be maintained by the business with various suppliers. The main suppliers will be as follows.

### Supplier 1

| | |
|---|---|
| Name: | Rossi Coffee Importers |
| Location: | interstate |
| Duration: | eight years |
| Supplies: | coffee beans |
| Supply terms: | COD |

### Supplier 2

| | |
|---|---|
| Name: | The Grocery Wholesaling Co. |
| Location: | local area |
| Duration: | six years |
| Supplies: | drinks, meats and vegetables |
| Supply terms: | COD, quantity discounts |

### Supplier 3

| | |
|---|---|
| Name: | Bill's Bakery Shop |
| Location: | local area |
| Duration: | five years |
| Supplies: | breads, sweets |
| Supply terms: | COD |

## C.2 Purchasing policies

Items will regularly be purchased according to requirements. Orders will be communicated to suppliers by issuing signed purchase orders. Supplier payments will be made after receiving suppliers' invoices. Food supplies will be handled and stored in a healthy manner.

## C.3 Purchasing controls

The following purchasing controls will be maintained to ensure purchasing activities are carried out efficiently and effectively:

- daily purchasing of perishable food supplies to ensure fresh food quality
- regularly checking perishable food supplies for freshness
- analysing gross profit margins in annual profit reports to determine the acceptability of supply prices
- reviewing supply terms and supplier performance half-yearly.

# D. PERSONNEL

## D.1 Management details

The operation will be managed by the proprietor, Tina Coffey, whose relevant personal details are as follows.

*Relevant experience:*
- six years' experience as waiter
- two years' experience as restaurant cashier
- one year's experience of making coffee.

*Relevant training/qualifications:*
- hospitality operations diploma from TAFE college
- small business management certificate from TAFE college.

In Year 1, the proprietor intends to undertake a series of day-long training seminars relating to 'law for food sellers'. The proprietor will draw $2000 per calendar month from the business. This amount will be sufficient to meet the proprietor's monthly personal expenses.

## D.2 Organisation structure

The proposed staff organisation structure for each of the next three years is as follows.

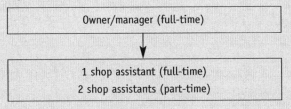

```
┌─────────────────────────────────────────┐
│        Owner/manager (full-time)         │
└─────────────────────────────────────────┘
                    │
                    ▼
┌─────────────────────────────────────────┐
│        1 shop assistant (full-time)      │
│        2 shop assistants (part-time)     │
└─────────────────────────────────────────┘
```

*Job profile: Owner/manager*
Full-time—70 hours p.w. (Year 1), 60 hours p.w. (Year 2), 50 hours p.w. (Year 3)

*Job duties:*
- serving customers
- purchasing supplies
- record-keeping
- banking takings
- supervising staff.

*Job profile: Shop assistant*
Full-time—30 hours p.w.                     Part-time—12 hours p.w.

*Job duties:*
- serving customers
- cleaning premises.

*Job attributes:*
- school certificate
- minimum three years' experience as waiter
- pleasant, outgoing and communicative.

*Remuneration:*
- full-time—$19 000 gross p.a. start (plus bonuses)
- part-time—$9000 gross p.a. start (plus bonuses).

## D.3 Staffing strategies
The staffing policies that will be adopted to keep staff motivated and productive are as follows:
- an initial three-month probation period for new employees
- remunerating staff at competitive, above-award rates
- increasing remuneration by 4% p.a.
- providing an incentive scheme of bonus payments based on sales turnover
- creating a pleasant work environment with adequate facilities and amenities
- adopting a friendly, informal leadership style where decision-making is delegated within defined limits
- providing initial induction training for new employees
- training and impressing employees in pleasant and courteous customer service
- adopting hygenic work practices, including wearing gloves, for handling food
- regular health and safety audits of the workplace.

## D.4 Professional advisers
The following business advisers will be used:
- Qualified accountant (and tax agent):    Tim Lane, My-Suburb
- Solicitor:    John Kandos, My-Suburb
- Insurance broker    Jack Hardy, My-Suburb
- Bank:    Commercial Bank, My-Suburb

Annual membership of the Retail Traders' Association will be maintained.

## D.5 Personnel controls
Overall labour productivity will be measured annually to identify any labour performance problems that may occur in the operation. For these purposes, labour productivity will be measured as the relationship between sales and labour costs in each relevant period. Key aspects of individual job performance will also be evaluated after a three-month probation period for new employees and at six-monthly intervals for existing employees. Employee job evaluation will be conducted face to face to receive feedback.

The proprietor will directly supervise employees and the handling of cash to prevent the occurrence of staff dishonesty.

# E. FINANCIAL

## E.1 Personal financial position

The current personal financial position of Tina Coffey is shown as follows.

| Statement of personal net worth at start of Year 1 | |
|---|---:|
| | **$** |
| **Personal assets** (current selling value) | |
| Real estate | 120 000 |
| Motor vehicle | 15 000 |
| Furniture and contents | 12 000 |
| Investments | 46 000 |
| | 193 000 |
| *less* **Personal liabilities** (current balance owing) | |
| Mortgage | 20 000 |
| Credit card | 1 000 |
| | 21 000 |
| **Personal net worth** | **$172 000** |

| Statement of current monthly personal expenses | |
|---|---:|
| **Expenses** | **$** |
| Mortgage payment | 200 |
| Credit card payment | 50 |
| Food | 500 |
| Household consumables | 15 |
| Clothing | 30 |
| Motor vehicle running costs | 500 |
| Rates | 100 |
| Electricity and telephone | 100 |
| Health insurance | 80 |
| School fees | 200 |
| Child care costs | 100 |
| Entertainment | 75 |
| Other living expenses | 50 |
| **Total monthly personal expenses** | **$2000** |

## E.2 Establishment costs

|  | Estimated cost $ |
|---|---|
| Purchase price of business | *95 000 |
| Initial supplies | 500 |
| Lease costs | 800 |
| Registrations, permits and approvals | 1 000 |
| Records and stationery | 300 |
| Insurances | 1 800 |
| Advisers' fees | 700 |
| Borrowing costs | 900 |
| **Total establishment costs** | $101 000 |

| * Comprising: | $ |
|---|---|
| Goodwill | 75 000 |
| Equipment furniture and fittings | 20 000 |
| | $95 000 |

## E.3 Borrowing requirements
The borrowing amount required is calculated as follows.

| Total establishment costs | $101 000 |
|---|---|
| *less* Personal capital | $46 000 |
| Borrowing amount required | $55 000 |

Details of the loan sought are:

| Date required: | start of Year 1 |
|---|---|
| Loan type: | business term loan |
| Loan amount: | $55 000 |
| Loan period: | five years |
| Repayment method: | monthly, by principal and interest |
| Interest rate basis: | fixed interest |
| Loan purpose: | to buy business |

## E.4 Financial forecasts

### Forecast monthly sales statements

Products—beverages and light snacks

| Month | Seasonality factor % | Year 1 $ | Year 2 $ | Year 3 $ |
|---|---|---|---|---|
| July | 7 | 16 287 | 16 674 | 17 091 |
| August | 8 | 18 613 | 19 056 | 19 533 |
| September | 10 | 23 267 | 23 820 | 24 416 |
| October | 10 | 23 267 | 23 820 | 24 416 |
| November | 11 | 25 593 | 26 202 | 26 858 |
| December | 11 | 25 593 | 26 202 | 26 858 |
| January | 10 | 23 267 | 23 820 | 24 416 |
| February | 8 | 18 613 | 19 056 | 19 533 |
| March | 7 | 16 287 | 16 674 | 17 091 |
| April | 6 | 13 960 | 14 292 | 14 650 |
| May | 6 | 13 960 | 14 292 | 14 650 |
| June | 6 | 13 960 | 14 292 | 14 650 |
| **Totals** | **100%** | **$232 667** | **$238 200** | **$244 162** |

### Forecast profit statements

| | Year 1 $ | Year 2 $ | Year 3 $ |
|---|---|---|---|
| Income | | | |
| Sales | 232 667 | 238 200 | 244 162 |
| *less* Drinks and food purchases | 93 067 | 95 280 | 97 665 |
| GROSS PROFIT (at 60%) | 139 600 | 142 920 | 146 497 |
| *less* OPERATING EXPENSES | | | |
| Advertising and promotions | 100 | 104 | 108 |
| Advisers' fees | 700 | 416 | 433 |
| Bank charges | 1 200 | 312 | 324 |
| Depreciation | 3 000 | 3 000 | 3 000 |
| Electricity | 1 800 | 1 872 | 1 947 |
| Insurances | 1 800 | 1 872 | 1 947 |

| | | | |
|---|---|---|---|
| Interest paid | 4 400 | 3 681 | 2 905 |
| Legal fees | 1 000 | 1 040 | 1 082 |
| Rent | 26 000 | 27 040 | 28 122 |
| Stationery | 300 | 312 | 324 |
| Telephone | 1 200 | 1 248 | 1 298 |
| Wages (gross) | 37 000 | 38 480 | 40 019 |
| Wages on-costs | 11 100 | 11 544 | 12 006 |
| Other expenses | 500 | 520 | 541 |
| *Total operating expenses* | *90 100* | *91 441* | *94 056* |
| **NET PROFIT before tax** | **$49 500** | **$51 479** | **$52 441** |

*Assumptions:*
- No allowance is made for GST.
- Drink and food supplies are at constant levels.
- Depreciation is 15% p.a. of the original cost of long-term assets.
- Interest paid rate is 8% p.a.
- 'Wages' exclude owner's drawings.
- 'Wages on-costs' comprise superannuation, workers' compensation insurance, bonuses, training costs and staff amenities for employees.
- 'Wages on-costs' are 30% of wages.
- Unless determinable, each cost is increased by 4% p.a.

| **Break-even sales** | | | |
|---|---|---|---|
| | **Year 1** | **Year 2** | **Year 3** |
| | $ | $ | $ |
| Estimated sales | 232 667 | 238 200 | 244 162 |
| Variable costs | 93 067 | 95 280 | 97 665 |
| Fixed costs | 90 100 | 91 441 | 94 056 |
| **Break-even point for sales** | **$150 167** | **$152 402** | **$156 760** |

*Assumptions:*
- Drinks and food purchases are variable costs.
- All operating costs are fixed costs.
  *(See Chapter 7 for how to calculate break-even sales.)*

## Forecast capital expenditure statements

| Date and type of expenditure | | Year 1 $ |
|---|---|---|
| 1/7/Year 1—equipment, furniture and fittings | | 20 000 |
| 1/7/Year 1—purchased business goodwill | | 75 000 |
| | **Year 1 total** | **$95 000** |
| | | Year 2 $ |
| | **Year 2 total** | – |
| | | Year 3 $ |
| | **Year 3 total** | – |

## Forecast cash flow statements

| | Year 1 $ | Year 2 $ | Year 3 $ |
|---|---|---|---|
| Cash position—start of year | 0 | 25 516 | 31 442 |
| CASH RECEIPTS | | | |
| Cash sales | 232 667 | 238 200 | 244 162 |
| Cash from debtors | – | – | – |
| Capital contributions | 46 000 | – | – |
| Borrowings | 55 000 | – | – |
| *Total cash receipts* | *333 667* | *238 200* | *244 162* |
| *less* CASH PAYMENTS | | | |
| Drinks and food purchases | 93 067 | 95 280 | 97 665 |
| Operating expenses | 82 700 | 84 760 | 88 151 |
| Loan repayments | 13 384 | 13 384 | 13 384 |
| Capital expenditure | 95 000 | – | – |
| Owner's drawings | 24 000 | 24 000 | 24 000 |
| Taxation | – | 14 850 | 15 444 |
| *Total cash payments* | *308 151* | *232 274* | *238 644* |
| **NET CASH FLOW** | **$25 516** | **$5 926** | **$5 518** |
| Cash position—end of year | $25 516 | $31 442 | $36 960 |

*Assumptions:*

- 100% of annual sales are cash sales.
- Purchases and operating expenses are paid for in cash.
- Operating expenses paid exclude depreciation and interest.
- Loan repayments include principal and interest.
- Income tax (at 30%) on annual net profit is paid in the following year.

| Forecast financial position statements | | | |
|---|---|---|---|
| | Year 1 | Year 2 | Year 3 |
| | $ | $ | $ |
| ASSETS | | | |
| Short-term assets | | | |
| Cash | 25 516 | 31 442 | 36 960 |
| Stock (at cost) | – | – | – |
| Debtors | – | – | – |
| *Subtotal* | *25 516* | *31 442* | *36 960* |
| Long-term assets | | | |
| Equipment, furniture and fittings (at cost) | 20 000 | 20 000 | 20 000 |
| *less* Accumulated depreciation | (3 000) | (6 000) | (9 000) |
| Purchased business goodwill | 75 000 | 75 000 | 75 000 |
| *Subtotal* | *92 000* | *89 000* | *86 000* |
| TOTAL ASSETS | 117 516 | 120 442 | 122 960 |
| *less* LIABILITIES | | | |
| Short-term liabilities | | | |
| Overdraft | – | – | – |
| Creditors | – | – | – |
| *Subtotal* | – | – | – |
| Long-term liabilities | | | |
| Term loan | 46 016 | 36 313 | 25 834 |
| *Subtotal* | *46 016* | *36 313* | *25 834* |
| TOTAL LIABILITIES | 46 016 | 36 313 | 25 834 |
| **NET ASSETS** | **$71 500** | **$84 129** | **$97 126** |

*Assumptions:*

- Long-term assets are shown at original cost.
- The term loan is a reducing-balance loan.

| Key financial ratios | | | |
| --- | --- | --- | --- |
| | Year 1 | Year 2 | Year 3 | Industry average |
| **Profitability ratios:** | | | | |
| Gross profit margin | 60% | 60% | 60% | 60% |
| Wage costs to sales ratio | 16% | 16% | 16% | 22% |
| Rent to sales ratio | 11% | 11% | 12% | 15% |
| Operating expenses to sales ratio | 39% | 38% | 39% | 42% |
| Net profit margin | 21% | 22% | 21% | 18% |
| **Financial position ratio:** | | | | |
| Debt ratio | 39% | 30% | 21% | 39% |

## E.5 Financial records

A business bank account will be operated at the Commercial Bank, My-Suburb. All receipts and payments will be processed through the account.

A manual system of financial records will be established and maintained. These records include:

- *source documents:* cash register rolls, deposits slips, cheque butts and bank statements
- *cash journal books:* cash receipts journal, cash payments journal and petty cash book
- *secondary books*: sales register, time and wages book.

Internal controls will be adopted to ensure the accuracy of financial records. These include:

- having only the proprietor sign cheques
- crossing cheques drawn with 'not negotiable'
- banking takings daily
- paying suppliers' invoices by cheque
- preparing monthly bank reconciliations to check cashbook totals with bank statement balances.

## E.6 Business insurances

The following insurances will be maintained by the business:

- workers' compensation insurance (compulsory under law)
- business contents insurance
- plate glass insurance
- public liability insurance
- sickness/accident insurance (for proprietor).

An annual check of operating risks will be conducted to design risk-prevention measures and determine insurance needs.

## E.7 Financial controls

The following financial controls will be used to monitor and evaluate the financial performance of the operation.

- *Profit control.* Detailed profit results will be reported annually. Profit results will be compared with corresponding forecasts by applying variance analysis. Any unsatisfactory variances identified will be corrected by appropriate follow-up actions.
- *Cash flow control.* Cash flows of the operation will be closely monitored by the preparation of monthly cash flow reports. Unsatisfactory cash flow results identified will be rectified by taking appropriate corrective action.
- *Financial position control.* The total debt of the business will be reviewed annually by preparing an annual report of the financial position.

# F. OPERATIONAL REVIEW

## Operational review schedule

Years—Year 1, Year 2 and Year 3

| Control action | Frequency | Review date | Person responsible |
|---|---|---|---|
| **Marketing controls:** | | | |
| Analyse sales results | Quarterly | End of quarter | Proprietor |
| Conduct customer satisfaction surveys | Half-yearly | End of half-year | Proprietor |
| Review marketing program | Annually | End of year | Proprietor |
| **Purchasing controls:** | | | |
| Check purchases | Daily | On each day | Shop assistant |
| Analyse gross profit margins | Annually | End of year | Proprietor |
| Review suppliers | Half-yearly | End of half-year | Proprietor |
| **Personnel controls:** | | | |
| Analyse labour productivity | Annually | End of year | Proprietor |
| Evaluate job performance | Half-yearly | End of half-year | Proprietor |
| Supervise employees | Daily | On each day | Proprietor |
| **Financial controls:** | | | |
| Evaluate profit performance | Annually | End of year | Proprietor |
| Evaluate cash flow results | Monthly | End of month | Proprietor |
| Review financial position | Annually | End of year | Proprietor |
| Check operating risks | Annually | End of year | Insurance broker |

## Supporting documents

Attachment A—Detailed financial statements for last year

Attachment B—ABS industry statistics

Attachment C—Menu showing products and prices

**SAMPLE PLAN**

**2**

[show any business logo]

**PRIVATE AND CONFIDENTIAL**

# Business Plan of Kate's Bush Tours

for Year 1, Year 2 and Year 3

Prepared by: Kate Busby

Completion date: 1/7/Yr 1

Email address: kbusby@mymail.com

# CONTENTS

Page number

**BUSINESS GOAL STATEMENT** 3

**A.    BUSINESS PROFILE** 4

A.1    Business activity 4

A.2    Ownership structure 4

A.3    Business name 4

A.4    Business location 4

A.5    Entry strategy 4

A.6    Legal requirements 4

A.7    Business objectives 5

**B. MARKETING** 6

B.1    Environmental trends 6

B.2     Industry conditions 6

B.3    Services 7

B.4    Competitors 7

B.5    Target customers 7

B.6    Marketing strategies 8

B.7    Marketing controls 9

**C. PURCHASING** 11

C.1    Suppliers 11

C.2    Purchasing policies 11

C.3    Purchasing controls 12

**D. PERSONNEL** 13

D.1    Management details 13

D.2    Organisation structure 13

D.3    Professional advisers 13

**E. FINANCIAL** 14

E.1    Personal financial position 14

E.2    Establishment costs 15

E.3    Borrowing requirements 15

E.4    Financial forecasts 16

E.5    Financial records 20

E.6    Business insurances 20

E.7    Financial controls 21

**F. OPERATIONAL REVIEW** 22

SUPPORTING DOCUMENTS

# BUSINESS GOAL STATEMENT

My business goal is to establish the operation and sell
it for a fair goodwill value worth at least $100 000 by the
end of Year 5.

# A. BUSINESS PROFILE

## A.1 Business activity
The proposed business will be a service provider of one-day sightseeing tours to areas around My-Town—a township in Central Australia.

## A.2 Ownership structure
The business will be operated as a sole trader by Kate Busby. The proprietor has chosen to operate as a sole trader to have complete freedom to implement her own ideas for developing the business.

## A.3 Business name
The business will trade under the registered name of 'Kate's Bush Tours'.

The business website is <www.katestours.com.au>.

## A.4 Business location
The operation will be based at the proprietor's home at 104 Browser Road, My-Town. The business portion of the premises comprises a home office (20 m$^2$) and a garage (36 m$^2$) for storing the passenger-carrying vehicle. The business premises are in a centralised position in My-Town, located half a kilometre from the CBD.

The township of My-Town is in Central Australia and has a population of 9384. The town has five hotels, six motels, one hotel/motel and two caravan/camping parks, as well as a wide assortment of restaurants and cafés. The town is surrounded by scenic national parks, which attract sightseers and campers every year. There are also rivers and billabongs in the general area with good fishing. The town has all the modern facilities and amenities. There are also good transport links to the town. There is an interstate railway and a national highway passing through the town, as well as an airport servicing interstate flights.

## A.5 Entry strategy
The business will be started up as a new operation. The reason for starting up as a new business is because there are few competitors based in the area and the tourism industry is growing rapidly (particularly overseas travellers). The proposed date of commencement of business is 1 July, Year 1.

## A.6 Legal requirements
The legal requirements to operate the business are:
- business name registration with the Australian Securities and Investments Commission

- home business use permit from the local council
- driver's licence for passenger-carrying vehicle from state roads and traffic authority
- ABN registration (for GST) with the Australian Taxation Office
- entry permit to national parks from National Parks and Wildlife Authority.
  Legal requirements will be met before business commences.

## A.7 Business objectives

The key objectives of the business for the next three years are summarised as follows:

|  | Year 1 | Year 2 | Year 3 |
|---|---|---|---|
| **Marketing:** | | | |
| Sales turnover | $92 000 | $99 000 | $108 000 |
| **Personnel:** | | | |
| Number of personnel (full-time equivalents) | 1 | 1 | 1 |
| **Financial:** | | | |
| Net profit | $32 000 | $40 000 | $46 000 |
| Net cash flow | $57 000 | $17 000 | $21 000 |
| Debt ratio | 48% | 44% | 40% |

# B. MARKETING

## B.1 Environmental trends

Research and analysis of the general business environment identifies the following opportunities and challenges for the business in the next three years.

### Opportunities:
- A steady increase in the general population is expected.
- Overseas travel interest in Australia is growing.
- There is increasing desire for leisure time.
- People are taking earlier retirements.
- There is greater environmental awareness and appreciation.
- Rapid development is occurring in communications technology.

### Challenges:
- slowdown in world economy
- likely increases in interest rates
- likely introduction of new business taxes
- a more litigious society
- increased consumer protection laws
- erratic changes in climate and weather patterns.

The conclusion reached from the environmental analysis is that there are opportunities for the business that will support the growth in sales forecasts. These environmental trends will influence the selection of marketing strategies for the business.

## B.2 Industry conditions

Statistics from Tourism Research Australia show that the number of overseas tourists visiting Australia has been increasing steadily by an average of 4% p.a. for the past five years. This growth trend is expected to continue for the forseeable future. Last year, about 36% of overseas tourists visited the Central Australia region. The highest proportions of overseas visitors to this region were Asian tourists and backpackers. This is expected to continue for the next three years.

Information obtained from the local tourist information centre also shows that the number of visitor inquiries last year was 30% more than five years previously. About 70% of last year's inquiries were from interstate retirees. The number of interstate visitors to the area is expected to increase in the next three years. It is not expected that there will be any significant change in the supply of tourism services in the region during the next three years.

Industry conditions will influence the selection of marketing strategies for the business.

## B.3 Services

The business will offer day-long sightseeing tours by mini-bus for small groups of ten or fewer people. The sightseeing tours will be conducted in the naturally picturesque area around My-Town in Central Australia. Passengers will be picked up from their accommodation and returned there after a full day of touring. The tour package will include food and non-alcoholic drinks being served at barbecue and picnic stops. Tours will also stop at pre-arranged souvenir shops and roadside cafés. At the start of each tour, tourists will be given an attractively presented itinerary with a map that can be kept as a souvenir of the trip.

## B.4 Competitors

Through direct observation, one competitor has been identified that will compete directly with the business.

### Competitor 1

Name:              Bluey's Outback Tours
Location:          interstate
Duration:          two years
Personnel:         five employees (full-time equivalents)

*Strengths:*
- professional presentation
- new air-conditioned buses
- large capital backing.

*Weaknesses:*
- low market exposure
- no local knowledge or community involvement
- high prices.

It is expected that more direct competitors will emerge in the three-year period ahead as more opportunities arise from increasing tourism. Competitor observations form the basis for designing competitive advantage strategies to follow.

## B.5 Target customers

The main customer groups that have been targeted by the business are Asian tourists, overseas backpackers and interstate retirees. Target customer groups will remain the same during the period of the plan, unless changed in the annual marketing review.

### Target customer group 1: Asian tourists

*Personal characteristics:*

- 20–40 years old, predominantly couples, Asian residents, adventurous, curious, working class, middle to high incomes, average education.

*Relevant wants:*

- scenic tours, information about areas, friendly and courteous service.

### Target customer group 2: Overseas backpackers

*Personal characteristics:*

- 18–35 years old, couples and singles, mainly from Europe and the United Kingdom, adventurous, active and energetic, open-minded, environmentally aware, health-conscious, students or wage earners, low to middle incomes, well educated.

*Relevant wants:*

- scenic sights, outdoor activities, affordable prices.

### Target customer group 3: Interstate retirees

*Personal characteristics:*

- over 55 years old, interstate urban dwellers, conservative, adventurous, active retirees, outdoors oriented, bargain conscious, low to middle incomes.

*Relevant wants:*

- convenient sightseeing, amenities and facilities, pleasant outings, affordable prices.

Statistics show that the size of these target customer groups is growing annually (see section B.2, 'Industry conditions'). A random sample of 100 people from the target customer groups in the area was surveyed for attitudes to day-long sightseeing tours in Central Australia. Survey results have been taken into account in selecting marketing strategies for the business.

## B.6 Marketing strategies

The business will adopt a customer-oriented approach in the marketing of its services. Any marketing strategy selected will focus on satisfying the relevant wants of the target customer groups.

### Services:

- offering day-long mini-bus sightseeing tours within four hours' travelling time of My-Town
- providing a barbecue lunch with damper, billy tea and drinks
- providing stopovers at souvenir shops and roadside cafés
- providing an attractive itinerary guide to tour participants as an information brochure and trip memento.

### Prices:

- services offered for an all-inclusive price at competitive rates
- discounts for group bookings
- bookings to be pre-paid
- cancellation fee applies for terminated bookings.

### Distribution:

- services provided from base of home location
- business availability times, six days a week—8 a.m. to 6 p.m.
- answering machine installed and mobile telephone and email used for customer access.

### Image:

- clean and tidy personal and vehicle presentation
- projection of Australiana themes
- friendly, helpful and courteous attitudes.

### Promotions:

- *Yellow Pages* advertising in major urban centres
- mobile sign on vehicle
- regular advertising in travel journals and magazines
- networking with travel agents
- circulating brochures to city hotels and travel agents
- advertising on the internet
- sponsorship of local area tourist promotion campaigns.

### Competitive advantages:

- providing a friendlier and more courteous service than competitor
- multilingual speaking skills
- local area knowledge
- offering Australiana dining experiences in the tour package
- offering more affordable prices than competitor
- using a more effective promotional campaign than competitor.
  Competitive advantages are expected to be sustainable in the long term.

## B.7 Marketing controls

Marketing strategies will be adaptable to change if business conditions change or new opportunities emerge.

A booking and sales register will be maintained to record bookings and sales. Recorded sales results and the effectiveness of promotions will be analysed quarterly by comparison with corresponding targets. Customer satisfaction surveys will also be conducted after every tour to survey customers for their responses to marketing strategies.

The marketing program will be reviewed annually. This will involve a new analysis of the operating environment followed by the design of a new marketing program.

# C. PURCHASING

## C.1 Suppliers

The following suppliers will be used by the business.

### Supplier 1

| | |
|---|---|
| Name: | Judd's Wholesale Meat Supplies |
| Location: | local area |
| Duration: | 22 years |
| Supplies: | barbecued meat |
| Supply terms: | COD, quantity discounts |

### Supplier 2

| | |
|---|---|
| Name: | Bess's Grocery Shop |
| Location: | local area |
| Duration: | sixteen years |
| Supplies: | fruit, vegetables, teas, coffee, drinks and cooking supplies |
| Supply terms: | COD |

### Supplier 3

| | |
|---|---|
| Name: | Reddy's Printery |
| Location: | local area |
| Duration: | eight years |
| Supplies: | itinerary guides and maps |
| Supply terms: | COD |

### Supplier 4

| | |
|---|---|
| Name: | Nilsen's Auto Parts |
| Location: | local area |
| Duration: | thirteen years |
| Supplies: | vehicle parts and spares |
| Supply terms: | COD |

## C.2 Purchasing policies

Quality food supplies from established and reliable local suppliers will be purchased for each trip. Food supplies will be handled and stored in a healthy manner.

## C.3 Purchasing controls

The following purchasing controls will be maintained to ensure purchasing activities are carried out efficiently and effectively:

- daily purchasing of perishable food supplies to ensure fresh food quality
- regularly checking perishable food supplies for freshness
- reviewing supplier performance half-yearly.

# D. PERSONNEL

## D.1 Management details

The operation will be managed by the proprietor, Kate Busby, whose relevant personal details are as follows.

*Relevant experience:*
- five years' experience as tour guide
- seventeen years living in local area.

*Relevant training/qualifications:*
- tourism operations diploma from TAFE college
- small business management certificate from TAFE college
- speaks several languages fluently.

In Year 1, the proprietor intends to undertake a six-month tourism marketing course by correspondence. During Year 2, the proprietor also intends to undertake a nine-week (part-time) diesel engine maintenance course at the local TAFE college.

The proprietor will draw $1500 per calendar month in Year 1 and $1800 per calendar month in Years 2 and 3 from the business. These amounts will be sufficient to meet the proprietor's monthly personal expenses.

## D.2 Organisation structure

The proprietor will be the sole employee of the business for the next three years.

*Job profile—Owner/manager*
Full-time—60 hours p.w.

*Job duties:*
- driving tour vehicle
- purchasing supplies
- cooking
- maintaining tour vehicle
- banking takings
- record-keeping and administration.

## D.3 Professional advisers

The following business advisers will be used:
- Qualified accountant (and tax agent):  Ken James, My-Town
- Solicitor:                              Diane Chool, My-Town
- Insurance broker:                       Tom Smithers, My-Town
- Bank:                                   Commercial Bank, My-Town

Annual membership of the local Chamber of Commerce will be maintained.

# E. FINANCIAL

## E.1 Personal financial position

The current personal financial position of Kate Busby is shown as follows.

| Statement of personal net worth at start of Year 1 | |
|---|---|
| | $ |
| **Personal assets** (current selling value) | |
| Real estate | 140 000 |
| Motor vehicle | 8 000 |
| Furniture and contents | 14 000 |
| Investments | 50 000 |
| | 212 000 |
| *less* **Personal liabilities** (current balance owing) | |
| Mortgage | 8 500 |
| Credit card | 500 |
| | 9 000 |
| **Personal net worth** | **$203 000** |

| Statement of current monthly personal expenses | |
|---|---|
| **Expenses** | $ |
| Mortgage payment | 300 |
| Credit card payment | 50 |
| Food | 400 |
| Household consumables | 10 |
| Clothing | 20 |
| Motor vehicle running costs | 400 |
| Rates | 60 |
| Electricity and telephone | 85 |
| Health insurance | 70 |
| Other living expenses | 50 |
| **Total monthly personal expenses** | **$1445** |

## E.2 Establishment costs

Establishment costs to set up the operation are as follows.

|  | Estimated cost |
|---|---:|
|  | $ |
| New 4WD mini-bus (carries ten passengers) | 50 000 |
| Office machines | 6 000 |
| Registrations permits and licences | 2 000 |
| Records and stationery | 600 |
| Insurances | 2 800 |
| Initial promotions | 6 000 |
| Advisers' fees | 600 |
| First three months of operating expenses | 16 900 |
| Drawings (first three months) | 4 500 |
| Borrowing costs | 1 000 |
| **Total establishment costs** | **$90 400** |

## E.3 Borrowing requirements

The borrowing amount required is calculated as follows.

| | |
|---|---|
| Total establishment costs | $90 400 |
| *less* Personal capital | $40 400 |
| Borrowing amount required | $50 000 |

Details of the loan sought are:

| | |
|---|---|
| Date required: | start of Year 1 |
| Loan type: | business term loan |
| Loan amount: | $50 000 |
| Loan period: | five years |
| Repayment method: | monthly, by interest only (principal repayable at end of period) |
| Interest rate basis: | fixed interest |
| Loan purpose: | to buy motor vehicle |

# E.4 Financial forecasts

| **Forecast monthly sales statements** | | | | |
|---|---|---|---|---|
| **Service—Sightseeing tours** | | | | |
| **Month** | **Seasonality factor** | **Year 1** | **Year 2** | **Year 3** |
| | **%** | **$** | **$** | **$** |
| July | 3 | 2 760 | 2 970 | 3 240 |
| August | 3 | 2 760 | 2 970 | 3 240 |
| September | 11 | 10 120 | 10 890 | 11 880 |
| October | 12 | 11 040 | 11 880 | 12 960 |
| November | 14 | 12 880 | 13 860 | 15 120 |
| December | 14 | 12 880 | 13 860 | 15 120 |
| January | 14 | 12 880 | 13 860 | 15 120 |
| February | 13 | 11 960 | 12 870 | 14 040 |
| March | 6 | 5 520 | 5 940 | 6 480 |
| April | 4 | 3 680 | 3 960 | 4 320 |
| May | 3 | 2 760 | 2 970 | 3 240 |
| June | 3 | 2 760 | 2 970 | 3 240 |
| **Totals** | **100%** | **$92 000** | **$99 000** | **$108 000** |

| **Forecast profit statements** | | | |
|---|---|---|---|
| | **Year 1** | **Year 2** | **Year 3** |
| | **$** | **$** | **$** |
| INCOME | | | |
| Sales | 92 000 | 99 000 | 108,000 |
| *less* OPERATING EXPENSES | | | |
| Advertising and promotions | 6 000 | 3 500 | 3 640 |
| Advisers' fees | 600 | 400 | 416 |
| Bank charges | 1 400 | 416 | 433 |
| Commissions paid | 2 000 | 2 080 | 2 163 |
| Consumables | 7 800 | 8 420 | 8 914 |
| Depreciation | 8 400 | 8 400 | 8 400 |
| Home office expenses | 200 | 208 | 216 |
| Insurances | 2 800 | 2 912 | 3 028 |
| Interest paid | 4 000 | 4 000 | 4 000 |

| | | | |
|---|---|---|---|
| Legal fees | 2 000 | 2 080 | 2 163 |
| Motor vehicle running costs | 20 948 | 22 542 | 24 592 |
| Stationery | 600 | 624 | 649 |
| Telephone | 2 600 | 2 704 | 2 812 |
| Other expenses | 500 | 520 | 541 |
| *Total operating expenses* | *59 848* | *58 806* | *61 967* |
| **NET PROFIT before tax** | **$32 152** | **$40 194** | **$46 033** |

*Assumptions:*
- No allowance is made for GST.
- 'Consumables' comprise food supplies.
- Depreciation is 15% p.a. of the original cost of long-term assets.
- Interest paid rate is 8% p.a.
- 'Motor vehicle running costs' comprise petrol, repairs and maintenance, registration and insurance and road tax.
- unless determinable, each cost is increased by 4% p.a.

| Break-even sales | | | |
|---|---|---|---|
| | **Year 1** | **Year 2** | **Year 3** |
| | $ | $ | $ |
| Estimated sales | 92 000 | 99 000 | 108 000 |
| Variable costs | – | – | – |
| Fixed costs | 59 848 | 58 806 | 61 967 |
| **Break-even point for sales** | **$59 848** | **$58 806** | **$61 967** |

*Assumptions:*
- No costs are variable costs.
- All operating costs are fixed costs.
  *(See Chapter 7 for how to calculate break-even sales.)*

**Forecast capital expenditure statements**

| | **Year 1** |
|---|---|
| **Date and type of expenditure** | **$** |
| 1/7/Year 1—Mini-bus | 50 000 |
| 1/7/Year 1—Office machines | 6000 |
| **Year 1 total** | **$56 000** |

|  | Year 2 |
| --- | --- |
|  | $ |
| Year 2 total | – |
|  | Year 3 |
|  | $ |
| Year 3 total | – |

| Forecast cash flow statements | | | |
| --- | --- | --- | --- |
|  | Year 1 | Year 2 | Year 3 |
|  | $ | $ | $ |
| Cash position—start of year | 0 | 56 952 | 74 300 |
| CASH RECEIPTS |  |  |  |
| Cash sales | 92 000 | 99 000 | 108 000 |
| Cash from debtors | – | – | – |
| Capital contributions | 40 400 | – | – |
| Borrowings | 50 000 | – | – |
| *Total cash receipts* | *182 400* | *99 000* | *108 000* |
| *less* CASH PAYMENTS |  |  |  |
| Operating expenses | 47 448 | 46 406 | 49 567 |
| Loan repayments | 4 000 | 4 000 | 4 000 |
| Capital expenditure | 56 000 | – | – |
| Owner's drawings | 18 000 | 21 600 | 21 600 |
| Taxation | – | 9 646 | 12 058 |
| *Total cash payments* | *125 448* | *81 652* | *87 225* |
| **NET CASH FLOW** | **$56 952** | **$17 348** | **$20 775** |
| Cash position—end of year | $56 952 | $74 300 | $95 075 |

*Assumptions:*
- 100% of annual sales are cash sales.
- Operating expenses are paid for in cash.
- Operating expenses paid exclude depreciation and interest.
- Loan repayments include interest only.
- Income tax (at 30%) on annual net profit is paid in the following year.

| **Forecast financial position statements** | | | |
|---|---|---|---|
| | **Year 1** | **Year 2** | **Year 3** |
| | **$** | **$** | **$** |
| ASSETS | | | |
| Short-term assets | | | |
| Cash | 56 952 | 74 300 | 95 075 |
| Stock (at cost) | – | – | – |
| Debtors | – | – | – |
| *Subtotal* | *56 952* | *74 300* | *95 075* |
| Long-term assets | | | |
| Motor vehicle (at cost) | 50 000 | 50 000 | 50 000 |
| *less* Accumulated depreciation | (7 500) | (150 00) | (22 500) |
| Office machines (at cost) | 6 000 | 6 000 | 6 000 |
| *less* Accumulated depreciation | (900) | (1 800) | (2 700) |
| *Subtotal* | *47 600* | *39 200* | *30 800* |
| TOTAL ASSETS | 104 552 | 113 500 | 125 875 |
| *less* LIABILITIES | | | |
| Short-term liabilities | | | |
| Overdraft | – | – | – |
| Creditors | – | – | – |
| *Subtotal* | – | – | – |
| Long-term liabilities | | | |
| Term loan | 50 000 | 50 000 | 50 000 |
| *Subtotal* | *50 000* | *50 000* | *50 000* |
| TOTAL LIABILITIES | 50 000 | 50 000 | 50 000 |
| **NET ASSETS** | **$54 552** | **$63 500** | **$75 875** |

*Assumptions:*
- Long-term assets are shown at original cost.
- The term loan is an interest only loan.

| Key financial ratios | | | | |
|---|---|---|---|---|
| | Year 1 | Year 2 | Year 3 | Industry average |
| **Profitability ratios:** | | | | |
| Advertising to sales ratio | 7% | 4% | 3% | 4% |
| Motor vehicle running costs to sales ratio | 23% | 23% | 23% | 23% |
| Operating expenses to sales ratio | 65% | 59% | 57% | 61% |
| Net profit margin | 35% | 41% | 43% | 39% |
| **Financial position ratio:** | | | | |
| Debt ratio | 48% | 43% | 39% | 54% |

## E.5 Financial records

A business bank account will be operated at the Commercial Bank, My-Town. All receipts and payments will be processed through the account.

A manual system of financial records will be established and maintained. These records include:

- *source documents:* sales receipts, deposit slips, cheque butts and bank statements
- *cash journal books:* cash receipts journal, cash payments journal and petty cash book
- *secondary book:* bookings and sales register.

Internal controls will be adopted to ensure the accuracy of financial records. These include:

- using standardised pre-numbered source documents in consecutive number sequence
- issuing source documents in triplicate form
- crossing cheques drawn with 'not negotiable'
- banking takings daily
- paying suppliers' invoices by cheque
- preparing monthly bank reconciliations to check cashbook totals with bank statement balances.

## E.6 Business insurances

The following insurances will be maintained by the business:

- comprehensive motor vehicle insurance
- business contents insurance
- professional indemnity insurance
- sickness/accident insurance (for proprietor).

An annual check of operating risks will be conducted to design risk-prevention measures and determine insurance needs.

## E.7 Financial controls

The following financial controls will be used to monitor and evaluate the financial performance of the operation.

- *Profit control.* Detailed profit results will be reported quarterly. Profit results will be compared with corresponding forecasts by applying variance analysis. Any unsatisfactory variances identified will be corrected by appropriate follow-up actions.
- *Cash flow control.* Cash flows of the operation will be closely monitored by the preparation of monthly cash flow reports. Unsatisfactory cash flow results identified will be rectified by taking appropriate corrective action.
- *Financial position control.* The total debt of the business will be reviewed annually by preparing an annual report of the financial position.

# F. OPERATIONAL REVIEW

### Operational review schedule

Years—Year 1, Year 2 and Year 3

| Control action responsible | Frequency | Review date | Person responsible |
|---|---|---|---|
| **Marketing controls:** | | | |
| Analyse sales results | Quarterly | End of quarter | Proprietor |
| Conduct customer satisfaction survey | Daily | On each day | Proprietor |
| Review marketing program | Annually | End of year | Proprietor |
| **Purchasing controls:** | | | |
| Checking perishable supplies | Daily | On each day | Proprietor |
| Review suppliers | Half-yearly | End of half-year | Proprietor |
| **Financial controls:** | | | |
| Evaluate profit performance | Quarterly | End of quarter | Proprietor |
| Evaluate cash flow results | Monthly | End of month | Proprietor |
| Review financial position | Annually | End of year | Proprietor |
| Check operating risks | Annually | End of year | Insurance broker |

## *Supporting documents*

Attachment A—Tourism Research Australia tourism statistics

Attachment B—Personal survey results

[show any business logo]

**PRIVATE AND CONFIDENTIAL**

# Business Plan of Mike's Building Co. Pty Ltd

for Year 1, Year 2 and Year 3

Prepared by: Mike Naylor

Completion date: 1/7/Yr 1

Email address: mnaylor@mymail.com

# CONTENTS

Page number

**BUSINESS GOAL STATEMENT**                                    **3**

**A.     BUSINESS PROFILE**                                    **4**

A.1    Business activity                                        4
A.2    Ownership structure                                     4
A.3    Business name                                           4
A.4    Business location                                       4
A.5    Business history                                        4
A.6    Legal requirements                                      4
A.7    Business objectives                                     5

**B. MARKETING**                                               **6**

B.1    Environmental trends                                    6
B.2    Industry conditions                                     6
B.3    Services                                                7
B.4    Competitors                                             7
B.5    Target customers                                        8
B.6    Marketing strategies                                    9
B.7    Marketing controls                                     10

**C. PURCHASING**                                             **11**

C.1    Suppliers                                              11
C.2    Purchasing policies                                    12
C.3    Purchasing controls                                    12

**D. PERSONNEL**                                             **13**

D.1    Management details                                     13
D.2    Organisation structure                                 13
D.3    Staffing strategies                                    15
D.4    Professional advisers                                  15
D.5    Personnel controls                                     16

**E. FINANCIAL**                                             **17**

E.1    Personal financial position                            17
E.2    Borrowing requirements                                 18
E.3    Financial forecasts                                    18
E.4    Financial records                                      22
E.5    Business insurances                                    23
E.6    Financial controls                                     23

**F. OPERATIONAL REVIEW**                                    **24**

SUPPORTING DOCUMENTS

# BUSINESS GOAL STATEMENT

The business goal of the company is to maintain positive
annual net cash flows during the next three years.

# A. BUSINESS PROFILE

## A.1 Business activity

The existing business is a service provider of building services specialising in the construction of small 'specified plan' homes for customers on suburban blocks of land.

## A.2 Ownership structure

The business is operated as a small proprietary company by Mike Naylor, who is the sole director of and shareholder in the company. The proprietor chooses to operate as a company because of the risks inherent in operating in the cyclical building industry. In the event of a sudden business downturn, personally owned assets are protected from creditors because they are separate from the business assets owned by the company.

## A.3 Business name

The company trades under its own name, 'Mike's Building Co. Pty Ltd'.

The business website is <www.mikesbuilding.com.au>.

## A.4 Business location

The operation is based at the proprietor's home at 64 Carpenter Place, My-Suburb—a suburb of My-City—which is also the registered address of the company. The business portion of the premises comprises a home office (15 m$^2$) and a secure garage (40 m$^2$) for storing tools and job materials.

## A.5 Business history

The business is an existing operation that began four years ago. The history of business growth is summarised by the following results.

| Year | Annual sales turnover | Annual net profit |
| --- | --- | --- |
| 4 years ago | $248 320 | $4966 |
| 3 years ago | $307 006 | $6140 |
| 2 years ago | $392 186 | $5882 |
| 1 year ago | $408 320 | $5920 |

## A.6 Legal requirements

The legal requirements to operate the business are:
- builder's licence from National Occupational Licensing Authority
- home business use permit from local council
- company registration with the Australian Securities and Investments Commission
- ABN registration (for GST and PAYG tax) with the Australian Taxation Office

- building approval from the local council for each construction job.

  Legal requirements will continue to be met during the course of the operation.

## A.7 Business objectives

The key objectives of the business for the next three years are summarised as follows.

|  | Year 1 | Year 2 | Year 3 |
|---|---|---|---|
| **Marketing:** | | | |
| Sales turnover | $422 000 | $357 000 | $294 000 |
| **Purchasing:** | | | |
| Average gross profit margin | 57% | 57% | 57% |
| **Personnel:** | | | |
| Labour productivity ratio (i.e. sales : labour cost) | $2.03 : $1 | $2.11 : $1 | $2.25 : $1 |
| Number of personnel (full-time equivalents) | 5 | 4 | 3 |
| **Financial:** | | | |
| Net profit | $5 000 | $5 000 | $7 000 |
| Net cash flow | $14 000 | $15 000 | $17 000 |

# B. MARKETING

## B.1 Environmental trends

Research and analysis of the general business environment identifies the following opportunities and challenges for the business in the next three years.

*Opportunities:*
- A steady increase in the general population is expected.
- More people are investing in real estate.
- There are rising levels of immigration.
- Easing of regulatory red tape for small business has occurred.
- There is growing acceptance of medium- and high-density housing.

*Challenges:*
- likely slowdown in general economic activity
- likely future increases in interest rates
- rising levels of household debt
- likely introduction of new taxes
- increased consumer protection laws
- more environmental protection laws.

The conclusion reached from the environmental analysis is that there are challenges for the business to overcome if sales forecasts are to be maintained. These environmental trends will influence the selection of marketing strategies for the business.

## B.2 Industry conditions

The business operates in a cyclical industry. The housing construction industry regularly fluctuates between periods of high activity and low activity in the cycle.

In My-City, construction activity for residential housing has been increasing rapidly for the past three years. The last three years has also been a period of low interest rates, which has contributed to the growth in construction activity. During this period, ABS statistics for the region show:
- the number of construction businesses operating has increased by an average of 6% p.a.
- the number of new housing dwellings constructed has increased by an average of 5% p.a.
- the number of home loans approved has increased by an average of 9% p.a.

The strong growth trend in housing construction is expected to continue in Year 1 before a housing industry downturn begins at the start of Year 2. By this time, there will be an over-supply of housing and possible interest rate rises.

The industry downturn is expected to last for about three years. During this period, there will be a reduction in the number of building operations and limited land available for building due to the amount of construction activity in previous periods.

Industry conditions will influence the selection of marketing strategies for the business.

## B.3 Services

The business will continue to specialise in the building of 'specification type' homes for customers. Services will be expanded to include home renovations in Year 2 and home repairs and maintenance in Year 3.

Services are to be increased because of the expected slowdown in housing construction activity. It is expected that less income will be generated by building new houses. To compensate for this, extra income is expected to be generated in Years 2 and 3 from the expansion of services into home renovations and repairs.

The contribution of each service to annual sales turnover is expected to be as follows.

| Services | Year 1 | Year 2 | Year 3 |
|---|---|---|---|
| | % | % | % |
| Constructing homes | 100 | 82 | 67 |
| Renovating homes | – | 18 | 28 |
| Home repairs | – | – | 5 |
| **Totals** | **100%** | **100%** | **100%** |

## B.4 Competitors

Through direct observation, many competitors have been identified that compete directly with the business. The two main competitors that specialise in constructing similar types of homes to the business are as follows.

### Competitor 1

Name:          The Betta Building Co.
Location:      local area
Duration:      six years
Personnel:     six employees (full-time equivalents)

*Strengths:*

- quality workmanship
- well-known business
- network of good contacts.

*Weaknesses:*
- high overheads
- unpleasant tradespeople employed
- slow completion of jobs.

### Competitor 2

| | |
|---|---|
| Name: | Ossie's Homes Pty Ltd |
| Location: | local area |
| Duration: | 26 years |
| Personnel: | eighteen employees (full-time equivalents) |

*Strengths:*
- quick completion of jobs
- fluent in several foreign languages
- heavy advertising.

*Weaknesses:*
- high overheads
- large capital investment
- unfriendly attitudes.

It is expected that there will be a reduction in the number of competitors in the three-year period ahead as the housing industry slowdown sets in. Competitor observations form the basis for designing competitive advantage strategies to follow.

## B.5 Target customers

The main customer group that will continue to be targeted by the business is first-home buyers. Target customers will be expanded from Year 2 onwards to include young families who are currently home owners.

Target customers will remain the same during the period of the plan, unless changed in the annual marketing review.

### Target customer group 1: First-home buyers

*Personal characteristics:*
- 20–36 years old, couples, modern tastes, bargain-conscious, working class, dual incomes, home seekers.

*Relevant wants:*
- a new home, affordable prices, contemporary designs.

### Target customer group 2: Young families

*Personal characteristics:*
- 26–40 years, couples with two or more young children, money-conscious, single-income family, low to middle incomes, current home owners.

*Relevant wants:*
- modern, spacious living, affordable prices.

These target customers are to be found across the metropolitan area of My-City, within a 40 kilometre radius of the business location. Relevant demographic statistics obtained from the ABS show that the number of target customers in the metropolitan area has increased by 21% in the last ten years. Statistical projections indicate that these growth trends are likely to continue in the future.

## B.6 Marketing strategies

The business will adopt a customer-oriented approach in the marketing of its services. Any marketing strategy selected will focus on satisfying the relevant wants of the target customer groups.

*Services:*
- constructing new homes
- renovating existing homes
- home repairs and maintenance
- guaranteeing workmanship.

*Prices:*
- services competitively priced
- progress payments received for construction, renovation and repair jobs (e.g. a third upfront, a third one month later, a third three months later)
- legally approved standard building contracts used.

*Distribution:*
- services provided from base of home location
- jobs carried out across the metropolitan area
- business availability times, Mondays to Saturdays (inclusive)—6 a.m. to 6 p.m.
- free quotations at customer's premises
- mobile telephone used for customer access.

*Image:*
- professional, friendly and courteous service
- quality workmanship.

### Promotions:

- *Yellow Pages* advertising
- regular advertising in local newspapers
- mobile vehicle signs
- developing a network of business contacts.

### Competitive advantages:

- having lower overheads than competitors
- having more affordable prices than competitors
- providing a friendlier and more courteous service than competitors
- faster completion of jobs than competitors.

  Competitive advantages are expected to be sustainable in the long term.

## B.7 Marketing controls

Marketing strategies will be adaptable to change if business conditions change or new opportunities emerge.

Recorded sales results and the effectiveness of promotions will be analysed quarterly by comparison with corresponding targets. Quarterly sales performance will also be graphed and compared with targets to identify sales trends. After the completion of each job, customer satisfaction surveys will be conducted to survey customers for their responses to marketing strategies.

The marketing program will be reviewed annually. This will involve a new analysis of the operating environment followed by the design of a new marketing program.

# C. PURCHASING

## C.1 Suppliers

Existing supply relationships will be maintained with large, established and reliable suppliers for building supplies.

### Supplier 1

| | |
|---|---|
| Name: | Tierney's Roofing Supplies |
| Location: | local area |
| Duration: | eight years |
| Supplies: | roofing supplies |
| Supply terms: | COD |

### Supplier 2

| | |
|---|---|
| Name: | Blake Bros Timber Merchants |
| Location: | local area |
| Duration: | 22 years |
| Supplies: | timber supplies |
| Supply terms: | COD, quantity discounts |

### Supplier 3

| | |
|---|---|
| Name: | Clifton's Plumbing Supplies Pty Ltd |
| Location: | local area |
| Duration: | fourteen years |
| Supplies: | plumbing supplies |
| Supply terms: | COD |

### Supplier 4

| | |
|---|---|
| Name: | Mansons Electrical Wholesalers |
| Location: | local area |
| Duration: | 28 years |
| Supplies: | electrical supplies |
| Supply terms: | COD, quantity discounts |

### Supplier 5

| | |
|---|---|
| Name: | Complete Hardware Supplies Ltd |
| Location: | local area |
| Duration: | 32 years |
| Supplies: | tools, general hardware |
| Supply terms: | seven days' credit, prompt payment discount, quantity discounts |

## C.2 Purchasing policies

Supplies will be purchased according to job requirements.

## C.3 Purchasing controls

The following purchasing controls will be maintained during the period of the business plan to ensure that purchasing activities are carried out efficiently and effectively:

- issuing purchase orders signed by the director for purchases from suppliers
- checking purchase orders against deliveries and suppliers' invoices
- reviewing supply terms and supplier performance half-yearly.

# D. PERSONNEL

## D.1 Management details

The operation will be managed by Mike Naylor, the sole director of the company. Mike Naylor's relevant personal details are as follows.

*Relevant experience:*
- sixteen years' experience as a carpenter
- four years' experience as a builder.

*Relevant training/qualifications:*
- carpenter's licence
- builder's licence
- small business management certificate from TAFE college.
  Mike Naylor will not undertake any training or qualifications in the next three years.
  As an employee director of the company, Mike Naylor will continue to receive a wage of $40 000 gross p.a. for each year. This amount will be sufficient to meet the director's monthly personal expenses.

## D.2 Organisation structure

The proposed staff organisation structure for each of the next three years is as follows.

*Job profile: Director*
Full-time—50 hours p.w.

*Job duties:*
- doing quotations
- dealing with customers
- supervising building work
- buying job materials
- arranging tradespeople
- inspecting properties.

*Job profile: Subcontract tradesperson*
Full-time—35 hours p.w.

*Job duties:*
- doing building or repair work.

*Job attributes:*
- qualified tradesperson
- minimum three years' experience as tradesperson
- easygoing, reliable and cooperative.

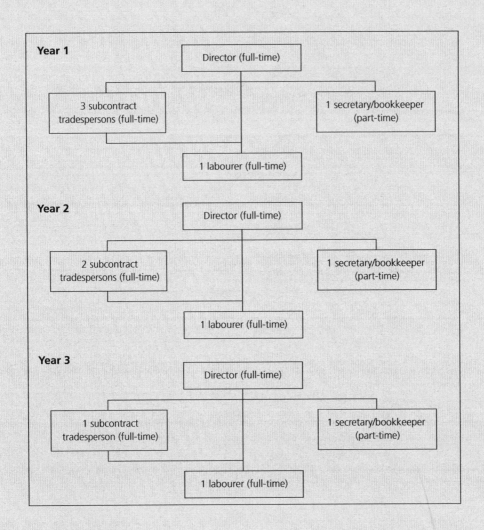

*Remuneration:*
- $40 000 gross p.a. at start.

### *Job profile: Secretary/bookkeeper*
Part-time—15 hours p.w.

*Job duties:*
- record-keeping and administration
- paying wages and bills
- receiving incoming calls
- banking.

*Job attributes:*
- minimum five years' experience in record-keeping
- trustworthy, accurate and organised.

*Remuneration:*
- $12 000 gross p.a. at start.

### Job profile: Labourer
Full-time—30 hours p.w.

*Job duties:*
- performing general labouring work
- doing errands.

*Job attributes:*
- physically fit and strong
- reliable and cooperative.

*Remuneration:*
- $18 000 gross p.a. at start.

## D.3 Staffing strategies
The policies that will be adopted to keep workers motivated and productive are as follows:
- an initial three-month probation period for new workers
- remunerating workers at competitive, above-award rates
- increasing remuneration by 4% p.a.
- adopting an authoritarian leadership style where centralised decisions are made to ensure deadlines are met for job completion
- requiring workers to use appropriate safety wear and follow safe work systems
- regularly monitoring health and safety conditions at job sites
- regularly supervising workers.

## D.4 Professional advisers
The following business advisers will be used:
- Qualified accountant (and tax agent):   Craig Watts, My-Suburb
- Solicitor:   Jocelyn Cheung, My-Suburb
- Insurance broker:   Tracey Henson, My-Suburb
- Bank:   Commercial Bank, My-Suburb

Annual membership of the Master Builders Association will be maintained.

## D.5 Personnel controls

Overall labour productivity will be measured annually to identify any labour performance problems that may occur in the operation. For these purposes, labour productivity will be measured as the relationship between sales and labour costs in each relevant period. Key aspects of individual job performance, including health and safety awareness, will also be evaluated after a six-month probation period for new employees and at six-monthly intervals for existing employees. Employee job evaluation will be conducted face to face to receive feedback. Job work will also be checked daily.

The director or secretary/bookkeeper will handle the cash of the business to prevent the occurrence of staff dishonesty.

# E. FINANCIAL

## E.1 Personal financial position

The current personal financial position of Mike Naylor is shown as follows.

| Statement of personal net worth at start of Year 1 | |
|---|---:|
| | **$** |
| **Personal assets** (current selling value) | |
| Real estate | 340 000 |
| Motor vehicle | 35 000 |
| Furniture and contents | 40 000 |
| Investments | 160 000 |
| | 575 000 |
| *less* **Personal liabilities** (current balance owing) | |
| Mortgage | 12 000 |
| Credit card | 1 000 |
| | 13 000 |
| **Personal net worth** | **$562 000** |

| Statement of current monthly personal expenses | |
|---|---:|
| **Expenses** | **$** |
| Mortgage payment | 150 |
| Credit card payment | 50 |
| Food | 600 |
| Household consumables | 15 |
| Clothing | 40 |
| Motor vehicle running costs | 500 |
| Rates | 120 |
| Electricity and telephone | 100 |
| Health insurance | 65 |
| Entertainment | 200 |
| Other living expenses | 100 |
| **Total monthly personal expenses** | **$1940** |

## E.2 Borrowing requirements

A bank business overdraft will continue to be maintained with a limit of $20 000. The overdraft will be reviewed annually. The purpose of the overdraft is to meet short-term operating expenses and provide a source of contingency funds for the business.

## E.3 Financial forecasts

### Forecast monthly sales statements

Services—building construction

| Month | Seasonality factor % | Year 1 $ | Year 2 $ | Year 3 $ |
|---|---|---|---|---|
| July | 6 | 25 342 | 21 422 | 17 610 |
| August | 8 | 33 789 | 28 563 | 23 480 |
| September | 10 | 42 237 | 35 704 | 29 351 |
| October | 10 | 42 237 | 35 704 | 29 351 |
| November | 9 | 38 013 | 32 133 | 26 415 |
| December | 8 | 33 789 | 28 563 | 23 480 |
| January | 6 | 25 342 | 21 422 | 17 610 |
| February | 8 | 33 789 | 28 563 | 23 480 |
| March | 10 | 42 237 | 35 704 | 29 351 |
| April | 10 | 42 237 | 35 704 | 29 351 |
| May | 9 | 38 013 | 32 133 | 26 415 |
| June | 6 | 25 343 | 21 420 | 17 611 |
| **Totals** | **100%** | **$422 368** | **$357 035** | **$293 505** |

*Assumption:*
• Sales are recognised when building contracts are signed before commencement of jobs.

### Forecast profit statements

| | Year 1 $ | Year 2 $ | Year 3 $ |
|---|---|---|---|
| INCOME | | | |
| Sales | 422 368 | 357 035 | 293 505 |
| *less* Job materials purchases | 181 618 | 153 525 | 126 207 |
| GROSS PROFIT (at 57%) | 240 750 | 203 510 | 167 298 |

*less* OPERATING EXPENSES

| | | | |
|---|---:|---:|---:|
| Advertising and promotions | 3 000 | 3 120 | 3 245 |
| Advisers' fees | 1 500 | 1 560 | 1 622 |
| Bank charges | 500 | 520 | 541 |
| Depreciation | 5 250 | 5 250 | 5 250 |
| Hire fees | 1 000 | 1 040 | 1 082 |
| Home office expenses | 600 | 624 | 649 |
| Insurances | 4 800 | 4 992 | 5 192 |
| Interest paid | 500 | 500 | 500 |
| Legal fees | 800 | 832 | 865 |
| Loose tools replaced | 1 500 | 1 500 | 1 500 |
| Motor vehicle running costs | 5 000 | 5 200 | 5 408 |
| Repairs and maintenance—equipment | 1 000 | 1 040 | 1 082 |
| Stationery | 500 | 520 | 541 |
| Subcontract payments (gross) | 120 000 | 80 000 | 40 000 |
| Telephone | 1 800 | 1 872 | 1 947 |
| Wages (gross) | 70 000 | 71 200 | 72 448 |
| Wages on-costs | 17 500 | 17 800 | 18 112 |
| Other expenses | 500 | 520 | 541 |
| *Total operating expenses* | *235 750* | *198 090* | *160 525* |
| **NET PROFIT before tax** | **$5 000** | **$5 420** | **$6 773** |

*Assumptions:*
- No allowance is made for GST.
- Job materials are purchased according to job requirements.
- Depreciation is 10% p.a. of the original cost of long-term assets.
- Interest paid rate is 8% p.a.
- 'Motor vehicle running costs' comprise petrol, repairs and maintenance, and registration and insurance.
- 'Wages on-costs' comprise superannuation, workers' compensation insurance and staff amenities for employees.
- 'Wages on-costs' are 25% of wages.
- Unless determinable, each cost is increased by 4% p.a.

## Break-even sales

|  | Year 1 | Year 2 | Year 3 |
|---|---|---|---|
|  | $ | $ | $ |
| Estimated sales | 422 368 | 357 035 | 293 505 |
|  |  |  |  |
| Variable costs | 181 618 | 153 525 | 126 207 |
| Fixed costs | 235 750 | 198 090 | 160 525 |
| **Break-even point for sales** | **$413 596** | **$347 526** | **$281 623** |

*Assumptions:*
- Job materials purchases are variable costs
- All operating costs are fixed costs.
  *(See Chapter 7 for how to calculate break-even sales.)*

## Forecast capital expenditure statements

| **Date and type of expenditure** | **Year 1** |
|---|---|
|  | $ |
| **Year 1 total** | – |
|  | **Year 2** |
|  | $ |
| **Year 2 total** | – |
|  | **Year 3** |
|  | $ |
| **Year 3 total** | – |

## Forecast cash flow statements

|  | Year 1 | Year 2 | Year 3 |
|---|---|---|---|
|  | $ | $ | $ |
| Cash position—start of year | (17 810) | (4 071) | 10 845 |
| CASH RECEIPTS |  |  |  |
| Cash sales | 140 789 | 119 009 | 97 832 |
| Cash from debtors | 285 068 | 243 772 | 202 228 |
| Capital contributions | – | – | – |
| Borrowings | – | – | – |
| *Total cash receipts* | *425 857* | *362 781* | *300 060* |

*less* CASH PAYMENTS

| | | | |
|---|---|---|---|
| Job materials purchases | 181 618 | 153 525 | 126 207 |
| Operating expenses | 230 500 | 192 840 | 155 275 |
| Capital expenditure | – | – | – |
| Taxation | – | 1 500 | 1 626 |
| *Total cash payments* | *412 118* | *347 865* | *283 108* |
| **NET CASH FLOW** | **$13 739** | **$14 916** | **$16 952** |
| Cash position—end of year | ($4 071) | $10 845 | $27 797 |

*Assumptions:*
- Existing overdraft at start of Year 1 is $17 810.
- Existing debt at start of Year 1 is $47 136 to be collected as follows:

| | |
|---|---|
| July | $24 328 |
| August | $13 685 |
| September | $9 123 |
| Total | $47 136 |

- Sales are collected by progress payments—a third upfront, a third one month later, a third three months later.
- Purchases and operating expenses are paid for in cash.
- Operating expenses paid exclude depreciation.
- Operating expenses paid include interest on overdraft.
- Income tax (at 30%) on annual net profit is paid in the following year.
- No income tax is paid in Year 1.

| Forecast financial position statements | | | |
|---|---|---|---|
| | **Year 1** | **Year 2** | **Year 3** |
| | **$** | **$** | **$** |
| ASSETS | | | |
| Short-term assets | | | |
| Cash | – | 10 845 | 27 797 |
| Stock (at cost) | – | – | – |
| Debtors | 47 136 | 43 646 | 36 892 |
| *Subtotal* | *47 136* | *54 491* | *64 689* |
| Long-term assets | | | |
| Equipment (at cost) | 20 000 | 20 000 | 20 000 |
| *less* Accumulated depreciation | (10 000) | (12 000) | (14 000) |
| Motor vehicle (at cost) | 32 500 | 32 500 | 32 500 |

| | | | |
|---|---:|---:|---:|
| *less* Accumulated depreciation | (16 250) | (19 500) | (22 750) |
| Loose tools (at cost) | 10 000 | 10 000 | 10 000 |
| *Subtotal* | *36 250* | *31 000* | *25 750* |
| TOTAL ASSETS | 83 386 | 85 491 | 90 439 |
| *less* LIABILITIES | | | |
| Short-term liabilities | | | |
| Overdraft | 4 071 | – | – |
| Creditors | – | – | – |
| *Subtotal* | *4 071* | – | – |
| Long-term liabilities | | | |
| Term loan | – | – | – |
| *Subtotal* | – | – | – |
| TOTAL LIABILITIES | 4 071 | – | – |
| **NET ASSETS** | **$79 315** | **$85 491** | **$90 439** |

*Assumption:*

- Loose tools are not depreciated—instead, the cost of replacements is shown as an operating expense.

| Key financial ratios | | | | |
|---|---|---|---|---|
| | Year 1 | Year 2 | Year 3 | Industry average |
| **Profitability ratios:** | | | | |
| Gross profit margin | 57% | 57% | 57% | 57% |
| Labour costs to sales ratio | 49% | 47% | 44% | 47% |
| Operating expenses to sales ratio | 56% | 55% | 55% | 56% |
| Net profit margin | 1% | 2% | 2% | 2% |
| **Financial position ratio:** | | | | |
| Debt ratio | 5% | – | – | 15% |

# E.4 Financial records

A business bank account will continue to be operated at the Commercial Bank, My-Suburb. All receipts and payments will be processed through the account. A manual system of financial records will continue to be maintained. These records include:

- *source documents:* sales quotations, sales invoices, sales receipts, purchase orders, deposit slips, cheque butts and bank statements
- *cash journal books:* cash receipts journal, cash payments journal and petty cash book
- *secondary books:* subcontractors payment book, time and wages book.

Internal controls will be adopted to ensure the accuracy of financial records. These include:

- using standardised pre-numbered source documents in consecutive number sequence
- issuing source documents in triplicate form
- having only the director sign cheques and purchase orders
- checking purchase orders against suppliers' invoices
- crossing cheques drawn with 'not negotiable'
- paying suppliers' invoices by cheque
- preparing monthly bank reconciliations to check cashbook totals with bank statement balances.

## E.5 Business insurances

The following insurances will be maintained by the business:

- workers' compensation insurance (compulsory under law)
- comprehensive motor vehicle insurance
- public liability insurance
- professional indemnity insurance.

An annual check of operating risks will be conducted to design risk-prevention measures and determine insurance needs.

## E.6 Financial controls

The following financial controls will be used to monitor and evaluate the financial performance of the operation.

- *Profit control.* Detailed profit results will be reported quarterly. Profit results will be compared with corresponding forecasts by applying variance analysis. Any unsatisfactory variances identified will be corrected by appropriate follow-up actions.
- *Job cost control.* Job costs will be monitored and controlled by maintaining a cost summary record for each job.
- *Cash flow control.* Cash flows of the operation will be closely monitored by the preparation of monthly cash flow reports. Unsatisfactory cash flow results identified will be rectified by taking appropriate corrective action.
- *Debtor control.* A debtor control system will be adopted in which jobs will only be carried out for approved customers. Progress payments will be monitored by preparing monthly aged debtor schedules and a standardised collection procedure will be followed for overdue progress payments.
- *Financial position control.* The total debt of the business will be reviewed annually by preparing an annual report of financial position.

# F. OPERATIONAL REVIEW

## Operational Review Schedule

### Years—Year 1, Year 2 and Year 3

| Control action | Frequency | Review date | Person responsible |
|---|---|---|---|
| **Marketing controls:** | | | |
| Analyse sales results | Quarterly | End of quarter | Director |
| Analyse sales trends | Quarterly | End of quarter | Director |
| Conduct customer satisfaction surveys | Per job | At completion of job | Director |
| Review marketing program | Annually | End of year | Director |
| **Purchasing controls:** | | | |
| Check deliveries | Daily | On each day | Director |
| Review supply terms and supplier performance | Half-yearly | End of half-year | Director |
| **Personnel controls:** | | | |
| Analyse labour productivity | Annually | End of year | Director |
| Evaluate job performance | Half-yearly | End of half-year | Director |
| Check job work | Daily | On each day | Director |
| Check cash handling | Daily | On each day | Director and secretary/bookkeeper |
| **Financial controls:** | | | |
| Evaluate profit performance | Quarterly | End of quarter | Director |
| Monitor job costs | Daily | During jobs | Director |
| Evaluate cash flow results | Monthly | End of month | Director |
| Analyse debtor positions | Monthly | End of month | Secretary/ bookkeeper |
| Review financial position | Annually | End of year | Director |
| Check operating risks | Annually | End of year | Insurance broker |

*Supporting documents*

Attachment A—Detailed financial statements for last year

Attachment B—ABS housing industry statistics

Attachment C—Standard building contracts

24/24

# APPENDIX 1
# Assessment activities

This appendix has assessment activity suggestions for teachers to administer to students. The activities include assessment criteria and rating scales.

The suggested assessment activities are:

Activity 1: Completed written business plan *(compulsory)*
Activity 2: Verbal presentation of business plan *(compulsory)*
Activity 3: Operational review schedule *(optional)*
Each assessment activity is shown on a separate page for teachers to copy.

# COMPULSORY ACTIVITY 1: COMPLETED WRITTEN BUSINESS PLAN

## To do

Prepare a written business plan for a three-year period for any operation. The plan must be presented in the structured format shown in Table 8.1.

STUDENT'S NAME .......................................................

## Assessment criteria

Your business plan will be assessed using the following criteria and rating scale.

| | Rating Scale | | | | |
|---|---|---|---|---|---|
| Assessment criteria | Unsatis-factory (4 marks) | Average (6 marks) | Good (7 marks) | Very good (8 marks) | Excellent (10 marks) |
| **Information quality:** | | | | | |
| Relevance | _____ | _____ | _____ | _____ | _____ |
| Accuracy | _____ | _____ | _____ | _____ | _____ |
| Currency | _____ | _____ | _____ | _____ | _____ |
| **Presentation quality:** | | | | | |
| Clarity and understandability | _____ | _____ | _____ | _____ | _____ |
| Structured format | _____ | _____ | _____ | _____ | _____ |
| Comprehensive coverage | _____ | _____ | _____ | _____ | _____ |
| Consistency and coordination | _____ | _____ | _____ | _____ | _____ |
| **Viability quality:** | | | | | |
| Acceptable objectives | _____ | _____ | _____ | _____ | _____ |
| Anticipated growth | _____ | _____ | _____ | _____ | _____ |
| Sound analysis | _____ | _____ | _____ | _____ | _____ |

The rated marks are tallied to calculate a score out of a possible total of 100 marks.

## Results interpretation

85 marks or more—the plan quality is sound.
70 to 84 marks—the plan is acceptable but could be improved.
50 to 69 marks—the plan definitely needs improvement.
49 marks or below—the plan must be reattempted.

## Additional comments

## COMPULSORY ACTIVITY 2: VERBAL PRESENTATION OF BUSINESS PLAN

### To do

Verbally present your written business plan before submitting it for assessment. Assume your presentation will be to a prospective lender.

The verbal presentation should be between five and ten minutes.

STUDENT'S NAME ........................................................

PRESENTATION DATE AND TIME ........................................................

### Assessment criteria

Your verbal presentation will be assessed using the following criteria and rating scale, but will not be scored.

| | Rating scale | |
|---|---|---|
| **Assessment criteria** | **Unsatisfactory** | **Satisfactory** |
| Demonstration of business knowledge | _____ | _____ |
| Logical presentation sequence | _____ | _____ |
| Focus on key aspects | _____ | _____ |
| Clear and coherent presentation | _____ | _____ |

This verbal presentation is a prerequisite for your written business plan to be assessed.

### Verbal presentation guidelines

- State your overall business goal.
- Briefly describe your business activity and ownership structure.
- Briefly indicate what products/services will be sold.
- Outline the market your business will be selling to (i.e. type of target customers and market area).
- Indicate anticipated business growth over the next three years in financial terms (i.e. annual turnover, annual net profit).
- Briefly comment on the net cash flows of your business over the next three years.
- Specify the type, amount and use of borrowed funds required (if applicable).

*Note:* It is important to ensure that your presentation is coherent in the limited time available.

## OPTIONAL ACTIVITY 3: OPERATIONAL REVIEW SCHEDULE

### To do

Prepare a schedule showing when you will use your business controls to review the performance of each function of your operation. Include in the schedule who will be responsible for the review action. For guidance, use the structured format shown in Table 8.4.

STUDENT'S NAME ........................................................

### Assessment criteria

Your operational review schedule will be assessed using the following criteria and rating scale.

| | Rating scale | |
|---|---|---|
| **Assessment criteria** | **Unsatisfactory** | **Satisfactory** |
| Adequacy of business controls | _____ | _____ |
| Comprehensiveness of controls | _____ | _____ |
| Suitability of review times | _____ | _____ |
| Presentation format | _____ | _____ |
| Appropriate delegation of responsibility | _____ | _____ |

## Additional comments

# APPENDIX 2
# The environmentally friendly small business

There are many ways in which a small business can become more environmentally friendly in its operation. The benefits of being a 'greener' business can include:

- greater business owner satisfaction
- lower business costs
- healthier and more productive employees
- growing customer appreciation.

An environmentally friendly enterprise adopts practices that reduce greenhouse gas emissions, conserve water or otherwise help sustain the natural environment.

Environmentally sustainable business practices that can be implemented by any small business include these areas: motor vehicle usage, office power usage, materials usage and water conservation.

## MOTOR VEHICLE USAGE

- Reduce the usage of motor vehicles.
- Regularly service motor vehicles.
- Use motor vehicles with smaller engine sizes.
- Use biofuel alternatives (e.g. ethanol) made from food waste.

## OFFICE POWER USAGE

- Use natural (not electrical) lighting whenever possible.
- Turn off lights at night (without compromising security).
- Turn off power points at wall when office equipment is not in use.
- Use more energy-efficient machines, equipment and appliances.
- Use compact fluorescent (not incandescent) light globes.
- Sign up for green power.
- Regularly clean air-conditioning ducts.
- Moderate air-conditioning temperature settings.
- Lower the heating temperature.
- Open windows, where possible (to reduce air-conditioning usage).
- Encourage staff to dress appropriately for the weather.

## MATERIALS USAGE

- Raise awareness to reduce wastage generally.
- Print double-sided.
- Choose paperless options (e.g. electronic bank statements, online invoices, email).
- Use recycled paper.
- Use recycled ink cartridges.
- Recycle paper, bottles and glass.
- Use recyclers for trade waste.
- Use biodegradable packaging.
- Use office furniture and fittings made with recycled materials and non-toxic finishes.
- Buy recycled raw materials (without compromising quality).
- Buy goods made from recycled materials.

## WATER CONSERVATION

- Install rainwater tanks linked to stormwater runoffs.
- Install water-saving plumbing (e.g. water-saving taps, flush-saving toilets, green showerheads).
- Use water conscientiously.

You should organise an energy audit for your business at regular intervals to review energy and water usage.

# ANSWERS
# Quick quizzes

## Chapter 1
1. A    2. D    3. B    4. C    5. C    6. C    7. B    8. B    9. C    10. A    11. A    12. B
13. B    14. B    15. C

## Chapter 2
1. B    2. A    3. C    4. A    5. A    6. C    7. D    8. D    9. C    10. B

## Chapter 3
1. C    2. B    3. C    4. B    5. A    6. C    7. C    8. D    9. D    10. A    11. D    12. A
13. B    14. C    15. C    16. B    17. D    18. C    19. B    20. C

## Chapter 4
1. B    2. C    3. B    4. A    5. C    6. C

## Chapter 5
1. D    2. B    3. B    4. B    5. B    6. A    7. D    8. C    9. A    10. B

## Chapter 6
1. A    2. D    3. B    4. D    5. A    6. B    7. B    8. A    9. D    10. C

## Chapter 7
1. B    2. D    3. C    4. A    5. B    6. C    7. B    8. B    9. C    10. A
11. B    12. B    13. A    14. C    15. D    16. D    17. C    18. C    19. B    20. A

## Chapter 8
1. A    2. C    3. B    4. D    5. E    6. D    7. A    8. D    9. C    10. B

# GLOSSARY
# Business planning terms

**ABN** Australian Business Number

**ABS** Australian Bureau of Statistics

**ASIC** Australian Securities and Investments Commission

**asset** any form of property owned by a business

**ATO** Australian Taxation Office

**award** a legally enforceable order of an industrial relations tribunal specifying minimum pay rates and employment conditions for a job classification

**balance sheet** *see* 'financial position statement'

**benchmark** a guiding norm to be measured against

**BLIS** Business Licence Information Service

**break-even analysis** finding the level of sales required where no profit or loss is made

**break-even point** the level of sales where no profit or loss is made

**business activity** a description of a selling activity (e.g. retailing)

**business control** a check or evaluation method used to monitor business performance

**business cycle** the regular periodic fluctuations which occur in the general level of economic activity

**business offer** the combination of marketing strategies that comprise what a business has to offer customers

**business operation** a systematic organisation of resources to sell goods or services regularly for profit-making purposes

**business plan** a formal written plan for the long-term development of a business operation

**business proposition** *see* 'business offer'

**capital expenditure** an outlay for a long-term asset

**cash flow statement** a financial statement summarising the receipts and payments of the business for a period

**cash position** the amount of cash surplus (or deficiency) at a point in time

**component plan** a plan for a function (e.g. section) of the business operation

**contingency plan** a plan of possible responses to unfavourable results

**contribution margin** the excess of sales over variable costs for a period

**corrective action** action taken to rectify an unsatisfactory result detected

**CPI** Consumer Price Index

**current asset** *see* 'short term asset'

**current liability** *see* 'short term liability'

**customer base** the existing customers of the business

**customer-oriented** being sensitive and responsive to customers' needs

**customer profile** a detailed description of the characteristics and relevant wants of a defined customer group

**debt ratio** the total liabilities of a business expressed as a percentage of its total assets at a point in time

**demographic statistics** statistics on the population number or characteristics for a given area

**depreciation** the estimated rate of wear and tear for using a long-term asset (e.g. plant and equipment)

**desk top research** collecting and analysing published information

**direct observation** observing and listening to people directly

**drawings** the cash taken by a business proprietor from the business

**economic performance indicators** variables which measure the general level of economic activity (e.g. growth in GDP)

**EEO** equal employment opportunity

**entry barrier** a legal or competitor obstacle which prevents business entry into an industry

**entry strategy** a method of commencing a business in the industry

**environmental scanning** a comprehensive examination of factors in the general business environment

**environmental trend** a favourable or an unfavourable change in the general business environment

**financial performance statement** *see* 'profit statement'

**financial position statement** a financial statement showing assets and liabilities at a point in time which enables net assets to be calculated

**financial ratio** a measure of the relationship between specific items found in a financial statement

**financial report** a report of past financial results for a period

**financial year** the annual period, usually between 1 July and the next 30 June

**fixed costs** business running costs that remain constant regardless of sales volume

**forecast** a financial estimate used in a financial plan

**GDP** gross domestic product

**goal** a desired outcome

**goodwill** established business reputation

**gross profit** a profit calculation represented by sales minus cost of goods sold

**gross profit margin** the percentage of gross profit in each sales dollar

**hazard** anything in the workplace that has the potential to cause harm

**human resources** the physical labour used in a business operation

**image** an appearance to outsiders

**income statement** *see* 'profit statement'

**industry conditions** demand and supply conditions existing in an industry

**internal control** a safeguard designed to protect the accuracy of business records

**JIT** just-in-time inventory system

**job performance** the efficiency and effectiveness of an employee in a job role

**job profile** a detailed description of duties, attributes and remuneration for a job role

**labour productivity** refers to the relationship between business output and labour input for a period

**leadership** to direct and influence personnel

**liability** a debt owed by a business to an outsider

**long term** a period in excess of twelve months ahead

**long-term asset** a physical asset owned for more than twelve months ahead

**long-term liability** an obligation which is repayable in more than twelve months

**market** customers

**marketing** the process of giving customers what they want

**marketing mix** *see* 'business offer'

**marketing strategy** any business activity intended to create sales

**net assets** calculated by total assets minus total liabilities at a point in time

**net profit** a profit calculation represented by gross profit minus operating expenses

**niche market** an untapped specialised segment of the total market

**NOLA** National Occupational Licensing Authority

**non-current asset** *see* 'long-term asset'

**non-current liability** *see* 'long-term liability'

**normal profit** the minimum acceptable profit required for a business operation to be viable

**objective** a set target to achieve

**operating capability** the capacity of an operation to achieve an intended outcome

**operating environment** the external and internal environment in which a business operates

**operating expenses** the recurring costs (except for stock costs) in running an operation

**operating function** an internal function found in a business operation

**operating structure** an organised operating framework through which business activities can be carried out

**operational plan** *see* 'business plan'

**operational review schedule** a schedule showing when business controls will be used to review operational performance

**organisation structure** the organisation of human resources in a business operation

**outcome** a result achieved after carrying out a plan

**overdraft** a line of credit allowing a bank account to be overdrawn up to a limit

**overheads** *see* 'fixed costs'

**ownership structure** the form of legal ownership a business operates under

**PAYG** pay as you go

**performance** a result

**primary research** gathering information directly from the source

**procurement plan** a plan to obtain resources

**product mix** the relative quantities of each product (or service) type for sale

**product range** the range of different products (or services) to be sold

**profit statement** a financial statement of income and expenses showing the measurement of profit for a period

**promotion** any way of informing customers about the business offer

**promotion mix** the combination of promotion methods used

**ratio analysis** financial analysis of the relationship between items in financial statements

**resource** an input used in a business operation to generate income

**risk** an event that can cause financial loss (e.g. burglary, fire)

**safety audit** an examination of the workplace to find hazards

**sales performance** sales results for a period

**schedule** the timing of actions

**secondary research** collecting information that is already published

**segmentation** categorising potential customers into distinct customer groups with common characteristics

**short term** a period of up to twelve months ahead

**short-term asset** a physical asset owned for up to twelve months ahead

**short-term liability** an obligation which is repayable within twelve months

**situational analysis** an examination of the internal and external operating environments

**skills audit** identifying current skills and qualifications of employees

**solvency** the ability of a business to repay its debts

**strategic planning** planning business activities to achieve specified objectives

**strategy** a planned action chosen from competing alternatives to achieve a stated objective

**supporting document** a document included as an attachment to the business plan

**survey** a set of specific questions to ask people for their responses

**SWOT analysis** analysing the business's strengths, weaknesses, opportunities and threats (or challenges) to the business in the operating environment

**target** *see* 'objective'

**target customer** a customer group that is the focus of marketing strategies

**task analysis** an analysis of the work required to perform a job role

**TFN** Tax File Number

**title page** the front cover sheet of a formal business plan

**trend** an improving or declining result over time

**variable costs** business running costs that change proportionally with changes in sales volume

**variance analysis** a form of business control which involves comparing a result with its corresponding target for a period to find unfavourable discrepancies

**wage on costs** additional costs incurred due to wage costs (e.g. employee superannuation)

**WHS** Work Health and Safety

# Index

Page numbers in italics denote illustrations or tables

**A**

absenteeism, 111
accident/injury register, 114
accountant, 115, *116*
accounting software, 154
accumulated depreciation, 146–7
action plan
  procuring resources, 175, *176*
  setting up, for, 173, *174*
administrative expenses, 126–7
advertising forms, 69, *69*
after-sales service, 63, 64
ageing population, 52
anti-discrimination legislation, 108
approvals, 30
assessment activities, 253–6
  completed written business plan, 254
  operational review schedule, 256
  verbal presentation of business plan, 255
asset(s), 146–7
  depreciation of, 141, 145, 146–7
  examples of, 163–4
  long-term (non-current), 136, 146–7, 163, 174
  net, 146, 164
  personal, 130, *131*, 159
  sales of, 144
  short-term (current), 146, 163
  total, 147, 164
assumptions in forecasting, 141, 145–6, 148
audits
  safety, 114
  skills, 112
Austrade, 47
Australian Bureau of Agricultural and Resource
  Economics and Sciences, 47
Australian Bureau of Statistics (ABS), 10, 45–6,
  51, 54, *55*, 60, 93, 141
Australian Business Number (ABN), 31

Australian Chamber of Commerce and Industry, 47
Australian Competition and Consumer
  Commission (ACCC), 88
Australian Customs Service, 32, 47
Australian Government Treasury, 47
Australian Quarantine and Inspection Service, 32,
  47
Australian Securities and Investments
  Commission (ASIC), 21, 22, 30
Australian Taxation Office (ATO), 31, 93, 150
authoritarian leadership, 112, 113, *113*
award minimums, 109

**B**

balance sheet, 40, 41
bank(s)
  commercial lending, 136, *136*, 171
  professional advice from, 115, *116*
  statistical information from, 47
bank account, 153, 164
bank overdraft, 145
banking record, of stock purchases, 99
base prices, 64, 65
batch production, 87
benchmarks, 148, 150, 156
booms, 9, *10*, 12
borrowing requirements, 134–6. *see also* loan(s)
  business plan, purpose of, 4, 105, 129, 142, 169
  examples of, 160, 199, 221, 246
borrowings, 145
  investments, versus, 135, *135*
brands, product, 62
break-even analysis, 126–9
  examples of, 162, 201, 223, 248
break-even point, 128
budget information, 47
building application (BA), 30
building services, licensing of, 27

Bureau of Meteorology, 47
business activity, 18–19
    examples of, 18, 35, 188, 210, 232
    general level of, 8, 10–11, 27, 50, 51. *see also*
        economic performance indicators
business controls, 177
business costs. *see* cost(s)
business cycle, 8–12, *10*, 26
business expansion, 12, 134–5
business goal(s), 5
business goal statement, 169
    examples of, 187, 209, 231
business history, *18*, 25, *25*
business image, 67–8
    examples of, 193, 215, 237
Business Licence Information Service (BLIS), 27
business location. *see* location
business name, *18*, 22–4, 30
    examples of, 35, 188, 210, 232
    national names register, 22, 30
business objective. *see* objective(s)
business offer (proposition), 61–2, *62*
business operation
    characteristics of, 3
    functions. see operating functions
business performance, forecasts of. *see* financial
    forecasts
business plan
    components of, 6–8, *7*, 169
    defined, 3
    evaluation of, 171, 254
    format of, 8, *9*, 169, *170*
    implementation of, 172–6, *173*
    presentation of, 169–71, 254, 255
    sample. *see* sample business plans
business planning
    benefits of, 4
    personal attributes for, 13
    process of, 6, 6–8
    reasons for, 3–4
business profile
    examples of, 35–6, 188–90, 210–11, 232–3
    guidelines, 18–37
    outline, 18, *18*, *170*
business proposition (offer), 61–2, *62*
business publications, 47, 53
business regulation, 22, 27–32, 53
    examples of, 36, 189, 210–11, 232–3
business resources
    gathering information about, 175
    procuring, 173–5, *161*

business start-up. *see* start-up business
buyers, nature of, 54
buying an existing business, 26, *28*
    establishment costs, *133–4*

**C**
capital expenditure, 142, 145
    defined, 141
    long-term assets, for, 136, 141–2
    personal, 130
capital expenditure forecasts, 141–2
    examples of, 162, 202, 223–4, 248
carrying costs, 98
cash discounts, 66
cash flow
    net, 41, 124, 143, *143*, 145, 163
    unsatisfactory, responsive actions to, *179*
cash flow controls, 157–8
    examples of, 165, 205, 227, 251
cash flow forecasts, 142–6, 172
    examples of, 163, 202–3, 224, 248–9
cash flow reports, 157
cash flow statement, 40, 142, 143–6, *143*
cash journal books, *153*, 154
cash on delivery (COD), 97
cash payments, 145, 163
cash position
    closing, 143, 145, 163
    opening, 143–4, 163
cash receipts, 143, *143*, 144–5, 163
cash recording system, 153, *153*
casual employees, 106
channels of distribution, 67, *67*
cheque account, 154, 164
closing cash position, 143, 145, 163
collection agency websites, 30
commercial lending market, 136, *136*, 171–2
company (small), 21–2, *23*
    owner's drawings, 141
    registration of, 32
competitive advantage, 70–1
    examples of, 193, 215, 238
competitive pricing, 65, 93
competitors, *51*, 55, 57–8, 71
    examples of, 76, 191–2, 213, 235–6
completed written business plan, 3, 7, *7*, 168–81,
    254
component plan, preparation of, 169
consignment supplies, 97
consumer confidence, 11
Consumer Price Index (CPI), 141

consumer protection authorities, 27, *29*
consumer protection legislation, 53
consumer spending levels, 11
contingency plan, 177–80, *178*, *179*
continuous production, 87
contractionary trends, 9, *10*
contractors, independent, 106, *107*
contribution margin, 127
convenience samples, 43
Corporations Act 2001, 21
corrective actions, 180, *180*
   example of, 180–1
cost(s)
   carrying, 98
   establishment, 132–4, *132–4*, 134
   examples of, 160, 199, 221
   estimating, 126–7
   expansion, 134–5
   fixed, 127, 128
   forecasting, 140–1
   lease, *133*
   sales, 139–40, *139–40*
   supplies, 93, 97. *see also* purchasing plan
   variable, 127
council approval/permits, 30
cover sheet (title page), 169, *170*
   examples of, 185, 207, 229
credit mix, 65
credit terms, 65, 97
cultural trends, 52
current (short-term) assets, 146–7, 163
current (short-term) liabilities, 146, 147, 148, 164
current operation, reviewing, 40–1
customer(s)
   forms of payment, 65
   target. *see* target customers
customer database analysis, 45
customer grouping, 54, 58
   examples of, 54, 192
customer-oriented, 62, 77
customer referrals, 69
customer satisfaction surveys, *74*, 75
customer service, 63–4, 70

**D**
database analysis, 43, 45
debt ratio, 41, *149*, 150, 164
debtor collection, 157
debtor control system, 157, 251
debtor monitoring, 157
debtor selection, 157

delegation, 113, 114, 173
delivery decisions, 66
demand, seasonal, 85, 98, 138
   examples of, 200, 222, 246
demand conditions, 54–5
demand patterns, 54–5
democratic leadership, 112, 113–14, *113*
demographic factors, 51–2
demographic statistics, 42, 46, 47, 51–2, 59
depreciation, 141, 145, 147
   accumulated, 146–7
design/style, product, 62
desktop research, 43, 44, 53
development application (DA), 30
direct distribution methods, 67, *67*
direct observation, 43, 44, 53, 54, 55, 57
directors, 21, 22
discount policies, 66, 95, 97, 100
dishonesty by employee, prevention of, 117–19
distribution agreements, 97
distribution channels, 66–7, *67*
distribution strategies, 66–7
   examples of, 193, 215, 237
diversification, 56, 57, 64
domain name registration, 30
downward trends, 9, 12
drawings, 105, 131, 141, 145

**E**
economic activity, 51
economic factors, 10–11, 49, 51
economic performance indicators, 10–11 *10*, 45, 51
educational institutions, statistical information
   from, 48
employee(s). *see also* personnel plan; staffing
   strategies
   independent contractors, versus, 106, *107*
   motivation of, 111
   new. *see* new employees
   performance evaluation, 116–19, *118*
   recruitment of, 110–11
   training and development of, 112, *112*
employee dishonesty, prevention of, 117–19
employee protection laws, 106
employment alternatives, 106, *107*
employment conditions, 109
entry barriers, 55, 56
entry strategy, *18*, 25–7, *28*
   advantages and disadvantages of methods, *28–9*
   establishment costs, 132, *132–4*
   examples of, 36, 199

environmental scanning, 50–3
environmental trends, 50–3, *51*
   adaptability to, 177
   examples of, 75, 190, 212, 234
environmentally friendly business, 257–8
equal employment opportunity (EEO), 110
establishment costs, 132, *132*–4, 134–5
   examples of, 160, 199, 221
evaluation
   business plan, 171, 254
   work performance, 116–19, *118*
existing business, buying, 26, *28*
   establishment costs, 132, *133*–4
existing operation, reviewing, 40–1
expansionary trends, 9, *10*, 11–12
expenses. *see* operating expenses; personal
   expenses
external environment, 42, 177

**F**
factory plant and equipment, 83, *84*
   layout plan, 84, *84*, 90
factory registration, 31
financial controls, 153, 156–8, 172, *178*
   examples of, 165, 205, 227, 251, 252
financial expenses, 126–7
financial forecasts, 136, 137–52
   assumptions, 141, 145–6, 148
   capital expenditure, 141–2, *142*
   examples of, 162, 202, 223–4, 248
   cash flow, 142–6, *143*
   examples of, 163, 202, 224, 248–9
   examples of, 161–4, 200–4, 222–6, 246–50
   financial position, 146–8, *147*
   examples of, 203, 225, 249–50
   lender's scrutiny of, 172
   profit, 138–41, *140*
   examples of, 161–2, 200–1, 222–3, 246–7
   sales, 138, *138*
   examples of, 161, 200, 201, 222, 223, 246
financial measures, of labour productivity, 104, 116
financial objectives, 124–5
   examples of, 190, 211, 233
financial performance, unsatisfactory, responsive
   actions to, *179*
financial performance ratios, 148–50, *149*
financial performance review, 40–1
financial plan, 8, 123–65
   examples of, 159–65, 198–205, 220–7, 245–52
   guidelines, 129–58
   outline, 129, *130*, *170*

financial position
   personal, 130–1, *131*
   examples of, 159, 198, 220, 245
   unsatisfactory, responsive actions to, *179*
financial position controls, 158
   examples of, 165, 205, 227, 251
financial position forecasts, 146–8, *147*
   examples of, 203, 225, 249–50
financial position ratios, 137, *149*
   examples of, 164, 226, 250
financial position reports, 158
financial ratios, 148–50, *149*
   analysis of, 156, 158, 172
   examples of, 157, 164, 204, 226, 250
financial records, 153–4
   examples of, 164–5, 204, 226–7, 250–1
financial resources, 175
financial transactions, *153*, 154
fixed costs, 127, 128
fixed rate loans, 136
food businesses, permits for, 30
forecasts. *see* financial forecasts; *specific forecast*
foreign trade statistics, 45
format
   business plan, 8, 9, 169, *170*
   cash flow statement, 143, *143*
   financial position statement, 146, *147*
Franchise Council of Australia, 27
franchise outlet, obtaining, 26–7, *29*
   establishment costs, *134*
franchise system, *27*
funding sources, 135–6, *136*. *see also* borrowings;
   capital expenditure; investment

**G**
general business environment, 42, *42*, 50, 190
geographic area. *see* location
goal(s), 3, 5
goal statement, 169
   examples of, 187, 209, 231
goods and services tax (GST), 31, 53
goodwill, 26
*Google*, 47
government agencies, 47, 53. *see also specific
   agency*
graphing sales performance, 72, *73*
'green' business, 257–8
gross domestic product (GDP), *10*, 11
gross profit, 140
gross profit margin, 41, 93–4, *93*
   cost of sales and, 139–40

examples of, *93–4*, 94, 164
    ratio, 149, *149*, 149, 156, 164
guarantees, product/service, 62, 63

**H**
hazards, 114, *155*
headings, business plan, 169
health clearance permit, 30
history of business, *18*, 25, *25*
household expenditure statistics, 45
housing statistics, 45
human resources, 104, 173. *see also* employee(s);
    personnel plan

**I**
image strategies, 67–8
  examples of, 193, 215, 237
implementation of business plan, 172–6, *173*
import/export restrictions, 32, 47
incentives, 111
income, defined, 138, 139
income statement, 40, 41, 157
income tax, 31, 141, 145
independent contractors, 106, *107*
  employee, versus, 107
indirect distribution methods, 67, *67*
industrial awards, 108–9, 111
industry associations
  award information, 109
  membership, 115
  statistical information from, 47, 54
  work health and safety advice from, 114
industry averages
  benchmarks, 93, 148, 150, 156, 158
  profit margin, 93, 139
industry conditions, *51*, 54–6
  examples of, 76, 190, 212, 234–5
industry referrals for stock suppliers, 95
inflation rate, 141
information consultancies, 46
information gathering
  business cycle, 10–1
  business resources, 175
information processing, 53
information quality criteria, 171, 254
insurance, *155*, 155–6
  examples of, 165, 204, 226, 251
insurance agent/broker, 115, *116*
intellectual property registration, 32
interest paid, 145
internal controls, 154, 165

internal operation analysis, 42
Internet
  research, 47, 53, 95
  website presence, 30, 64
investment. *see also* capital expenditure
  borrowing, versus, 135, *135*
  rate of return on, 125
invoice, supplier's, 99
IP Australia, 32

**J**
JIT (just-in-time) inventory system, 98
job cost controls, 251
job description, 108, *109*
job needs, 105, 106–7
job performance evaluation, 117, *118*
job production, 87
job profiles, 105, 108–10
  examples of, 196–7, 241–3
job roles, allocation of, 107–8, *108*
job satisfaction, 111, 117
job specification, 108, *109*
job turnover, 111
joint venture, 20–1, *23*

**L**
labour performance evaluation, 116–19, *118*
labour productivity, 104, 111, 116–19, *117*
labour rates, 106
labour requirements, 173. *see also* employee(s);
    personnel plan; staffing strategies
layout plan, production process, 84–5, *84*, 90
leadership styles, 112–14, *113*
lease costs, *133*
lease terms, 25
legal liability
  company, 21
  joint venture, 20
  partnership, 20
  sole trader, 19
legal requirements, *18*, 27–32, 53
  checklist, *33*
  examples of, 36, 189, 210–11, 232–3
  manufactured products, 88
legislation
  anti-discrimination, 108
  employee protection, 106
liabilities, 147, 148
  examples of, 164
  legal. *see* legal liability
  liquor licence, 30

long-term (non-current), 146, 147, 148, 164
personal, 130, *131*, 159
short-term (current), 146, 147, 148, 164
total, 147, 164
libraries, statistical information from, 48
licences, 27, 30
loan(s). *see also* borrowing requirements
security for, 172
sources of, 136, *136*
types of, 136, *136*
loan application, using business plan for, 4, 105, 129, 142, 171–2
loan repayments, 135, 142, 145, 172
local council(s)
approval/permits, 27, 30
statistical information from, 47
location, *18*, 24–5
customer groups, 59
decisions about, 66
examples of, 35, 188, 210, 232
market size and, 54
long-term (non-current) assets, 136, 146–7, 163, 174
long-term (non-current) liabilities, 146, 147, 148, 164
long-term loans, 136
loyalty discounts, 66

**M**
management aims
benefits of business planning for, 4
financial performance, 124
marketing function, 48
personnel function, 104
production function, 83
purchasing function, 93
management details, 105
examples of, 119, 196, 219, 241
lender's scrutiny of, 172
management resources, 175
manufactured products, minimum standards, 88
market areas, 54, 60
market conditions, 54–5, 64, 67
market development, 64
market extension, 64
market penetration, 64
market segmentation, 57, 58–9
examples of, 60–1, 192
market size, 54
marketing controls, *51*, 72–5, *178*
examples of, 78–9, 193–4, 215–16, 228, 238, 252

marketing expenses, 126
marketing mix (business offer), 62, *62*
marketing objectives, 48–50
examples of, 189–90, 212, 233
marketing performance, unsatisfactory, responsive actions to, *179*
marketing plan, 7, 39–79
coordination with other plans, 83, 85, 94, 98, 104
examples of, 75–9, 190–94, 212–16, 234–8
guidelines, 50–79
outline, 50, *51*, *170*
marketing program review, 75
marketing strategies, *51*, 61–72. *see also specific strategy*
examples of, 77–8, 192–3, 214–15, 238
materials usage, 258
media coverage, 48, 53, 69
merit principle, 110
motor vehicle usage, 257
music copyright, 30

**N**
National Occupational Licensing Authority (NOLA), 27
natural environmental factors, 53
natural resources, 173
conservation of, 258
net assets, 146, 148, 164
net cash flow, 41, 124, 143, *143*, 145, 163
net profit, 41, 124, 138
before tax, 141, 162
net profit margin, *149*, 149–50, 164
net worth, personal, 130, *131*, 159
networking, 69–70
new employees
induction training, 112
performance evaluation, 117, *118*
probationary period, 111
termination of, 111
news media, 48, 69
niche market, 57
non-current (long-term) assets, 136, 146–7, 163, 174
non-current (long-term) liabilities, 146, 147, 148, 164
normal profit, 124, 125

**O**
objective(s), *18*, 32–5. *see also specific type of objective*
criteria for, 33–4, 49
defined, 32

examples of, 36, 189–90, 211, 233
goals, versus, 5
key, 32, *34*
office power usage, 257
opening cash position, 143,
opening times, 66
operating capability, 49, 50
operating environment, 40, 42, *42*
  analysis of, 42, *42*
  dynamic nature of, 42, 177
operating expense(s), 140–1, 161
  cash payments, versus, 145
  estimating, 126–7, 138, 141
  example of, 161
operating expense ratio, 138, 149, *149*, 156, 164
operating functions, 5–6, *6. see also specific
   function*
  managing, 5–6
  objectives for, 32–4
  plans for, 7, *7*
operating permits, 30
operating strategies, 175
operating strengths, 41
operating structure, setting up, *173*, 173, *174*
operating weaknesses, 41
operational plan. *see* business plan
operational review schedule, 177, *178*
  assessment activity, 256
  examples of, 206, 228, 252
organisation structure, 105–10, *108*
  examples of, 120, 196–7, 219, 241–3
output levels, 83, *83*, *85*, 85–6, 89
overdraft, 145
overheads (fixed costs), 127, 128
owner's drawings, 105, 131, 141, 145
ownership structure, *18*, 19–22, *20*
  advantages and disadvantages, 22, *23*
  examples of, 35, 188, 210, 232

**P**
packaging, product, 62
partnership, 19, *23*
partnership agreement, 19, *20*
part-time employees, 106
pay rates, 108
PAYG (Pay As You Go) system, 31, 126
payment(s)
  cash, 145, 163
  forms of, 65
  stock supplies, for, 98, 99, 145
payment discounts, 95, 97, 100

performance
  business, forecasts of. *see* financial forecasts
  personnel, 116–19
periodic stocktake, 158
permits, 27, 30, *33*
personal assets, 130, *131*, 159
personal attributes
  business planning, 13
  customer grouping by, 59
personal expenses statement, 131, *131*
  examples of, 159–60, 198, 220, 245
personal financial position, 130–1, *131*
  examples of, 159–60, 198, 220, 245
personal net worth, 130, *131*, 159–60
personal selling, 70
personal surveys. *see* surveys
personnel, defined, 104
personnel controls, *105*, 116–19, *178*
  examples of, 121, 197, 244, 252
personnel expenses, 126
personnel objectives, 104
  examples of, 189, 211, 233
personnel performance, unsatisfactory, responsive
   actions to, *179*
personnel plan, 8, 103–21. *see also* employee(s);
   staffing strategies
  coordination with other plans, 104
  examples of, 119–21, 196–7, 219, 241–4
  guidelines, 104–19
  outline, *105*, *170*
physical materials resources, 173
physical operation review, 40
physical product decisions, 62
plant and equipment, 83, *84*
  layout plan, 84, *84*, 90
political factors, 53
population samples, 43
population size/characteristics, 51–2
population statistics, 43, 45, 60
position. *see* location
pre-sales service, 63, 64
presentation of business plan, 169–71, 254, 255
presentation quality criteria, 171, 254
pricing strategies, 64–6
  examples of, 193, 215, 237
primary research, 43
private research organisations, 46
probation, 111
procurement plan, 173–5, *176*
product decisions, 62
  examples of, 76, 191

product development, 64
product mix, 56–7, *57*, 62
product range, 56–7, 62
product services, 63–4
product strategies, 62, 64
production, defined, 83
production capacity, *83*, 83–5, 89
production controls, *178*
production expenses, 126
production method, *83*, 87, 89
production output levels, 85–6, *86*, 89
production output schedule, *85*, 85–6
production performance, unsatisfactory,
    responsive actions to, *179*
production plan, 82–90
  coordination with other plans, 83, 85, 94, 98,
    104
  example of, 89–9
  guidelines, 83–90
  objectives, 83
  outline, 83, *83*, *170*
production process layouts, 84–5, *84*, 90
production quality controls, *83*, 88, 89
professional advisers, *105*, 115–16
  examples of, 115, 121, 197, 219, 243
  functions of, *116*
professional occupations, licensing boards, 30
profit
  calculation, example of, 125
  gross, 140
  net, 41, 124, 138
  before tax, 141, 162
  normal, 124, 125
  unsatisfactory, responsive actions to, *179*
profit controls, 156
  examples of, 165, 205, 227, 251
profit forecasts, 138–41, *140*
  examples of, 150–2, 161–2, 200–1, 222–3, 246–7
profit margin
  gross. *see* gross profit margin
  industry average, 93, 139
  net, *149*, 149–50, 164
profit reports, 156
profit statement, 40
profit target, 83, 124, 126, 128, 138
profitability ratios, 156
  examples of, 164, 226, 250
project production, 87
promotion mix, 68
promotion strategies, 68–9
  examples of, 193, 215, 238

promotional discounts, 66
public relations, 70
publicity, 69–70
purchase orders, 98, *99*
purchase price, *133*
purchasing controls, *95*, 100, *178*
  examples of, 101, 195, 218, 228, 240, 252
purchasing expenses, 126
purchasing objectives, 93–4
  examples of, 189, 233
purchasing outline, *170*
purchasing performance, unsatisfactory,
    responsive actions to, *179*
purchasing plan, 7, 92–101
  coordination with other plans, 95, 98, 104
  examples of, 100–1, 195, 217–18, 239–40
  guidelines, 94–100
  outline, 95, *95*
purchasing policies, *95*, 98–100
  examples of, 101, 195, 217, 240
purchasing procedures, 98–9

**Q**
quality
  business plan, 171
  product/service, 62, *63*
quality controls, production, *83*, 88, 89
quantitative information, 43
quantity discounts, 66, 95

**R**
receipts, 143, *143*, 144–5, 163
recessions, 9, *10*, 11
recordkeeping
  financial, 153–4
  examples of, 164–5, 204, 226, 250–1
  stock supplies, 158
recruitment, employee, 110–11
registration
  business name, 22, 24, 30
  company, 32
  domain name, 30
  factory, 31
  intellectual property, 32
  taxation, 31
  workplace agreement, 32
regulation of business, 22, 27–32, 53
  examples of, 36, 189, 210–11, 232–3
remuneration packages
  employee's, 108, *110*, 111
  owner's, 105, 124

research organisations, 46
research techniques, 43–5
Reserve Bank of Australia, 10, 47
resources
    conservation of, 258
    gathering information about, 175
    procuring, 173–5, *176*
returns, product, 62, 97
rewards, 111
risk allowance, 125
risk check, 156
*RP Data*, 46
running costs. *see* operating expenses

**S**
safety audit, 114
salary
    employee's, 108, *110*
    owner's, 105, 124
sales
    assets, of, 144
    cost of, 139–40, *13940*
    credit, 65
sales break-even point, 126
    examples of, 162, 201, 223, 248
sales forecasts, 138, *138*
    examples of, 161, 200, 222–3, 246
sales objective, 48–50, 83, 138
    example of, 49–50
sales performance, 41, 72–3
    graph, 72, *73*
sales receipts, 144–5, 163
sales register, 72, *73*
sample business plans
    Carla's Café, 184, 185–206
    Kate's Bush Tours, 184, 207–28
    Mike's Building Co. Pty Ltd, 184, 229–52
    summary of, 184
samples, population, 43
seasonal demand, 85, 98, 138
    examples of, 200, 222, 246
secondary books, 154
secondary research, 43
segmentation, 57, 58–9
    examples of, 60–1, 192–3
selling, personal, 70
selling activity, 18
selling agency agreements, 97
service products
    decisions about, *63*, *64*, 63–4
    defined, 63

examples of, 213, 235, 237
    mix of, 63–4, *63*, *64*
shareholders, 21
shifts, production, 87
short-term (current) assets, 146, 163
short-term (current) liabilities, 146, 147–8, 164
short-term loans, 136
short-term solvency ratio, *149*, 150
situational analysis, 6
skills audit, 112, *112*
sociocultural factors, 52
sole trader, 19, *23*
solicitor, 115, *116*
solvency ratio, *149*, 150
source documents, 154
specialisation, 56, 57
spending levels, 11
staff development, 112, *112*
staffing strategies, 104, *105*, 110–14. *see also*
        employee(s); personnel plan
    examples of, 121, 197, 243
start-up business, 25, 26, *28*
    business cycle and, 8–12, 26
    establishment costs, *132–3*, 160
statement of monthly personal expenses, 130, *131*,
        159–60
    examples of, 198, 220, 245
statement of personal net worth, 130, *131*
    examples of, 198, 220, 245
statistical information, 43
    examples of, 45–6
    sources of, 45–8
stock, trading, *96*, 126, 133, 136, 173
stock control, 158
stock levels, 98
stock records, 159
stock supplies, 93, 94–7. *see also* purchasing plan
    payments for, 97, 99–100, 145, 162
stockouts, 98
stocktakes, periodic, 158
strategic planning process, 6–7, *6*
strategy
    entry. *see* entry strategy
    marketing. *see* marketing strategies
    operating, 175
    staffing. *see* staffing strategies
subheadings, business plan, 169
superannuation contributions, 111
suppliers, *95*, 95–7, *96*
    examples of, 100–1, 195, 217, 239
supplier's invoice, 99

supplies
  availability of, 55, 56
  sources of, 95, *96*
supply conditions, 55–6
supporting documents, 169, 171
  examples of, 206, 228, 252
surveys, 43, *44*
  customer groups, 59
  customer satisfaction, *74*, 75
  participation discounts, 66
SWOT analysis, 42

**T**
target. *see* objective(s)
target customers, *51*, 58–61
  examples of, 77, 192, 213–14, 236–7
  public relations and, 70
target segments, 59–61
tax(es), 53
  goods and services (GST), 53
  income, 31, 141, 145
  net profit before, 141, 162
tax agent, 115, *116*
tax file number, 31
taxation registration, 31
technological factors, 52
telephone directories
  *Yellow Pages*, 47, 48, 55, 57, 95, 115
termination of employment, 111
time factors
  opening hours, 66
  owner's work hours, 104
  production process, 87
  setting objectives, for, 34
title page, 169, *170*
  examples of, 185, 207, 229
total assets, 146, 147
total liabilities, 146, 148
total production capacity, 86, *86*
Tourism Research Australia, 47, 212

trade discounts, 66
trade waste, 30
trademarks, 32
trading name, *18*, 22, 24, 30
  examples of, 35, 188, 210, 232
trading stock, *96*, 126, 133, 136, 173
training, employee, 112, *112*

**U**
uneconomic idle capacity, point of, 86, *86*
unsatisfactory performance, responsive actions to,
  178, *179*
upward trends, 9, 11–12

**V**
variable costs, 127
variable rate loans, 136
variance analysis, 156
verbal presentation of business plan, 255
viability quality criteria, 171, 254
visual observation of stock levels, 158

**W**
wage on-costs, 106, *107*, 126, 141, 145, *162*
warranties, product, 62, 97
waste permit, 30
water conservation, 258
website presence, 30, 64
work health and safety (WHS)
  authorities, 30, *31*, 114
  compliance, 114
  policies, *114*
work performance evaluation, 116–19, *118*
workplace agreement, 32, 109
  registration of, 32
workplace hazards, 114
written presentation of business plan, 169–71, 254

**Y**
*Yellow Pages*, 47, 48, 55, 57, 95, 115

Printed in Great Britain
by Amazon.co.uk, Ltd.,
Marston Gate.